Public Administration and Law

PUBLIC ADMINISTRATION AND PUBLIC POLICY
A Comprehensive Publication Program

Executive Editor

JACK RABIN
Graduate Program for Administrators
Rider College
Lawrenceville, New Jersey

Other volumes in preparation

Public Administration and Law

Bench v. Bureau in the United States

DAVID H. ROSENBLOOM
Department of Public Administration
The Maxwell School
Syracuse University
Syracuse, New York

MARCEL DEKKER, INC.   New York and Basel

Library of Congress Cataloging in Publication Data

Rosenbloom, David H.
    Public administration and law.

    (Public administration and public policy ; 14)
    Includes index.
    1. Administrative law—United States. 2. Judicial
review of administrative acts—United States. 3. Public
administration—United States. I. Title. II. Series.
KF5402.R67 1983   342.73'06   82-24193
ISBN O-8247-1791-0   347.3026

MARCEL DEKKER, Inc.

270 Madison Avenue, New York, New York 10016

Current printing (last digit):
10 9 8 7 6 5 4 3 2 1

PRINTED IN THE UNITED STATES OF AMERICA

For Deborah Diane Goldman

Preface

Until very recently, the study of public administration in the United States tended to diminish the importance of law. Indeed, the first American textbook on public administration, Leonard White's *Introduction to the Study of Public Administration* (1926),* was explicit in its assumption that ". . . the study of administration should start from the base of management rather than the foundation of law, and is therefore more absorbed in the affairs of the American Management Association than in the decisions of the courts" (vii-viii). True, as regulatory administration became more pronounced and controversial, greater attention was paid to administrative law. But for the most part, law, and especially constitutional law, was considered tangential to public administration.

Today, this traditional outlook is undergoing radical change. As the judiciary became heavily involved in many dimensions of public administration, the decisions of the courts became far too important to overlook. The judiciary emerged as a partner in public administration, but the study of law within the context of public administration has lagged behind. Administrative law, as traditionally conceived, is too narrow in its concerns to comprehend fully the contemporary relationship between public administration and law. Similarly, a case approach or law school approach emphasizing the development of legal concepts and up-to-the-minute rulings is also inadequate. What is needed is an approach that places the study of law squarely within the context of public administration, focuses on constitutional law and values, and also explains the radical expansion of the judicial role in public administration. That is the task of this book.

Specifically, the impact of public law on public administration is considered from the perspectives of four contexts in which individuals interact with public

*New York: Macmillan.

agencies: these are as clients, as public employees, as captives (prisoners and those confined to public mental health facilities), and as litigants against public administrators or public bureaucracies. Since the 1950s, the rights of individuals in each of these contexts have been dramatically expanded by judicial decisions. By focusing on these contexts of interaction, it is possible to contrast administrative values with judicial and constitutional values. This approach is beneficial because it facilitates public administrators' understanding of the broad concerns of constitutional law and the ways in which the Constitution acts as a constraint on their official actions.

This book is informed by the underlying thesis that there has been a judicial response to the rise of the contemporary administrative state. This response is rooted in the judiciary's concern for its own position in an increasingly bureaucratized government. It culminates in judicial activity that forces public administrators to be responsive to judges' decrees and values. Thus, this study is an ambitious attempt to reformulate the way in which public law is taught to students and practitioners of public administration. It seeks to impart a broad understanding of judicial and legal activity in the realm of public administration that will outlast the immediacy of specific court decisions.

The author of any book analyzing legal developments of a contemporary nature runs substantial risks. Courts are not wholly predictable. Different judges come to different conclusions. Whether various trends will continue into the future is often obscure. Nevertheless, by adopting an institutional perspective, fundamental aspects of the courts' activities become understandable. This book seeks to demonstrate that the federal judiciary has established sufficient leverage and control over public administration to secure itself a place of rough coequality with the other branches of government in the contemporary American administrative state. Whether the judiciary will seek to assert a measure of supremacy in the future is debatable. Recent decisions by the Supreme Court in some areas, especially those affecting the rights of captives, suggest that it may be signaling a halt to ever-increasing judicial activity in public administration. Yet, the forest should not be mistaken for the trees. It is highly unlikely that the judiciary will forfeit its *potential* to intervene in public administration, even if used more sparingly in the future. Nor will it cease to force public administrators to be responsive to its values.

The format of this book is as follows: Chapter 1 analyzes the rise of the administrative state, its impact on government in the United States, and its effect on the quality of democratic citizenship; Chapter 2 considers the federal judiciary, its place in the separation of powers, and its initial reactions to the emergence of the full-fledged administrative state; Chapters 3–6 analyze the rights of clients, public employees, captives, and antagonists (litigants) of the contemporary administrative state; and, Chapter 7 concludes the study with a broad consideration of the impact of the judicial response to the rise of the administrative state upon constitutional government and public administration.

Acknowledgments

This book grew out of a course on public administration and law that I taught at Syracuse University's Maxwell School. Students in three successive classes are to be thanked for pushing me beyond normal bounds to refine my ideas and strengthen my support for them. My colleagues at Maxwell were highly supportive during the often difficult times while the book was being written. Special thanks are due to Dean Guthrie Birkhead and Professors Bernard Jump and James D. Carroll. Also to be thanked are Gregory Lewis and David Sadofsky for their critical reading of the manuscript. A very special intellectual debt is owed to Deborah D. Goldman for assistance in researching, formulating, and presenting the ideas contained herein. Her collaboration has been invaluable. Thanks are also due to Professor Jack Rabin and Marcel Dekker for their commitment to the project at an early stage and their continued support of it. Finally, Leah and Sarah Rosenbloom are to be thanked for bearing some of the burdens of this work.

David H. Rosenbloom

Contents

1

The Rise of the American Administrative State: Some Issues

"The growth of the civil service system already has limited the ability of elected politicians to effect political change" (*Branti v. Finkel*, 1980:530). With these words, Supreme Court Justice Lewis Powell succinctly captured the essential problem of the rise of the administrative state. Political power and influence devolve into the hands of quasi permanent, unelected, and somewhat apolitically appointed administrative functionaries. By many accounts, they frequently frustrate the will of elected officials, make a great deal of public policy, and control the pace and tone of its implementation. Among other elements, administrators' power and influence rest upon their insulation from the electoral system, specialized expertise, and secure tenure. Unlike elected officials, they are not generally considered to be representatives of the citizenry and are only tenuously connected to the electorate at large. Consequently, the rise of administrative power has diminished the political importance of elections, the electorate, and ultimately, the citizenry as a whole. This fact of contemporary political life in the United States is hardly controversial: In 1973, 65 percent of the public and 57 percent of a sample of elected officials agreed that "the trouble with government is that elected officials have lost control over the bureaucrats, who really run the country" (U.S. Congress, 1973:Part 2, p. 115; Part 3, p. 61). However, the bureaucratization of American government continues to raise a host of perplexing political and constitutional issues.

The Historical Rise of the Administrative State

Politically, the twentieth century has been epitomized by the "bureaucratization of the world" (Jacoby, 1973). Virtually everywhere one looks, whether in the Western, Eastern, or Third Worlds, political life is strongly influenced, if not actually dominated, by public bureaucrats and the agencies in which they work. Ironically, as public bureaucracy has grown, so has public denunciation of it. Political authorities everywhere, it seems, are frustrated by the power of public bureaucrats. Nor do ordinary citizens appear to be happier with the growth of administrative power. Indeed, in many political systems, institutional arrangements have been established to deal with their complaints. Why has bureaucracy proliferated? What accounts for its tendency to engulf and dominate an increasing number of political, economic, and social activities?

There is, of course, no easy answer to these questions. In the view of some, bureaucratization can be considered an almost immutable historical trend. There is much to recommend such an interpretation. One of the outstanding facts of contemporary political life is the great similarity among the governmental structures of diverse societies. As Ferrel Heady (1966:23) observes,

> A necessary consequence of hierarchy and specialization in large-scale organization is an orderly arrangement of units into successively larger and more inclusive groupings. This process of departmentalization has occurred in a remarkably uniform way in countries that vary greatly in their political orientation and in other aspects of their administrative systems. The basic unit is the department or ministry, with each one representing a major organizational subdivision of administration. Chapman identifies five "primordial fields of government"—foreign affairs, justice, finance, defense and war, and internal affairs—represented in Europe's past by primary ministries with origins dating back to the Roman system of administration. With the growth of governmental responsibilities and services, new ministries emerged from what had been the residual category of internal affairs, adding new ministries in such fields as education, agriculture, transport, trade, and more recently, social security and health. The contours of the sphere of governmental activities in each country will certainly affect the number and missions of the central ministries, but the impression one gets from reviewing rosters of ministries in many countries is one of uniformity or close similarity rather than of wide variation.

In general, nations will have somewhere in the range of 12 to 30 ministries or cabinet departments, depending on a number of factors including the degree of governmental penetration of the society and the nature of political parties and political coalitions. In addition to ministries or departments, governmental structures contain any number of organizational subunits. B. Guy Peters (1978:110) addresses the bases upon which these are commonly organized.

> The purposes served are clearly the most frequent basis of organization, as departments or ministries of defense, education, and health would indicate.

Organization by process is more commonly found at subministerial levels, with divisions or bureaus of accounting, legal services, engineering, and the like. Types of persons or things dealt with would include organizations such as the Veterans Administration in the United States, similar organizations in other countries, the Bureau of Indian Affairs, and the various boards and commissions for (or against) foreign workers in European countries. Finally, the area served is frequenty used as an organizational principle at the subdepartmental level, as in the use of regional offices, but may also be institutionalized at the departmental level, as in the Scottish and Welsh Offices in the United Kingdom.

Indeed, as Heady and Peters suggest, the commonalities in governmental structures are so overwhelming as to require some explanation.

In general, there are four types of theoretical approaches explaining the rise of the administrative state. These are largely complementary, rather than mutually contradictory, and together they explain a great deal about the development of contemporary public administration.

The Development of the Public Service State

Contemporary public administration can be understood as an outgrowth of the concept of the state as an organization providing public services. Although sometimes taken for granted today, the emergence of this concept was revolutionary and brought about major political and constitutional changes in Western nations. In discussing the development of the public service state in Western Europe, Ernest Barker (1966:4) points out that "When we go back to 1660 . . . [t]he State is not regarded as a legal association, united in a common scheme of rights and duties which requires the discharge of public services." Rather, there were several other prevalent conceptions, including the state as a family, as property, and as society. In Barker's view,

> This confusion of the idea of the state with notions of Family, Property, and general Society was generally characteristic of Europe about 1660; and the confusion still survived under Louis XIV, and into the eighteenth century. So long as it persists, it complicates and checks the development of a pure and specific administration of public services. The disengaging of the idea of the State, as a service-rendering organization for the protection of rights and enforcement of duties, is the prior condition of such a development (Barker, 1966:5-6).

Thus, it is only after the emergence of the *concept* of the public service state that a public service or administrative state becomes common.

Barker analyzes the development of the Western European public service state in some detail. No such discussion is necessary in the context of the United States, for as Louis Hartz (1955) has argued what was revolutionary in Europe was sometimes accepted by common consensus in the United States. Thus, the present constitutional government is overwhelmingly based on the concept of the state as a public service rendering organization. It is common to point out that the Founding Fathers seemed to have no concept of public administration and made little provision for the establishment of an administrative apparatus. However, they clearly believed that the purpose of government included the provision of public services. Indeed, the Preamble to the Constitution identifies the promotion of "the general welfare" as a fundamental objective of the government it establishes. That government is also given power to regulate commerce among the states, with foreign nations, and with Indian tribes. It is authorized to coin money, regulate its value, establish standard weights and measures, and to establish post offices and post roads. In addition, it is empowered "To promote the Progress of Science and useful Arts, by securing for limited Times to Authors and Investors the exclusive Right to their respective Writings and Discoveries." Furthermore, the government was specifically conceived to "establish Justice, insure domestic Tranquility, and provide for the common defence." A government charged with such functions, conceptualized in such a fashion, would almost inevitably develop a large administrative component. A public service state cannot exist without a public service.

However, the situation is somewhat more complex than Barker's approach suggests. The public service state and what could be called the *regulatory* or *control* state are thoroughly intertwined. It is not too much to say that one person's service is generally another's control. Much is in the perspective and the definition. For example, to take the consitutional functions mentioned previously, although each can be seen as service rendering, each also involves control. Thus, although regulating commerce, coinage, and weights and measures clearly provides a public service, by definition, such regulation also serves a control function. Patents and copyrights may promote the general welfare, but they also regulate the use of authors' and inventors' works. Along with the creation of the post office came its monopoly to deliver the mail. Establishing justice has entailed establishing prisons; providing for the common defense has involved conscription. Going beyond these specific constitutional bounds, it can be seen that the government rarely provides a pure service: the receipt of benefits, such as welfare or public housing, often entails meeting eligibility requirements as a means of regulating behavior and morality; governmental licenses and franchises require that certain standards be adhered to; and, the use of public property is conditioned upon various types of behavior. The intermixing of governmental service and control functions raises complex and important constitutional issues which are addressed in Chapter 3. Here, it is enough to say that in the view of some, such as Ralph Hummel (1977), the point of the public service state is not actually public service, but rather control.

Thus, to a considerable extent service and control turn out to be two sides of the same coin. When a government engages in rendering public services, it is likely also to engage in regulation or control. Regulation and control, on the other hand, may also render a service to some segment of the population, although in totalitarian nations with a small ruling elite, this segment may be very small indeed. The concept of the state as an instrument of control lies within the confines of the concept of the state as an organization for the rendering of public service. This concept also promotes the growth of public administration, and does so in a very specific way. Ralph Hummel (1977:28) reflects a classical view of bureaucracy in writing that ". . . bureaucracy is a control instrument and a control instrument without compare." When societies turn to control, they inevitably seem to rely increasingly upon bureaucratization. Before returning to this theme, it is desirable to examine related theories of the rise of the administrative state.

Societal Pressures for Governmental Expansion

Several theorists have stressed the extent to which external forces place pressures upon government to expand its administrative component. The difference between this approach in explaining the emergence of the administrative state and the theory discussed previously is subtle: it has much to do with whether the state is thought of as legitimately proactive in providing services, or is viewed as a service provider in a narrow realm and as a last resort. Perhaps the best known approach to administrative growth that stresses external forces is encompassed in *Wagner's Law.*

Adolph Wagner, a German economist, attempted to explain the tendency for public spending to increase at a rate faster than the rise in community economic output generally. He found this tendency in both complex and developing industrial nations, regardless of the political characteristics of their regimes. His conclusions can be distilled as follows:

1. "Government expands in order to control and coordinate the many antagonistic sectors of an increasingly complex society" (Wade and Curry, 1970: 78).
2. As "the size of industrial units increases," because of the disappearance of less efficient firms from the economy, "the response of government is again one of intervention. . . . The government's purpose in intervening is to maintain social stability, either by expanding controls over private industry or by taking over the property and management of industry itself" (Wade and Curry, 1970:78).

3. Demands and needs for certain social services such as education arise, and given the costs and collective benefit of underwriting such services, government often seeks to provide them.
4. The scale of certain tasks is so great that only government can procure the resources required. A contemporary example might be the exploration of space.

Wagner's Law has been subject to a considerable criticism and, strictly speaking, it applies only to government expenditures as opposed to the growth of government employment itself. However, discussions pertaining specifically to the latter tend to identify similar factors. For instance, Donald Warwick (1975: 7-8) delineates the following sources of administrative growth.

1. "Population growth increases the normal administrative demands made on governments—for police and fire protection and record-keeping, for example. Public employment expands to meet these demands."
2. In complex societies, ". . . there is rising pressure for the government to act as agent of the public welfare and the arbiter of private conflicts."
3. As the concentration of corporate power increases, "governmental bureaucracies arise to: (1) provide the political and economic stability needed to protect the investments of the corporate giants; (b) protect the interests of society against the corporations; (c) prevent political chaos by mediating between large corporations and organized labor; or (d) act as agents to stimulate economic activity by corporations and channel it in constructive directions."
4. "The increasing specialization of knowledge favors the rise of a new 'managerial elite' in both the public and the private sectors. . . . Their presence in government swells the size of the public bureaucracy."
5. "Increased levels of abundance generate new demands for services typically provided by public organizations, including education, welfare, health, and recreation. In many cases no single arm of government is willing or able to take full responsibility for a given set of services. The action is divided among several agencies, with considerable duplication of effort and demands for interagency coordination."

Although discussing the growth of red tape, or governmental regulation, as opposed to growth in employment, Herbert Kaufman (1977: 29-30) translates the general concerns of Wagner and Warwick into the political context found in the United States. He explains that

Every restraint and requirement originates in somebody's demand for it. Of course, each person does not will them all; on the contrary, even the most broadly based interest groups are concerned with only a relatively small band of the full spectrum of governmental activities, and most interest groups are narrowly specialized rather than broadly based. So each constraint is the product of a fairly small number of claimants. But there are so many of us, . . . that modest individual demands result in great stacks of official paper and bewildering procedural mazes.

Or for that matter, greater numbers of public employees.

Like most other theorists of bureaucratic growth, Kaufman sees nothing malevolent about it. He attributes red tape, and therefore, by implication, administrative growth to "compassion." In this view, government grows as it seeks to protect people from one another, to alleviate distress, and to forestall systemic disruptions. Red tape and public bureaucracy are used to ensure that these purposes are actually served and that only those entitled to compassionate governmental treatment receive it.

This line of interpretation is largely consistent with the development of the concept of the state as a public service rendering organization. Once it was widely believed that the state could and should provide such services, pressures increased for it actually to do so. Again, however, Hummel's point that *control* will often be intermingled with *compassion* or public *service* should be borne in mind. This brings us to a consideration of the extent to which the organizational attributes of bureaucracy may foster its growth.

Organizational Attributes

There is a considerable body of theory that holds that the rise of the administrative state is partly due to the organizational characteristics of bureaucracy. According to this approach, bureaucracy, which is the dominant organizational form of the administrative state, is almost constantly expanding. It eventually entrenches itself to such an extent that the society as a whole becomes thoroughly *dependent* upon it. This view is best represented in the writings of Max Weber (1958:214).

The decisive reason for the advance of bureaucratic organization has always been its purely technical superiority over any other form of organization. The fully developed bureaucratic mechanism compares with other organizations exactly as does the machine with the non-mechanical modes of production.

Precision, speed, unambiguity, knowledge of the files, continuity, discretion, unity, strict subordination, reduction of friction and of material and personal costs—these are raised to the optimum point in the strictly bureaucratic administration. . . .

In this view, bureaucracy, once established, is continually called upon to perform an increasing number of tasks that require an evermore extensive degree of specialization.

There are several organizational attributes of bureaucracy that are especially crucial to its continual expansion. Among these are the following:

1. *Hierarchy.* Hierarchy is a ranking of roles and statuses. It promotes control of individuals within the bureaucratic organization, projects unity, and facilitates coordination. Those lower down in the organization are dependend upon those higher up for promotions and other rewards; frequently, they become psychologically dependent upon the superordinates as well.

2. *Specialization.* Specialization is differentiation of work and expertise. By creating a highly refined and often rational division of labor, bureaucratic organizations are able to develop a great deal of expertise in the performance of limited tasks among their employees. The expertise of the specialized bureaucrat may not be matched elsewhere in the society. This being the case, specialization often promotes unparalleled efficiency.

3. *Formalization.* Bureaucracies tend to stress formalized rules and communication. A great deal of communication is in writing. Employee tasks, obligations, and rights may be described elaborately in written detail. Memos take the place of oral communications, and bureaucrats may even write memos to the file, rather than to actual persons. The principal objectives of formalization are clarity and continuity.

4. *Merit-oriented personnel systems.* Bureaucratic organizations stress some concept of merit, or achievement, in their personnel decisions. Although actually defining and measuring *merit* is often extremely difficult, bureaucratic organizations seek to hire and promote those who are most likely to perform specific task requirements well. Seniority is sometimes used as a surrogate measure for merit, though often with obvious difficulties. Today, the merit orientation of public bureaucracies is sometimes taken for granted. However, it should be remembered that, historically, patronage has been a primary means of selecting public administrators.

5. *Nonmarketable output.* Public bureaucracies generally do not produce a product that can be freely bought and sold. Although price tags may be attached to bureaucratic services, they are not established by market mechanisms. Rather, they are budgetary devices or the result of monopolistic transactions. Agencies may show surpluses or deficits, but these are not to be confused with profit and loss. Nonmarketable output makes it very difficult to evaluate the performance of a bureaucratic organization or its individual workers (Downs, 1967:Chapter 4).

How do these attributes tend to promote bureaucratic expansion? Anthony Downs (1967:17) is among a group of theorists who offer some explanations.

Hierarchy creates a scarcity of positions at the top which can be mitigated somewhat by growth: "Growth tends to reduce internal conflicts in an organization
by allowing some (or all) of its members to increase their personal status without
lowering that of others. Therefore, organizational leaders encourage expansion
to maximize morale and minimize internal conflicts." Moreover, "the expansion
of any organization normally provides its leaders with increased power, income,
and prestige; hence they encourage its growth." *Specialization* can be further
refined through the creation of more positions: "Increasing the size of an organization may also improve the quality of its performance (per unit of output) and
its chances for survival." The *merit organization* of bureaucracies is enhanced by
growth because "an organization that is rapidly expanding can attract more capable personnel, and more easily retain its most capable existing personnel. . . ."
With regard to the absence of a *marketable* output, Downs observes that
"because there is no inherent *quid pro quo* in bureau activity enabling officials
to weigh the marginal return from further spending against its marginal cost, the
incentive structure facing most officials provides much greater rewards for
increasing expenditures than for reducing them." Greater expenditures are often
translated into a larger work force. To this list can be added *formalization*,
which creates a great deal of paperwork and the need for information processing,
storage, and retrieval systems that also promote an expansion of the number of
employees in bureaucratic organizations.

   In addition to these theories concerning the impact of the attributes of
bureaucratic organizations on their growth, there are a number of more popular
ideas concerning the behavior of such organizations. Perhaps best known is
Parkinson's Law: "Work expands so as to fill time available for its completion"
(1957:2). Parkinson predicted an annual growth rate of 5.17 to 6.56 percent
in the number of employees in bureaucratic organizations. Parkinson's law can
be augmented by Peter's Principle: "In a hierarchy every employee tends to rise
to his level of incompetence" (Peter and Hull, 1969:7). In other words, one is
promoted through the ranks of bureaucratic organizations until one can no
longer perform the required tasks of a position well. At that point, promotion
stops, and individuals remain in positions in which they are not fully competent.
One consequence of this would be to hire additional employees to do the work
of the incompetents. Of course, these theories are more notable for their levity
than accuracy, though they do contain some grains of truth.

Idiosyncratic Factors

A final theoretical approach to explaining the rise of the administrative state
stresses the importance of factors peculiar to the development of individual
political systems. James Q. Wilson (1975) is among those who propound this
approach. He criticizes theoretical approaches that stress the importance of
nongovernmental forces and the attributes of bureaucratic organizations: "Such

theories, both the popular and the scholarly, assign little importance to the nature of the tasks an agency performs, the constitutional framework in which it is embedded, or the preferences and attitudes of citizens and legislators" (80). In this view, only the most general outlines of administrative expansion can be explained by the broader theories. Nevertheless, almost all observers would agree that these theories do identify several preconditions for the more specific, idiosyncratic approach favored by Wilson. By the same token, Wilson's approach does supply an enlightening political context to the analysis of bureaucratic growth. For instance, it provides a convenient departure for a description of the development of the U.S. version of the administrative state.

The Rise of the American Administrative State

Although there are many ways of discussing the growth of the federal bureaucracy, Wilson (1975) convincingly argues that its rise to a position of centrality in the political system has been largely a result of a limited number of factors involving changing political attitudes. According to his analysis, until the Civil War the major source of bureaucratic growth was the expansion of the post office: "From 1816 to 1861, federal civilian employment in the executive branch increased nearly eight-fold (from 4,837 to 36,672), but 86 percent of this growth was the result of additions to the postal service" (82). The post-Civil War period, by contrast, was marked by a diversity of sources of bureaucratic growth. One was that ". . . government began to give formal, bureaucratic recognition to the emergence of distinctive interests in a diversifying economy" (88), including agriculture, labor, and commerce. This development, sometimes referred to as *clientelism*, has continued into the contemporary period. It contains within it a tendency continually to add agencies as a means of granting recognition and representation to emergent occupational and social groups. Today, for example, there are additional agencies dealing with the interests of medical practitioners, educators, and members of minority groups. In Wilson's view, "The New Deal was perhaps the high water mark of at least the theory of bureaucratic clientelism. Not only did various sectors of society, notably agriculture, begin receiving massive subsidies, but the government proposed, through the National Industrial Recovery Act, . . . to cloak with public power a vast number of industrial groupings and trade associations so that they might control production and prices in ways that would end the depression" (90).

Another source of bureaucratic expansion came from the society's desire to regulate various aspects of economic life. Wilson argues that regulatory bureaucracies were created during four main periods: these were 1887-1890,

1906-1915, the 1930s, and the latter part of the 1960s. Relying on the idiosyncratic approach, he concludes

> Each of these periods was characterized by progressive or liberal Presidents in office (Cleveland, T. R. Roosevelt, Wilson, F. D. Roosevelt, Johnson); one was a period of national crisis (the 1930s); three were periods when the President enjoyed extraordinary majorities of his own party in both houses of Congress: . . . and only the first period preceded the emergence of the national mass media of communication. These facts are important because of the special difficulty of passing any genuinely regulatory legislation. . . . Without special political circumstances . . . the normal barriers to legislation . . . may prove insuperable (96-97).

Wilson's interpretation is strengthened by the fact that the commonality of political circumstances surrounding the development of regulatory agencies has prevailed despite the disjunctive character of the areas being regulated. Thus, in the earliest period, interstate commerce (primarily railroads) and monopolies were the subjects of regulation; in the second period not only were some of these regulations strengthened, but the Pure Food and Drug Act and the Meat Inspection Act were passed to regulate the quality of these products being offered to consumers; in the 1930s, cosmetics, utilities, natural gas companies, securities, and the airline and the radio communication industries were added to the list of regulated areas as were private sector labor relations; and regulation in the 1960s tended to center upon environmental and safety concerns and the protection of racial and ethnic minorities.

The military establishment is another major source of bureaucratic expansion discussed by Wilson. Although the Departments of War and the Navy were created in the eighteenth century, the military establishment did not emerge as the federal government's single largest bureaucracy until after World War II. Since that time, the Department of Defense has employed as many as a third of all civilian federal workers. Interestingly, this means that approximately half of all civilian employees of the federal bureaucracy are located in two agencies; the Department of Defense and the post office.

Wilson's approach provides a rationale for the broad outlines of bureaucratic growth within the federal government; yet, it must be augmented by the other approaches. Together, these offer useful explanations of the causes and processes of the rise of the contemporary American administrative state. They suggest its inevitability, if not its specific form. At this point, it is desirable to turn briefly to a discussion of the structural nature of public bureaucracy in the United States before returning to some of the more perplexing issues presented by its rise to a position of great power in the political system.

Public Bureaucracy in the United States

Today, the federal bureaucracy employs about 2.8 million civilian employees. These workers are engaged in a host of occupations, divided among many organizational forms, and widely disbursed throughout the nation and the world. Table 1.1 presents the growth in federal employment from 1821-1979. Although the major reasons for the expansion of the bureaucracy have already been discussed, some further observations are in order. First, the bureaucracy has not grown in smooth, constant, or linear fashion. There have been a few periods of very rapid expansion. One was from 1871-1881 when the number of personnel doubled from about 50,000 to 100,000. To place this growth in perspective, it should be remembered that it took some 82 years for the federal bureaucracy to acquire 50,000 employees in its ranks in the first place. Much of the growth in the 1870s was in response to clientelism and the emergence of some early forms of regulation. The 1930s were another period of rapid expansion that occurred mainly in response to the economic crisis that had engulfed the nation. In the 1940s, the federal bureaucracy continued to grow rapidly in response to World War II and the cold war. The 1950s through the 1970s, on the other hand, were characterized by limited growth and even some shrinkage at various times. In part, this situation was caused by the federal government's increasing reliance on state administrators to implement federal programs. Indeed, during the same period, the number of employees of a typical state more

Table 1.1 Growth of Federal Employment

Year	Employees (No.)	Year	Employees (No.)
1821	6914	1911	395,905
1831	11,491	1921	561,143
1841	18,038	1931	609,746
1851	26,274	1941	1,437,682
1861	36,672	1951	2,482,666
1871	51,020	1961	2,435,808
1881	100,020	1971	2,862,926
1891	157,442	1979	2,763,000
1901	239,476	*1980*	2895866
		1986	3022189

Sources: Through 1951, U.S. Bureau of the Census and Social Science Research Council, *Statistical History of the United States from Colonial Times to the Present* (Stamford, Conn.: Fairfield Publishers, 1965), p. 710. Figures for 1961 and 1971 are from U.S. Civil Service Commission, *Annual Report*, pp. 78, 88, appendix A. The 1979 figure is from U.S. Bureau of the Census, *Statistical Abstract* (Washington, D.C.: Bureau of the Census, 1980), p. 279.

than doubled in size. Limited expansion of the federal bureaucracy during this period also appears to be due to an increasing tendency to contract out the work of federal agencies to private groups. By some estimates, as many as one million civilian nonfederal employees are actually doing government work. Still, it should be borne in mind that while there appears to be an inevitable tendency for public bureaucracies to increase their size, the process may be very uneven.

The number of personnel in a public service is but one measure of its size and one indicator of the tendency toward bureaucratization of government. The number of administrative organizational entities is another. However, precisely determining this number is an almost impossible task—much depends upon definition. In 1977, the *U.S. Government Organization Manual* showed 55 agencies in the executive branch of the federal government outside the Executive Office of the President and about a dozen within it. But to this figure could be added legislative agencies, such as the Congressional Budget Office, and judicial agencies, including the Administrative Office of the United States Courts. Moreover, various interagency committees, advisory commissions and other adjuncts of the federal bureaucracy could arguably be included in any totaling of its units. Consequently, figures pertaining to the number of federal agencies range from those presented in the *U.S. Government Organization Manual* to at least the 1900 that candidate Jimmy Carter promised during the 1976 campaign to transform into 200 (Nachmias and Rosenbloom, 1980:41).

Enumerating the units of the federal bureaucracy is further complicated by the existence of scores of semiautonomous bureaus. Although in a legal sense these may be subsumed under one department or agency or another, in practice they are often quite independent in their operations. For instance, the Federal Bureau of Investigation is part of the Department of Justice, but at various times it has manifested sufficient independence to be considered a separate force of its own. These definitional problems make it difficult to say with any precision how much the federal bureaucracy has grown in terms of the number of its organizational entities. However, one study (Kaufman, 1976), which excluded the Department of Defense, found that in 1973 the remaining cabinet departments and the Executive Office of the President contained 394 bureaus and that the number had increased from 175 in 1923.

What do all these employees and organizational entities do? Some answers are suggested by Figure 1.1 which presents a recent organizational chart of the federal bureaucracy. For the most part, the names of departments and agencies are suggestive of the functions Wilson mentions, namely defense, clientelism, and regulation. They clearly reflect the society's acceptance of the public service state and suggest the kind of roles undertaken by the federal government. Table 1.2 presents the occupations of white-collar federal employees. These are also suggestive of the kind of work performed by the federal bureaucracy.

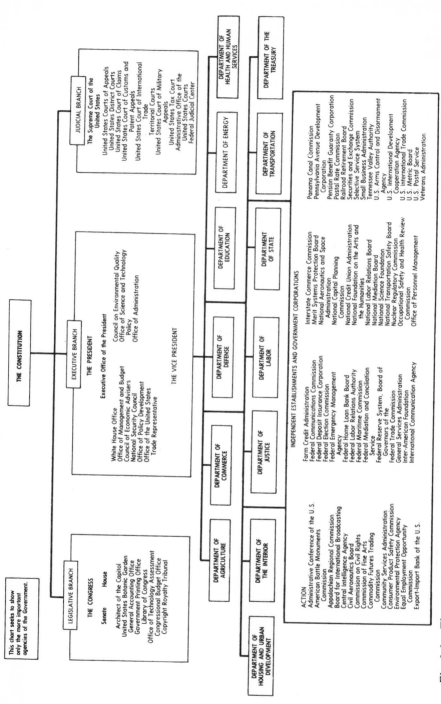

Fig. 1.1 The government of the United States. (From U.S. Government Manual, 1980–1981. U.S. Government Printing Office, Washington, D.C., 1981, p. 815.)

14

Table 1.2   White-Collar Full-Time Civilian Workers in the
Federal Government, by Major Occupational Group, 1978
(in Hundreds)

Occupational Group	
Postal	465.6
General administration, clerical, and office service	466.4
Engineering and architecture	154.2
Accounting and budget	125.8
Medical, hospital, dental, and public health	123.1
Supply	57.2
Business and industry	72.0
Legal and kindred	67.7
Personnel management and industrial relations	47.2
Physical sciences	43.0
Biological sciences	52.3
Investigation	48.8
Social sciences, psychology, and welfare	58.2
Transportation	44.4
Education	28.6
Quality assurance inspection and grading	18.9
Information and arts	20.9
Equipment, facilities, and service	14.4
Mathematics and statistics	14.8
Library and archives	9.8
Other	1.9

Source: U.S. Bureau of the Census, *Statistical Abstract* (Washington, D.C.:
Bureau of the Census, 1980), p. 284.

No discussion of public administration in the United States could possibly
avoid the myriad organizational forms found in the public sector. Bureaus may
be the working units of public bureaucracies, but they are grouped together in
a variety of different structures. Departments are often considered the most
important organizational entities. In general, their missions are broad and affect
most, if not all, segments of the public. Departments may be well-unified
organizational structures or they may be more like holding companies of disparate bureaus. There is obviously a great range in the number of employees
and budgets of the federal departments, as can be seen in Table 1.3. In addition
to departments, there are independent agencies. Generally, these are engaged in
regulatory functions, or have missions pertaining to a more limited number of

Table 1.3   Personnel and Budget of Cabinet Departments, 1978

Department	Personnel	Budget Outlays (in Billions)
Agriculture	114,000	$23
Commerce	39,000	5
Defense	982,000	105
Health, Education, Welfare	158,000	165
Housing and Urban Development	18,000	8
Interior	76,000	4
Justice	53,000	3
Labor	17,000	24
State	30,000	1
Transportation	74,000	14
Treasury	133,000	56
Energy	20,000	8

Source: U.S. Bureau of the Census, *Statistical Abstract* (Washington, D.C.: Bureau of the Census, 1978), pp. 280, 263. Budget figures are estimates.

people, such as veterans or minorities, or are engaged in administrative overhead functions, such as personnel management or supply. Corporations are another form of administrative unit. These are used where the government is providing a product or service that can be sold, such as insurance or electricity. Government corporations are distinct from other units in that they can generate their own revenues and, at least theoretically, need not rely upon legislative appropriations for their operating funds. Finally, public bureaucracies in the United States contain any number of advisory commissions, interagency and intergovernmental committees, and semipublic, semiprivate organizations, such as the Federal Reserve Banks.

As perplexing as the federal bureaucracy may be, there is a good deal more systematic knowledge of its structure and operations than exists concerning the state and local governmental bureaucracies. Although their remarkable growth during the past decades has been well documented, it has yet to be explained fully. Several factors appear to be at work, including the extent of federal spending within a state, the degree of its industrialization, and its population density (Rosenbloom and Bryan, 1981). The states range from about 9 public employees per 100 residents (Alaska) to 4.7 (Pennsylvania). While many of the functions they perform are similar to those performed by federal workers, state and local governments do not provide defense and postal services, whereas they do concentrate large numbers of employees in the areas of education and police and fire protection. State governments also maintain a number of mental health and penal institutions. These have emerged as highly problematic areas, as is discussed in Chapter 5.

Like the federal bureaucracy, state bureaucracies contain a variety of organizational forms and are frequently highly fragmented. Their number of units varies, but unlike the federal government many of them contain a large number of licensing boards. In the federal government, the president and vice president are the only elected officials in the executive branch. At the state level, by contrast, several executive branch officials may be elected, including department heads and commissioners of various types.

Both the federal and state governments have merit-oriented personnel systems. This is most pronounced at the federal level where it is estimated that roughly 90 percent of all civilian employees are covered by some form of merit protection. The extent of *actual* coverage at the state level is unknown, but by the 1970s 33 states had statewide merit arrangements (Shafritz et al., 1981:56). Generally speaking, merit protections enhance the power of public bureaucracies by making it difficult for political executives and politicians to fire employees and by promoting substantial expertise within the ranks of the civil service.

One additional characteristic of public bureaucracies in the United States should be stressed: they manifest a high degree of political fragmentation (Nachmias and Rosenbloom, 1980:Chapter 3). Their organizational units often have very unclear missions that cannot be operationalized in any precise fashion. For instance, they may be charged with regulating some aspect of economic life "in the public interest." They may also be charged with pursuing mutually contradictory objectives. Thus, the U.S. Department of the Interior is charged with assuring adequate resource development in order to meet the needs of national security and an expanding economy. But it is also supposed to maintain "productive capacity for future generations" (*U.S. Government Organization Manual*, 1973:251). Development and conservation of unrenewable resources are to be pursued at once! Matters become even more complex when, as is commonly the case, several agencies are pursuing complementary and contradictory missions at once. It is not unusual to find one agency charged with preservation of the environment, while another is seeking its development. Overlaps are especially pronounced in such areas as health, education, and equal opportunity. Often, the requirements of two or more federal agencies are not only at odds with one another, but also with state agencies dealing with the same policy area. All of this can be quite confusing and frustrating. It can serve to limit the potential for private and public action in the administrative state by making it difficult and time-consuming to get anything accomplished. Indeed, although they involved high human costs, the great developmental projects of the past, such as the transcontinental railroads and the Erie Canal, were undertaken without benefit of environmental impact statements or compliance with any formalized set of occupational safety, personnel, or labor relations requirements.

Fragmentation can also enhance the power of public bureaucracies by making it extremely difficult for outsiders to understand their operations and to control them. For instance, one of the major aspects of fragmentation has been the development of *iron triangles*, consisting of bureaucratic agency (or bureau), interest group, and legislative (sub)committee. Together, these elements develop a harmony of interest and an imperviousness to outside influence. Such triangles are often considered the basic policy-making blocks of American politics (Nachmias and Rosenbloom, 1980; Chapter 3). This brings us to a more general consideration of administrative power.

Administrative Power, Values, and Democratic Constitutionalism

Power

The rise of the administrative state places great power in the hands of administrative agencies and their personnel. This is especially true where public administration is bureaucratically organized, as Max Weber (1958:232-233) explains.

> Under normal conditions, the power position of a fully developed bureaucracy is always overtowering. The "political master" finds himself in the position of the "dilettante" who stands opposite the "expert," facing the trained official who stands within the management of administration. This holds whether the "master" whom the bureaucracy serves is a "people," equipped with the weapons of "legislative initiative," and the "referendum," and the right to remove officials, or a parliament, elected on a more aristocratic or more "democratic" basis and equipped with the right to vote a lack of confidence, or with the actual authority to vote it. It holds whether the master is an aristocratic, collegiate body, legally or actually based on self-recruitment, or whether he is a popularly elected president, a hereditary and "absolute" or a "constitutional" monarch.

Although the sources of bureaucratic power are numerous, as Weber indicates, expertise is of fundamental importance. Simply put, modern societies are dependent upon governmental bureaucrats for the formulation and implementation of public policy. Their independent power is both tolerated and granted because essentially, "government would come to a standstill if our 'closet statesmen' in the civil service suddenly started doing only what they were told" (Storing, 1964:152). Indeed, in Weber's view, "if the official stops working, or if his work is forcefully interrupted, chaos results, and it is difficult to improvise replacements from among the governed who are fit to master such chaos" (Weber, 1958:229). This is one reason why strikes by public employees are perceived as great threats to stability and are prohibited by law in many societies.

In sum, contemporary governments and societies find themselves highly dependent upon public bureaucrats, who supply expertise, continuity, and stability to governance. Bureaucrats do not simply carry out the commands of political superiors. They tend to frame the policy options available to political decision makers; they formulate a great deal of public policy on their own; they lobby for their proposals; and, they may block the implementation of policies to which they are opposed. As Hans Rosenberg (1958:1) describes the political impact of the rise of the administrative state:

All the states of the contemporary world, despite enormous differences in the moral, legal, and material basis of their authority and in the function, efficiency, control, and responsibility of governmental action, form part of a single political order. Everywhere government has developed into a big business because of the growing complexity of social life and the multiplying effect of the extension of the state's regulative functions. Everywhere government engages in service-extracting and service-rendering activities on a large scale. Everywhere the supreme power to restrain or to aid individuals and groups has become concentrated in huge and vulnerable organizations. For good or for evil, an essential part of the present structure of governance consists of its far-flung system of professionalized administration and its hierarchy of appointed officials upon whom society is thoroughly dependent. Whether we live under the most totalitarian despotism or in the most liberal democracy, we are governed to a considerable extent by a bureaucracy of some kind.

Values

As Weber, Rosenberg, and others observe, the political power of modern public bureaucracies is often at odds with other aspects of political systems. The conflict between bureaucratic organization on the one hand and regime values and governing processes on the other is perhaps nowhere greater than in democratic political systems. Simply put, bureaucracy and democracy stress different values and processes to the extent that the rise of the bureaucratized administrative state threatens the very fundamentals of democratic government. For instance, bureaucracy rests on hierarchy, seniority, command, unity, and differentiated expertise, whereas democracy stresses equality, rotation in office, freedom, pluralism, and the presumption that all citizens are sufficiently competent (i.e., expert) to take part in elections and politics. Moreover, democracy, taken literally, means rule by the people, whereas, taken in the same vein, bureaucracy means rule by bureaus or *desks*. These meanings are not insignificant; democracy stresses humanity while bureaucracy has come to stand for *dehumanization*.

Today, dehumanization is often referred to as impersonality. It is the elimination of emotions, personal biases, and idiosyncracies from the performance of individual bureaucrats. Max Weber (1958:216) referred to dehumanization as the "special virtue" of bureaucracy because, in his view, it vastly enhanced the rationality and efficiency of such organizations. Although some would contest this view today, it is still widely believed by organization theorists that "efficiency also suffers when emotions or personal considerations influence administrative decisions" (Blau and Meyer, 1971:9). Weber (1958:228) argued that dehumanization could turn the individual bureaucrat into a "cog," who could neither change the general direction the organization was taking nor manage to "squirm out" of it. But dehumanization not only applies to the employees of bureaucracies, it also defines the treatment of nonemployees who come into contact with such organizations. As Hummel (1977) observes, bureaucracies do not deal with "persons," rather they turn them into "cases." The case is then processed according to the formalized rules and regulations. Sometimes, as is discussed in Chapter 5, dehumanization goes so far as to actually involve the removal of *parts of the human body* that interfere with the efficient administration of mental health facilities and prisons. Even in the more common and less drastic instances of dehumanization, however, individuality is sacrificed to the objectives of procedural regularity and efficiency. In Hummel's words (1977: 21), "The bureaucrat has no time and no permission to become involved in the personal problems of clients. From his point of view the more he can depersonalize the client into a thing devoid of unique features the more easily and smoothly he will be able to handle the cases before him." Indeed, communication in bureaucracies can be between individuals and structures, between structures, or conceivably even between files. In the end, dehumanization creates a cultural conflict between bureaucracy and society that is ". . . between systems needs and human needs" (Hummel, 1977:56).

In the United States, the conflict between bureaucratic power and democratic constitutionalism is highly pronounced. In part, this is because whereas bureaucracy and public administrative theory generally stress dehumanization or impersonality in the quest for uniformity among individuals, the Constitution and much of the theory behind it seek to promote diversity among the citizenry. This is a theme which is stressed throughout Chapters 3, 4, and 5. Briefly, however, it should be pointed out here that American constitutional government is largely based on the theory that a large extended republic would promote and protect the development of a wide variety of diverse interests that, if properly channeled through government, would be made to check one another in such a fashion so as to advance the general public interest. As James Madison expressed this idea, "If you take a greater variety of parties and interests you make it less probable that a majority of the whole will have a common motive to invade the rights of other citizens; or if such a common motive exists, it will be more difficult for all who feel it to discover their own strength and to act in unison with each other" (*Federalist 10*; Rossiter, 1961:83). To the extent that the Madisonian theory is correct, diversity among the citizenry is crucial to the maintenance of constitutional democracy.

The Constitution seeks to provide representation to diverse interests. This is most evident in the bicameral legislature, in which each house was designed to represent different constituencies and was vested with both some overlapping and some different powers. A major purpose of this arrangement was to enable and motivate each house to act as a check on the other. In addition, many of the rights contained in the original Constitution and in the Bill of Rights serve to protect individuality and diversity among the population. For example, the guarantees of liberty, freedom of speech and press, and against search and seizure, protect individuals from governmentally enforced conformity and uniformity. Moreover, the guarantee of free exercise of religion and the prohibition of the establishment of religion bespeak of the desire to allow the maintenance and future development of diversity in a realm that has been critical to government and society throughout the ages.

The Separation of Powers and Representation

The rise of the administrative state has also placed great strains on the separation of powers and on the related representational scheme of the government. It is almost axiomatic that the government of the United States is one which relies on a system of far-reaching separation of powers in order to prevent the concentration of official authority in the hands of one group or a single political institution. Thus, James Madison (*Federalist 51*; Rossiter, 1961:321–322) wrote that the "great security against a gradual concentration of the several powers in the same department consists in giving to those who administer each department the necessary constitutional means and personal motives to resist encroachments of the others." The Constitution, at least at first consideration, is highly explicit concerning the separation of powers. For instance, Article I begins: "*All legislative Powers* herein granted shall be vested in a Congress of the United States . . ." (emphasis added); Article II, decrees that "The executive Power shall be vested in a President of the United States . . .;" and, Article III holds that "The judicial Power of the United States, shall be vested in one supreme Court, and in such inferior Courts as the Congress may from time to time ordain and establish." However, it is equally axiomatic that "there is no doubt that the development of the administrative agency in response to modern legislative and administrative need has placed severe strain on the separation-of-powers principle in its pristine formulation" (*Buckley v. Valeo*, 1976:280–281).

In this context, the conflict between consitutional government and the administrative state is one of both organization and values. American public administration now often combines elements of legislative, executive, and judicial powers. Although this tendency was perhaps always present, it was accelerated by the growth of regulatory administration since the 1880s and by the development of the full-fledged administrative state in the post-New Deal period. For instance, with regard to legislative functions, it has been observed that "the volume of legislative output of federal agencies far exceeds the volume of the legislative output of Congress" (Davis, 1975:8). Such legislation is embodied in the agency rule making, or the formulation of general standards applicable to an entire community (Woll, 1977:77). Rule making is a necessary response to the modern congressional tendency to delegate its own legislative powers to administrative agencies and Congress's inability or unwillingness to formulate precisely the objectives toward which such power should be used or the standards under which it should be applied. For example, the Federal Communications Act of 1934 authorizes the Federal Communications Commission (FCC) to issue "such rules and regulations and prescribe such restrictions and conditions, not inconsistent with law" as "public convenience, interest, or necessity requires." Nowhere, in the statute, however, is the public convenience, interest, or necessity defined in a fashion that would provide the FCC with substantive guidance or limit the scope of its rules. Nor do these terms have a specific meaning at common law or in everyday parlance. Its decisions, consequently, sometimes have the appearance of being based on whim (McConnell, 1966:285). Nor is the FCC in a unique situation by any means. Faced with a similarly unclear mission, a chairman of the Civil Aeronautics Board once exclaimed that "the philosophy of the . . . Board changes from day to day. It depends who is on the Board as to what the philosophy is" (McConnell, 1966: 286).

As is suggested by the lack of clarity in the legislative delegations of power to administrative agencies, administrative rule making is not just voluminous, it also reaches to some of the most crucial and controversial aspects of public policy. Perhaps the best contemporary example is affirmative action in public and private employment. Neither the Civil Rights Act of 1964 nor the Equal Employment Opportunity Act of 1972 defines *affirmative action* so as to mean the use of goals and timetables or quotas for the hiring, training, promotion, and retention of members of minority groups and women. Yet, despite a great deal of opposition, litigation, and public debate, the Equal Employment Opportunity Commission, an agency charged with implementing much of this legislation, has persisted in promoting and requiring the use of these techniques to the extent that they are now virtually synonymous with the term *affirmative action*. The tendency for controversial issues of public policy to be addressed so frequently by administrative agencies, with little or no concrete statutory guidance from Congress, suggests that the growth of legislative delegations can be explained in both political and administrative terms.

It is customary to consider delegations of legislative power to follow from the inherent virtues of the administrative process. Agency rule-making is far more flexible than the congressional, constitutional process for passing legislation. Congress is a fragmented body, with two houses doing much of the same work, though representing somewhat different constituencies. It does generate specialization through the committee system, but it remains primarily a body of generalists, who must address any number of complex issues of public policy in any given legislative session. (Some 20,000 bills may be introduced in a typical congressional session.)* In order to perform its functions better, Congress has added an increasing number of staff and created some administrative agencies of its own. Despite the expertise of these legislative functionaries, however, Congress may still lack adequate knowledge and be too fragmented to establish clear public policy objectives and standards for implementing them. What is an operational concept of the public interest, convenience, or necessity in broadcasting? How can equal employment opportunity be defined and implemented? These are questions requiring a great deal of time and detailed expertise to address well. Electoral pressures on the legislature and the likelihood that as conditions change new definitions and standards will have to be developed encourage Congress to delegate its authority to administrative agencies. These units, by contrast, have a relatively flexible rule-making procedure and their structures are often relatively fluid and relatively easily reorganized. They are also highly specialized and need not be concerned with several areas of public policy at once; and, they can correct their mistakes without going through the complexities of legislative process all over again. Consequently, despite the common view of administrative entrenchment, it is often easier for agencies to adapt to changing conditions (by modifying their rules) than it would be for Congress; and given their specialization and expertise, they may be less apt to make mistakes in the first place.

Another reason for the increasing tendency of Congress to delegate its authority to administrative agencies is far more political in nature. As Morris Fiorina (1977:43-46) explains, members of Congress may stand to lose more than they gain by addressing controversial issues of public policy in a precise fashion.

> From the standpoint of capturing voters, the congressman's lawmaking activities differ in two important respects from his porkbarrel and casework activities. First, programmatic actions are inherently controversial. Unless his district is homogeneous, a congressman will find his district divided on many major issues. Thus when he casts a vote, introduces a piece of nontrivial legislation, or makes a speech with policy content he

New York Times, December 3, 1978, p. 90. About 3000 were enacted.

will displease some elements of his district. . . . On such policy matters the congressman can expect to make friends as well as enemies. Presumably he will behave so as to maximize the former over the latter but nevertheless a policy stand will generally make some enemies. . . .

A second way in which programmatic activities differ from casework and the porkbarrel is the difficulty of assigning responsibility to the former as compared with the latter. No congressman can seriously claim that he is responsible for the 1964 Civil Rights Act, the ABM, or the 1972 Revenue Sharing Act. Most constituents do have some vague notion that their congressman is only one of hundreds and their senator is one of an even hundred. Even committee chairmen may have a difficult time claiming credit for a piece of major legislation. . . .

Overall then, programmatic activities are dangerous (controversial), on the one hand, and programmatic accomplishments are difficult to claim credit for, on the other.

Consequently, as Fiorina (1977:46) argues, the rise of the administrative state has been accompanied by "a change in the mix of congressional activities. Specifically, a lesser proportion of congressional effort is now going into programmatic activities and a greater proportion into pork-barrel and casework activities." Put plainly, members of Congress have developed an inclination to delegate not just authority, but also controversial political issues to public administrators. By so doing they not only avoid making enemies of those who would oppose their policy stands, but they also make friends of those constituents who seek their assistance in dealing with the bureaucratic rules and regulations they helped spawn. One need not go so far as to agree with Fiorina (1977: 48) that members of Congress "take credit coming and going," but their political interests in maintaining their incumbency are hardly antithetical to delegating legislative authority. Among the casualties, as Justice White pointed out in *Buckley v. Valeo* (1976), is the pure conception of the separation of powers.

Ironically, even the executive functions of federal agencies can raise important problems for the concept of the separation of powers. Public administration is generally considered to be an executive function concerned with the execution or implementation of the law. However, under the Constitution, the federal bureaucracy is largely dependent upon Congress for its organization, powers, budgets, staff, functions, and its internal workings with regard to a variety of processes including public personnel management. In fact, in the nineteenth century the notion that public administration should be dependent upon the legislature was so entrenched that in *Kendall v. U.S.* (1838) the Supreme Court declared that Congress could specifically direct the actions of individual public adminstrators.

It would be an alarming doctrine, that congress cannot impose upon any executive officer any duty they may think proper, which is not repugnant to any rights secured and protected by the constitution; and in such cases, the duty and responsibility grow out of and are subject to the control of law, and not to the direction of the President (524).

Indeed, although we now tend to think of the president as the head of the executive branch bureaucracy, his constitutional powers are meager compared to those of Congress. In specific terms, they amount to little more than the power to appoint department heads with the advice and consent of the Senate and to require the written opinions of these officials on occasion. More vaguely, the presidency may contain some inherent executive power and/or implied power to "take care that the laws be faithfully executed," but litigation over the past century has failed to clarify the extent of such powers.

In some areas, presidential powers vis- à-vis the federal bureaucracy have been augmented by congressional delegations of authority to initiate the reorganization of agencies and the impoundment of appropriations, to propound rules for personnel management, and to play an active role in budgeting. In addition, with congressional approval, a large Executive Office of the President has been established to assist in managing and directing the bureaucracy. The Office of Management and Budget and the White House Office have been particularly active in this regard and have provided the president with greater outreach into the administrative agencies. Nevertheless, a fundamental problem remains, as Peter Woll (1977:34) explains.

What the framers [of the Constitution] clearly failed to predict was the demise of local interest groups and the development of groups with a national orientation. The advantage of a republic because of the geographical dispersion of interests is no longer valid in the limitation of "faction." . . . The separation of powers system, by placing Congress in the position of an adversary of the President, motivates the legislature to place a significant portion of the administrative branch outside of the legal sphere of presidential control. In this manner, the separation of powers idea, instead of limiting governmental power, results in the relative independence of the administrative branch by displacing the most natural focal point of control. Because of the attachment between private clientele groups and public bureaucratic interest groups, the constitutional separation of powers often leads to an increase of "faction" in government.

Thus, there has been a tendency for administrative power to slip through the cracks in the scheme of the separation of powers. Although the nation looks to the president (and to presidential candidates) to manage the bureaucracy effectively, in truth the president's actual powers and influence over individual agencies will vary widely. Some agencies are much closer to Congress, some are relatively tightly controlled by the president, and some are almost wholly independent. Indeed, the Supreme Court once ruled that the head of the Federal Trade Commission "occupies no place in the executive department" (*Humphrey's Executor v. U.S.*, 1935:628).

This situation has been decried by many administrative theorists who would prefer to see all administrative operations except those of a judicial nature placed squarely under presidential authority. This ideal was put forward by Frank Goodnow in *Politics and Administration* as early as 1900. It has been echoed since by such bodies as the President's Committee on Administrative Management, which declared in 1937 that "any program to restore our constitutional ideal of a fully coordinated Executive Branch responsible to the President must bring within the reach of that responsible control all work done by these independent commissions which is not judicial in nature" (40-41). Yet, such administrative values notwithstanding, the political system as a whole seemed more inclined to favor Justice Brandeis's admonition that "The doctrine of the separation of powers was adopted by the Convention in 1787 not to promote efficiency but to preclude the exercise of arbitrary power. The purpose was not to avoid friction, but, by means of the inevitable friction incident to the distribution of the governmental powers among three departments, to save the people from autocracy" (*Myers v. U.S.*, 1926:293). The rise of the administrative state does do violence to the concept of the separation of powers, but by maintaining the separation of powers pertaining to its control, the nation is assured that no one branch of government will be able to use that administrative apparatus as a means of establishing its own autocratic dominance.

In addition, the ill-defined place of the bureaucracy under the Constitution often forces administrative agencies to seek support from a variety of sources, including Congress and its committees, the president and his aides, interest groups, and the general public. As Norton Long observes, the fragmented nature of power in the executive branch forces upon agencies ". . . a large share of responsibility for the public promotion of policy and even more in organizing the political basis for its survival and growth" (1949:259). As a result of this process, agencies often become quite representative of their constituencies, and, indeed, according to some observers the bureaucracy as a whole is more representative of the nation's population and organized interests than is the legislature (Krislov and Rosenbloom, 1981; Long, 1949:259; Davidson, 1967). Although some (Lowi, 1969) have opposed the shifting of representation from the legislature to the bureaucracy, others point out that it tends to tame the exercise of administrative power and often approximates the Madisonian ideal by pitting agency (faction) against agency (faction) (Woll, 1977; Nachmias and Rosenbloom, 1980).

Thus, the intermingling of legislative and executive power in federal public administration places great strains upon the traditional concept of separation of powers, and it tends to enhance administrative power. At the same time, however, it also tends to force administrative agencies to compete for support within the legislature, the executive branch, and the larger community, and in the process it often makes them representative of their constituencies. This situation is obviously highly complex, subtle, and constantly problematic. Further difficulty is added by the administrative exercise of judicial functions which has also created problems of control and a permanent sense of "crisis" (Freedman, 1978).

It has been maintained that the judicial activities of administrative agencies have a greater impact on the average citizen than the judicial activities of the courts themselves. Thus, Kenneth Davis (1975:7) writes

> The average person is much more directly and much more frequently affected by the administrative process than by the judicial process. The ordinary person probably regards the judicial process as somewhat remote from his own problems; a large portion of all people go through life without ever being a party to a lawsuit. But the administrative process affects nearly everyone in many ways nearly every day.

He goes on to point out that, among other elements of daily life, the judicial acitivities of administrative agencies affect the prices of utilities, those of various modes of transportation, the quality and safety of the foods and drugs the public consumes, and the nature of public broadcasting.

The exercise of judicial functions by bureaucratic agencies is an outgrowth of the administrative state. Yet, in a peculiar way, the intermingling of administrative and judicial functions predates the nation's widespread reliance on regulatory commissions. Peter Woll (1977:124) points out that "in the past the courts have exercised not only all judicial functions, but also what in modern terminology would be called administrative functions. For example, during the American colonial period and part of the nineteenth century the courts acted as rate-making bodies, setting tolls for public roads." The movement of such regulatory functions from the courts to administrative agencies has been part and parcel of the tendency for public bureaucracy to expand and to engulf an increasing number of aspects of public life. A main rationale for vesting what were once judicial functions in administrative agencies was the perceived advantage of such structures in terms of expertise, flexibility, and speed. Yet this aspect of the modification of the separation of powers, like the others, has not escaped serious criticism.

The combination of judicial and administrative functions in agency procedures has often been decried on the grounds that it promotes unfairness. James Freedman (1978:24) writes that

... the most dramatic departure that the administrative process has made from judicial norms has been in authorizing agencies to combine investigative, prosecuting, and adjudicatory functions in order to strengthen the coordinated development of regulatory policy. This means that an administrative agency has the opportunity to participate in each of the decisive stages of administrative lawmaking. It also means that an agency can act as investigator and prosecutor in issuing a complaint, and eventually as judge in deciding whether the allegations in the complaint have been proved at a hearing.

In short, a variety of biases can creep into the judicial functioning of administrative agencies. Politically, these have often reflected an interest in maintaining the power of established groups, such as industries ostensibly being regulated and dominant social groups.

Various efforts have been undertaken to control the exercise of judicial functions by administrative agencies. Foremost among these has been the enactment of the Administrative Procedure Act (1946), a development that is discussed in the next chapter. However, despite the act and related court decisions, the judicial functions of administrative agencies remain a source of constitutional difficulty.

Conclusion: Response to the Rise of the Administrative State

The comtemporary administrative state is highly problematic. Its development and growth seem almost inevitable, although its specific form varies with different political, economic, and social circumstances. Administrative agencies and public administrators possess considerable political power and influence. Administrative values differ from those of society generally. This is particularly true in nations with democratic political cultures. In the United States, the rise of the administrative state has placed great strains upon the scheme of the separation of powers. It has shifted representation away from elective officials and toward its own bureaus. As public bureaucracies and public administrators emerged as an independent force in the political system, and one so threatening to the power of elective officials and to democratic constitutionalism, it was inevitable that other major political power centers would respond.

To a large extent, the congressional response has already been discussed here and elsewhere (Nachmias and Rosenbloom, 1980). As Morris Fiorina (1977) and R. Douglas Arnold (1979) argue, members of Congress have sought to use bureaucratic agencies to promote their own incumbency. They have done so by vying for increasing shares of bureaucratic largess for their districts (pork-barrel projects) and by engaging their enlarged staffs in casework on behalf of constituents facing problems with administrative agencies. They have also increased specialization by subcommittees and have added more staff to assist in committee work. In addition, Congress has created new administrative units, such as the Congressional Budget Office and the Office of Technology Assessment, to assist it in coping with the expertise and power of the executive branch. It has also increased the size of older units, such as the General Accounting Office. Furthermore, Congress has become more reliant on the legislative veto as a means of checking agencies' use of delegated authority, and "sunset" provisions now appear more frequently in enabling legislation.

The net result of the legislative response to the rise of the administrative state is inherently debatable. Conventional political analysis holds that there is a harmony of interest between members of (sub)committees and the administrative agencies with which they deal. To the extent that this is true, legislative oversight of the administrative branch tends to be haphazard and pro forma in fashion. Members of Congress also tend to rely upon bureaucratic agencies for their continuing incumbency, as Fiorina and Arnold argue. Yet, the General Accounting Office and the Congressional Budget Office have had an impact on the legislature's ability to influence administrative agencies, and a new mood promoting a more adversial legislative stance toward the bureaucracy may be emerging (Orfield, 1975).

The presidential response has also been problematic and of questionable effectiveness. This too has been discussed at length elsewhere (Nachmias and Rosenbloom, 1980). Basically, the Executive Office of the President (EOP) was created in 1939 to provide the president with a few close aides to assist him in managing the large bureaucratic establishment that had developed during the New Deal. Eventually, however, the EOP itself grew to perhaps unmanageable proportions. It has become a miniaturized version of the larger executive branch bureaucracy and presents many of the same difficulties, including the devolution of political power and influence to the hands of unelected officials. As Thomas Cronin (1975:138) observes,

> The presidential establishment had become over the years a powerful inner sanctum of government isolated from the traditional checks and balances. Little-known, unelected, and unratified aides on occasion negotiate sensitive international commitments by means of executive agreements that are free from congressional oversight. With no semblance of public scrutiny other aides wield fiscal authority over billions of dollars. . . .

Nor it is clear that the EOP is satisfactorily controlled by the president, as Stephen Hess (1976:9) notes: "With the bureaucratizing of the presidency, it is hardly surprising that the White House fell heir to all the problems of a bureaucracy. . . ." Few would dispute Stephen Wayne's (1978:60) conclusion that "By the 1970s, [the EOP] had clearly become more than the president's personal office." However, equally clear, the development of the modern presidential establishment has not fully solved the problems of management presented by the rise of the administrative state.

> The bureaucracy, sometimes with Congress but often by itself, has frequently been able to resist and ignore Presidential commands. Whether the President is FDR or Richard M. Nixon, bureaucratic frustration of White House policies is a fact of life. Furthermore, the bureaucracy often carries out its own policies which are at times the exact opposite of White House directives. A classic case occurred during the India-Pakistan War in 1971 when the State Department supported India while the White House backed Pakistan (Woll and Jones, 1975:216–217).

The judiciary has also responded to the rise of the administrative state, but its response has gone largely unrecognized and misunderstood. Too often it has been considered within the narrow confines of traditional administrative law. Volumes have been devoted to the congressional and presidential reactions to the growth of bureaucracy, but little comprehensive and systematic analysis has been brought to bear on that of the judiciary. Ironically, however, the contemporary judicial response may be more effective than that of the other branches because it reaches deeper into the realm of public administration by requiring that public servants adhere to constitutional values and scrupulously avoid abridging the constitutional rights of the citizenry with whom they deal. The next chapter considers the nature of federal judicial power and the judiciary's early response to the rise of the administrative state. The remainder of the book is devoted to an analysis of its contemporary response to that phenomenon.

References

Arnold, R. Douglas, 1979. *Congress and the Bureaucracy*. New Haven, Conn.: Yale University Press.

Barker, Earnest, 1966. *The Development of Public Services in Western Europe, 1660–1930*. Hamden, Conn.: Archon Books.

Blau, Peter and Marshall Meyer, 1971. *Bureaucracy in Modern Society,* 2nd ed. New York: Random House.

Branti v. Finkel, 1980. 445 U.S. 506.

Buckley v. Valeo, 1976. 424 U.S. 1.

Cronin, Thomas, 1975. *The State of the Presidency.* Boston: Little, Brown.

Davidson, Roger, 1967. Congress and the executive: The race for representation. In A. DeGrazia (ed.), *Congress: The First Branch.* New York: Anchor.

Davis, Kenneth Culp, 1975. *Administrative Law and Government,* 2nd ed. St. Paul, Minn.: West Publishing.

Downs, Anthony, 1967. *Inside Bureaucracy.* Boston: Little, Brown.

Fiorina, Morris, 1977. *Congress: Keystone of the Washington Establishment.* New Haven, Conn.: Yale University Press.

Freedman, James, 1978. *Crisis and Legitimacy.* New York: Cambridge University Press.

Goodnow, Frank, 1900. *Politics and Administration.* New York: Macmillan.

Hartz, Louis, 1955. *The Liberal Tradition in America.* New York: Harcourt, Brace, and World.

Heady, Ferrel, 1966. *Public Administration: A Comparative Perspective.* Englewood Cliffs, N.J.: Prentice-Hall.

Hess, Stephen, 1976. *Organizing the Presidency.* Washington, D.C.: Brookings Institution.

Hummel, Ralph, 1977. *The Bureaucratic Experience.* New York: St. Martin's.

Humphrey's Executor v. United States, 1935. 295 U.S. 602.

Jacoby, Henry, 1973. *The Bureaucratization of the World.* Berkeley: University of California Press.

Kaufman, Herbert, 1976. *Are Government Organizations Immortal?* Washington, D.C.: Brookings Institution.

————, 1977. *Red Tape.* Washington, D.C.: Brookings Institute.

Kendall v. U.S., 1838. 12 Peters 524.

Krislov, Samuel and David H. Rosenbloom, 1981. *Representative Bureaucracy and the American Political System.* New York: Praeger.

Long, Norton, 1949. Power and administration. *Public Administration Review,* 9 (Autumn), 257–264.

Lowi, Theodore J., 1969. *The End of Liberalism.* New York: Norton.

McConnell, Grant, 1966. *Private Power and American Democracy.* New York: Knopf.

Myers v. U.S., 1926. 272 U.S. 52.

Nachmias, David and David H. Rosenbloom, 1980. *Bureaucratic Government, USA.* New York: St. Martin's.

Orfield, Gary, 1975. *Congressional Power.* New York: Harcourt, Brace, Jovanovich.

Parkinson, C. Northcote, 1957. *Parkinson's Law.* Boston: Houghton, Mifflin.

Peter, Lawrence and Raymond Hull, 1969. *The Peter Principle.* New York: William Morrow, 1969.

Peters, B. Guy, 1978. *The Politics of Bureaucracy.* New York: Longman.

Rosenberg, Hans, 1958. *Bureaucracy, Aristocracy, and Autocracy.* Boston: Beacon Press.

Rosenbloom, David H. and Frank Bryan, 1981. The size of state bureacracies. *State and Local Government Review, 13* (September), 115-123.

Rossiter, Clinton, ed., 1961. *The Federalist Papers.* New York: Mentor.

Rourke, Francis, ed., 1978. *Bureaucratic Power in National Politics.* Boston: Little, Brown.

Shafritz, Jay, Albert Hyde, and David H. Rosenbloom, 1981. *Personnel Management in Government,* 2nd ed. New York: Marcel Dekker.

Storing, Herbert, 1964. Political parties and the bureaucracy. In Robert A. Goldwin (ed.), *Political Parties, USA.* Chicago: Rand, McNally.

U.S. Congress, 1973. Senate Committee on Government Operations, Subcommittee on Intergovernmental Relations, Confidence and Concern: Citizens view American government. 93rd Congress, 1st Sess. (Dec. 3).

U.S. Government Organization Manual, 1973. Washington, D.C.: U.S. Government Printing Office.

U.S. President's Committee on Administrative Management, 1937. *Report.* Washington, D.C.: U.S. Government Printing Office.

Wade, L. and R. Curry, 1970. *A Logic of Public Policy.* Belmont, Calif.: Wadsworth.

Warwick, Donald, 1975. *A Theory of Public Bureaucracy.* Cambridge, Mass.: Harvard University Press.

Wayne, Stephen, 1978. *The Legislative Presidency.* New York: Harper and Row.

Weber, Max (1922), 1958. *From Max Weber: Essays in Sociology.* Translated and edited by H. H. Gerth and C. W. Mills. New York: Oxford University Press.

Wilson, James Q., 1975. The rise of the administrative state. *The Public Interest* 41 (Fall), 77–103.

Woll, Peter, 1977. *American Bureaucracy,* 2nd ed. New York: W. W. Norton.

Woll, Peter and Rochelle Jones, 1975. Bureaucratic defense in depth. In Ronald Pynn (ed.), *Watergate and the American Political Process.* New York: Praeger.

2
The Federal Judiciary and the Administrative State

The rise of the contemporary American administrative state altered the distribution of political power within the polity. The balance of power between elective officials and nonelective administrators changed. Extreme pressures were placed on the separation of powers and on the system of checks and balances as the executive branch became increasingly involved in policy making and exercising authority over the society. These developments were especially threatening to the position of the federal courts as a coequal branch of government. The other branches have far more direct constitutional authority to try to control public administrators and to make public bureaucracy a tool that works their will. Congress, for instance, is potentially very powerful according to constitutional theory because it has the authority to create agencies, positions, and missions, and to allocate funds for public administration. The president is somewhat weaker in this regard, but certainly any constitutional definition of the *executive power* would include authority to direct the actions of most federal administrators. The courts, however, seemed to have very little constitutional leverage concerning public bureaucracy. Indeed, the rise of the administrative state seemed to confirm Alexander Hamilton's view that judicial power was inherently limited and relatively weak:

> The judiciary . . . has no influence over either the sword or the purse; no direction either of the strength or of the wealth of the society, and can take no active resolution whatever. It may truly be said to have neither FORCE nor WILL but merely judgment; and must ultimately depend upon the aid of the executive arm even for the efficacy of its judgments (*Federalist 78*; Rossiter, 1961:465).

Thus, the rise of the administrative state confronted the judiciary with a serious dilemma. On the one hand, it could attempt to maintain its place in

33

the separation of powers by resisting the growth of administrative power. This would prevent the emergence in government of a new power center not readily amenable to judicial control. However, such a course was fraught with difficulty. It appeared to controvert historical and political development. It also proved politically untenable when the judiciary, and the Supreme Court in particular, seemed to be invoking hoary constitutional doctrines that frustrated the nation's recovery from the economic depression of the 1930s. On the other hand, accepting the agglomeration of power in the hands of public bureaucrats seemed certain to weaken the role of the judiciary in the political system. When the full-fledged administrative state materialized in the 1930s, it was unthinkable that the judiciary would or could play a substantial role in directing its activities. Yet, in the end, this is what occurred. The judiciary developed a means of protecting its status as a coequal branch of government by forcing the administrative state to respond to its direction and values. In the process, however, the role of the judiciary in the society underwent politically controversial change that threatens its position in another way.

Judicial Power

In order to understand the federal judiciary's response to the rise of the administrative state, it is necessary to consider the nature of judicial power and the ways in which it can be brought to bear upon public administrators. At the outset, it must be observed that this power has several paradoxical qualities. The federal judiciary is exceedingly powerful—so powerful in fact that some have come to fear "judicial supremacy" or "jurocracy," that is, rule by judges (Horowitz, 1977; Cramton, 1976; Berger, 1977). But it is also highly vulnerable to regulation by the other branches of government. Accordingly, the courts have historically tried to strike a balance between the full application of their powers and the exercise of restraint. Within this overall political framework, several aspects of judicial power stand out.

First, as Alexander Hamilton pointed out, judicial power is largely passive. The courts depend upon individuals or government agencies to bring cases before them. They cannot initiate cases and they do not give advisory opinions. Ultimately, therefore, their dockets are controlled by others, although the courts do have some freedom to choose among issues once cases are filed.

Similarly, judicial power is passive in terms of enforcement. The courts are dependent upon others for the execution of their decrees. Although rates of compliance may be high, ultimately the courts must rely upon other branches of government, primarily the executive, for implementation of their judgments. This is true even where the contempt power is invoked. As C. Herman Pritchett observed, "the judiciary must look to the executive and Congress for help in case of any real resistance to its orders. Whether apocryphal or not, Andrew Jackson's comment, 'John Marshall has made his decision, now let him enforce it,' reveals the hollowness of the Supreme Court's authority unless it is sustained by the support of its governmental colleagues and the backing of public opinion" (1977:83). The problem of enforcement is complicated by the Supreme Court's and the appellate courts' general reliance upon the district courts for effectuation of their decisions. Despite the hierarchical nature of the judiciary, district court judges possess considerable independence and either through misunderstanding or design they sometimes frustrate the will of their appellate colleagues.

Second, the federal judiciary is highly vulnerable to regulation by legislative enactment. Article III of the Constitution reads,

The judical Power of the United States, shall be vested in one supreme Court, and in such inferior Courts as the Congress may from time to time ordain and establish. The Judges, both of the supreme and inferior Courts, shall hold their Offices during good Behavior, and shall, at stated Times, receive for their Services, a Compensation, which shall not be diminished during their Continuance in Office.

. . . The judicial Power shall extend to all Cases, in Law and Equity, arising under this Constitution, the Laws of the United States, and Treaties made, or which shall be made, under their Authority;—to all Cases affecting Ambassadors, other public Ministers and Consuls;—to all Cases of admiralty and maritime Jurisdiction;—to Controversies to which the United States shall be a party;—to Controversies between two or more States. . . .

In all Cases affecting Ambassadors, other public Ministers and Consuls, and those in which a State shall be a Party, the supreme Court shall have original Jurisdiction. In all other Cases before mentioned, the supreme Court shall have appellate Jurisdiction, both as to Law and Fact, with such Exceptions, and under such Regulations as the Congress shall make.

Although Article III conveys great power to the judiciary, making it a separate, independent, and coequal constitutional branch of the government, it also makes the courts highly dependent upon Congress for their operation. There are several ways in which this is the case. One is that, with the exception of the Supreme Court, the entire court structure depends on congressional enactment. Presently that structure is comprised of a hierarchy reaching from U.S. magistrates through district courts, through courts of appeals, to the Supreme Court. There are also a number of specialized courts, such as the Court of Claims and the Court of Customs and Patent Appeals. But this structure has no particular constitutional stature and can be changed by the legislature. For instance, courts of appeals were not created until the 1890s, and the number of inferior courts has changed over time. In recent years, there has been some debate concerning the possibility of establishing a national court of appeals, which would be interposed between the Supreme Court and the 12 courts of appeals as a means of reducing the workload, and perhaps overall power, of the Supreme Court (Black, 1974).

Adjusting the number of courts and the relationships among them has substantial ramifications on the power of the judiciary and on its role in the political system. If there were too few courts, individuals seeking to assert their rights would have to turn to other forums or be prepared to wait very long periods before possibly achieving their objectives through litigation. A greater number of courts, on the other hand, encourages litigation and tends to involve the judiciary in a wider variety of political issues. The absence of appeals courts would drastically increase the workload of the Supreme Court, perhaps to the point at which it would have to change its mode of operation in order to keep up with its dockets.

Similarly, the number of judges and justices is fixed by law. Members of the judiciary cannot be removed from office except through impeachment, but positions can be reduced when vacancies occur. The number of judges can also be increased through legislation. Thus, Congress has the potential to regulate indirectly much of the workload of the federal court system—and such regulation would inevitably affect judicial roles, operations, and general quality of performance. Moreover, since the number of judges and justices can be increased, Congress and the president can potentially pack the federal judiciary with judges who are thought to support certain programs or policies. This, indeed, was exactly what President Franklin D. Roosevelt proposed with regard to the Supreme Court during 1937, after it declared a series of New Deal statutes to be unconstitutional. Such a step would not alter the power of the Court, but it could be used to change its political balance and thereby erode its political independence and functions in the system of checks and balances. Although Roosevelt's scheme was never enacted into law, it seems to have prompted one member of the Supreme Court, Owen Roberts, to switch his position on economic issues, which turned a bloc of four dissenters into a majority of five justices who were supportive of federal intervention in the economy (Pritchett, 1977:40).

Adjusting the number of justices on the Supreme Court is but one means of checking its activities. Another is to attempt to limit its jurisdiction. Unlike the federal courts generally, Article III provides the Supreme Court with very limited original jurisdiction and appears to allow Congress to regulate stringently its appellate jurisdiction. There is some dispute among legal scholars as to whether this would enable Congress to take away the Court's appellate jurisdiction in specific types of cases, such as those arising under the equal protection clause of the Fourteenth Amendment, or those dealing with abortion.

Nevertheless, over the years the mere existence of the possibility of amending the Court's jurisdiction in this way has prompted the introduction of several bills in Congress. In one such instance, *Ex Parte McCardle* (1869), the Supreme Court upheld the constitutionality of a congressional enactment depriving it of appellate jurisdiction after it had actually heard a case, but before rendering its decision. As part of a general legislative concern with the activities of the federal judiciary, and especially the Supreme Court, in the 1970s several bills were introduced in Congress to limit the Court's appellate jurisdiction in cases dealing with civil rights, school prayers, and abortion.

In addition, Congress controls the budget and staffing of the federal judiciary. Since the 1930s, the judicial branch has included a number of administrative organs, such as the Administrative Office of the United States Courts (1939) and the Federal Judicial Center (1967), to aid it in its administrative functions and research. In 1971, further assistance was authorized in the form of circuit court executives who manage many of the administrative aspects of the appeals courts. There is no doubt that these administrative arrangements have been valuable to the courts, and their abolition would be a severe sanction upon the judiciary. Similarly, many members of the federal judiciary have become dependent upon clerks for assistance in administrative matters, research, and opinion writing. Again, however, clerks have no constitutional stature and presumably can be eliminated through a reduction of the judiciary's budget.

Threats of this nature against the judiciary do not have to materialize in order for the courts to appreciate the efficacy of not provoking the legislature. Members of the judiciary understand their vulnerability to congressional sanction and overwhelmingly do not want to see the judicial branch damaged in an institutional sense. Consequently, from a historical perspective the courts have generally avoided long confrontations with the legislative branch. Rather, for the most part they have sought to find satisfactory compromises between the assertion of their powers and a desire to allow Congress to pursue the polices of its choosing.

It is not astonishing that the Founding Fathers considered the judiciary to be "beyond comparison the weakest" branch of the national government (*Federalist 78*; Rossiter, 1961:465). Indeed, given its passive nature and its vulnerability to checks by the legislature, it is more surprising that the federal judiciary ever emerged as a powerful and coequal branch of government at all. This is especially true as its constitutional powers are so limited. However, these powers were augmented almost at the outset by the Supreme Court itself under the chief justiceship of John Marshall (1803-1835). Yet, the fact that the Supreme Court had to go far beyond the actual wording of the Constitution in order to secure the judiciary's greatest powers also contributes to the courts' vulnerability. Returning to the thoughts of Hamilton, it has forced the judiciary to develop a high degree of legitimacy for its "mere judgment," and this, too, has served as an important check on the exercise of its powers.

A third aspect of judicial power, therefore, is that to a great extent it rests not directly on the language of the Constitution, but rather on decisions of the judiciary itself. It has not created its powers by fiat, but rather through the explication of constitutional law that reaches far beyond the specific words of the document itself. The process has been twofold. On the one hand, in order to exist, the powers had to be declared; on the other, the political system had to accept their legitimacy. It is in this context that Chief Justice John Marshall was so outstanding.

In some ways John Marshall was an unlikely candidate to augment drastically the development of judicial power. He was the fourth chief justice, and took over a court lacking in national prestige. He was appointed by President John Adams and assumed office after the nation's political mood had become decidedly anti-Federalist. His entire formal legal education has been described as consisting ". . . of a six-week lecture course given by George Wythe at William & Mary College in 1780, during which, if Marshall's notebook may be trusted, he devoted at least as much thought to the pursuit of his future wife, Polly Ambler (whose name was scrawled at prominent places throughout his law notes), as to the offerings of Mr. Wythe" (White, 1976:11). However, Marshall also appears to have had one of the keenest intellects among those in public life at a time when the nation's political leadership was characterized by much brilliance. In fact, Marshall's syllogistic reasoning was so powerful that Thomas Jefferson once noted that, "When conversing with Marshall, I never admit anything. So sure as you admit any position to be good, not matter how remote from the conclusion he seeks to establish, you are gone" (White, 1976:12).

It was precisely through reasoning of this type that Marshall was able to win agreement on the legitimacy and near inevitability of his opinions strengthening the powers of the federal courts. The leading example, of course, is *Marbury v. Madison* (1803) in which the Supreme Court, per opinion of Marshall, established its power to declare acts of Congress to be unconstitutional and therefore legally unenforceable. This remains the federal judiciary's greatest power, and is a peculiar one in that it enables the courts to determine what the polity can accomplish short of constitutional amendment. Thus, judicial review creates a measure of judicial supremacy—supremacy for a branch of government that is not elected, not intended to be representative, and somewhat insulated from politics through the secure tenure of its members. Moreover, it is a power that the Founding Fathers declined to provide explicitly to the courts. In fact, although Hamilton favored this power (*Federalist 78*; Rossiter, 1961), insofar as the Constitutional Convention considered it to be desirable, they discussed vesting it in a Council of Revision, which would include judicial and nonjudicial members (Solberg, 1958:78,97–101). Yet, Marshall announced the courts' power of judicial review of congressional enactments as though it were perfectly self-evident and incontrovertable:

It is emphatically the province and duty of the judicial department to say what the law is. Those who apply the rule to particular cases, must of necessity expound and interpret that rule. If two laws conflict with each other, the courts must decide on the operation of each.

So if a law be in opposition to the constitution; if both the law and the constitution apply to a particular case, so that the court must either decide that case conformably to the law, disregarding the constitution; or conformably to the constitution, disregarding the law; the court must determine which of these conflicting rules govern the case. This is the very essence of judicial duty.

If, then, the courts are to regard the constitution, and the constitution is superior to any ordinary act of the legislature, the constitution, and not such ordinary act, must govern the case to which they both apply (*Marbury v. Madison*, 1803:177).

The Marshall Court not only asserted its power of judicial review with regard to the acts of the national legislature, it also clearly asserted that power over the actions of the state governments. Thus, in *McCulloch v. Maryland* (1819) the Court struck down the constitutionality of a Maryland law taxing the politically unpopular, but nationally chartered, Bank of the United States. In the course of his decision, Marshall wrote: "If any proposition could command the universal assent of mankind, we might expect it would be this: that the government of the Union, though limited in its powers, is supreme within its sphere of action." As a result, the states lacked power "to retard, impede, burden, or in any manner control, the operations of the constitutional laws enacted by congress" (McCulloch v. Maryland, 1819:436). However, it was the Supreme Court's interpretation of the scope of national powers that was to serve as a limit on the constitutionality of state activities having such an effect.

Cohens v. Virginia (1821) presented a more explicit justification for federal review of state activities. There, Marshall had the occasion to reason that

The States are constituent parts of the United States. They are members of one great empire—for some purposes sovereign, for some purposes subordinate.

In a government so constituted, is it unreasonable that the judicial power should be competent to give efficacy to the constitutional laws of the legislature? That department can decide on the validity of the constitution or law of a State, if it be repugnant to the constitution or to a law of the United States. Is it unreasonable that it should also be empowered to decide on the judgment of a state tribunal enforcing such unconstitutional law? Is it so very unreasonable as to furnish a justification for controlling the words of the constitution?

We think it is not. We think that in a government acknowledgedly supreme, with respect to objects of vital interest to the nation, there is nothing inconsistent with sound reason, nothing incompatible with the nature of government, in making all its departments supreme, so far as respects those objects, and so far as is necessary to their attainment. The exercise of the appellate power over those judgments of the state tribunals which may contravene the constitution or laws of the United States, is, we believe, essential to the attainment of those objects (*Cohens v. Virginia*, 1821:412-414).

These and related Supreme Court decisions defined the scope of the judicial power conveyed by Article III of the Constitution. In truth, however, the Marshall Court expanded those powers well beyond the explicit words of that document, and despite the force of Marshall's reasoning his conclusions were not universally accepted as either inevitable or appropriate (White, 1976:Chapter 1). Given the judiciary's vulnerability to regulation by the legislature and the peculiar origin of its most far-reaching powers, the federal courts have historically been much concerned with generating a sense of legitimacy for their decisions.

The "mere judgment" which Hamilton attributed to the federal judiciary can be a very potent power when perceived as correct and legitimate by the political community. Otherwise, such judgments can be hollow indicators of the judiciary's fundamental weaknesses. Judicial opinions can fail to convey a sense of legitimacy for the courts' actions under a variety of circumstances. Their reasoning can be specious, they can reflect ideological biases that are inappropriate to the prevailing political climate, or they can appear to be acts of judicial aggrandizement by which the courts are encroaching on the legitimate spheres of the other branches of government or the states. In consequence, historically, the federal judiciary has sought to exercise a good measure of restraint in applying its powers. In the main, such restraint has taken two related forms. One has been a marked reluctance of the courts to challenge the will of a national majority *as represented in Congress*, and the other has been the self-imposition of legal doctrines limiting the application of judicial power.

The most acute and controversial assertion of judicial power occurs when the federal courts declare federal statutes to be unconstitutional. The exercise of federal judicial review over the states is less problematic because it seems to be a necessary feature of federalism under the U.S. system and because in overruling the actions of a state government the federal courts are not directly challenging the ostensible will of a national majority. Moreover, judicial review of acts of Congress is exceptionally antimajoritarian when the statute in question was passed by a Congress that is still in office, that is, prior to an election which could change the composition of its membership. Not surprisingly, in view of the nature of judicial power, therefore, there have been long periods in U.S. history when very few federal laws were declared unconstitutional. Only in about half the instances have such declarations occurred with regard to statutes that are less than four years old (Dahl, 1972:202). For instance, between 1789 and 1857 only two federal laws were declared unconstitutional. One was a section of the Judiciary Act of 1789 in *Marbury v. Madison* and the other was in *Dred Scott v. Sandford* (1857) in which the Missouri Compromise of 1820 was struck down and Congress was held to be without power to prohibit slavery in the territories of the United States. In another period, 1940-1964, only nine federal laws were declared unconstitutional. By comparison, during the latter period the federal courts voided 273 acts and ordinances of state and local governments (Ross, 1972:43).

Indeed, only in the period from 1890-1936 did the Supreme Court engage in a protracted battle against what appeared to a national majority. The fundamental issue at stake was "economic liberalism," and the Court stood firmly on the side of entrenched economic power in declaring the national government without power to regulate such aspects of the economy as child labor and workers' compensation. During this period, some 46 federal laws were declared unconstitutional. This vigorous use of judicial review provoked a long-term controversy that reached crisis proportions during the New Deal, when the Supreme Court declared 12 federal statutes unconstitutional (Dahl, 1972:202).

The decade of the 1930s was a period of crisis in the use of judicial review that demonstrated the limitations of the judiciary's powers vis-à-vis the other branches of the federal government. In a sense, the Court was given the choice of supporting New Deal legislation or being severely weakened in an institutional sense by the court-packing plan. Yet, historically, the outcome of this contest was far from unique. Robert Dahl observes that

> ... the Court rarely wins battles with the president and Congress on matters of major policy, particularly if successive presidents and Congresses continue to support the policy the Court has called unconstitutional. The Court wins skirmishes; in a long war it may win a battle; it does not win continuing wars with Congress. On this point the evidence is overwhelming. ...
>
> Where the Court confronts the major policies of a current president and Congress, it nearly always loses. In about two-thirds of the cases involving major policies of current lawmaking majorities, the Court's decision has, in effect, been reversed by congressional action—often simply by rewriting the law (Dahl, 1972:201-202).

The exercise of judicial restraint, therefore, is not simply a policy that can be considered appropriate in terms of democratic values, it may be a functional requirement through which the courts can maintain their legitimacy and institutional strengths.

The second form of restraint is partially a means of implementing the first. In order to avoid exercising judicial review in highly controversial areas, the courts have developed doctrines limiting their ability to hear and decide cases. These doctrines involve considerations of jurisdiction and justiciability, that is, the authority of the judiciary to hear the dispute and the matter of whether the dispute is suitable for judicial resolution. There are few, if any, hard and fast rules here, but in general such considerations enable the courts to generate a sense of legitimacy for their actions within the political community when they choose *not* to decide the constitutional merits of a controversial issue. Among the doctrines are the following.

1. Standing. In order for a federal court to have jurisdiction over a dispute, there must be an actual case or controversy brought before it. Thus, someone with standing to sue must file the case before the court. In terms of public law, at the very least, standing requires that one be able to show that the government perpetrated a particular injury upon him or her, or upon a class that the person bringing the case purports to represent. As is discussed in Chapter 6, the scope, uniqueness, and directness of the injury are considerations that may be raised in deciding whether the litigant possesses standing. Over the years, the courts have invoked the concept of standing in order to avoid rendering constitutional decisions on highly controversial matters.

2. Political questions. Even if one has standing to bring a case, the judiciary may avoid ruling on the issues raised on the grounds that they are essentially political questions that would be more appropriately resolved by the elected, that is, representative, branches of government. For example, in the past the political question doctrine was used to keep the federal judiciary out of the issue of legislative apportionment (*Colegrove v. Green*, 1946).

3. Mootness. In this instance, the courts may find that although a genuine case or controversy once existed, it has subsequently been dissipated through the course of events, such as the death of a party or resolution in another fashion. In such an event, a judicial decision could no longer affect the status or relationships of the parties in the case, and, therefore, the concept of judicial restraint holds that there is no need for a court to address the merits of the dispute. For example, in one of the more recent instances of mootness, the Supreme Court refused to reach the merits of an affirmative action scheme at a state law school on the grounds that the student bringing the suit was likely to graduate regardless of the Court's ruling (*DeFunis v. Odegaard*, 1974). Mootness was employed in this instance at a time when affirmative action was extremely controversial and while the nation appeared to be awaiting a definitive ruling from the Court on its constitutionality. Apparently, however, the Court was simply unwilling to provide one.

4. Ripeness. Whereas mootness suggests that the case has already been resolved, ripeness presents a situation in which the dispute is not yet ready for resolution in the judicial forum. In such instances, a genuine case or controversy presenting important legal or constitutional issues may be in the offing once a statute is enforced, but for one reason or another the courts may be so skeptical of the likelihood of enforcement that they are unwilling to address the legal issues presented. For instance, the concept of ripeness was discussed in the context of a state statute that prohibited the *use* of birth control devices. Some members of the Supreme Court reasoned that since the statute had not been enforced and appeared unenforceable without massive violations of the Fourth Amendment, the Court had no cause to consider whether the law as an unconstitutional abridgment of individuals' liberty (*Poe v. Ullman*, 1961).

The courts not only exercise judicial restraint through considerations of jurisdiction and justiciability, they also employ a kind of restraint when actually deciding the merits of cases.

1. Precedent. Reliance upon past precedent can constitute a form of judicial restraint. The deference accorded earlier decisions serves to promote the judiciary's legitimacy by making it appear that its members are bound by the rule of law and cannot simply make policy based upon their own ideological proclivities. Sometimes reliance on precedent is extreme to the point that it can be tantamount to the ". . . imprisonment of reason, . . ." as Justice Frankfurter once remarked (*U.S. v. International Boxing Club*, 1955:249). For instance, in a 1922 case the Supreme Court ruled that professional baseball was not a subject of interstate commerce and therefore not regulated by federal antitrust statutes (*Federal Baseball Club of Baltimore v. National League*). It reaffirmed this ruling in 1953 (*Toolson v. N.Y. Yankees*) and in 1972 (*Flood v. Kuhn*). In the interim, however, the Court ruled that boxing, football, and other professional sports were covered by the antitrust statutes (*U.S. v. International Boxing Club*, 1955; *Radovich v. National Foodball League*, 1957). This occurred despite Justice Frankfurter's dissenting admonition that "it would baffle the subtlest ingenuity to find a single differentiating factor between other sporting exhibitions, . . . and baseball" insofar as the relevant statutes were concerned (*U.S. v. International Boxing Club*, 1955:248). However, a majority of the Court in these cases argued that even though by more contemporary standards baseball would be interstate commerce, precedent should be relied upon until such time as Congress sought to abolish the special status for baseball through appropriate legislation.

Yet the judiciary's claim to rely upon precedent can sometimes be misleading. The simple fact of the matter is that precedents are often unclear or contradictory. Past decisions generally leave ample room for reinterpretation under present circumstances. Moreover, where a majority of the Supreme Court considers a past decision to be mistaken, it has shown a willingness to abandon it in short order. Thus, in 1940 the Court upheld the constitutionality of a require-ment that public school pupils salute the flag (*Minersville School District v. Gobitis*), but in 1943 it held a similar requirement elsewhere to be in violation of the First and Fourteenth Amendments (*West Virginia Board of Education v. Barnett*).

2. Statutory construction. The judiciary also employs a kind of restraint in construing statutes in the way most favorable to their constitutionality. In general, the judiciary works under the presumption that statutes are constitu-tional, and it rarely reaches out in a deliberate effort to read the law in question in such a fashion so as to find it unconstitutional.

3. Narrow opinions. Finally, the judiciary often exercises restraint by rendering the narrowest opinions possible, rather than by articulating compre-hensive constitutional doctrines in any given case. In this sense, judicial decision making is highly incremental, tied to the facts and circumstances actually before the court, and designed to resolve the particular dispute under litigation. As Alexander Bickel observed,

> Now, to say that any first case is always a poor one in which to pronounce new principles is no doubt an overgeneralization. And yet it is not far wrong. A sound judicial instinct will generally favor deflecting the prob-lem in one or more initial cases, for there is much to be gained from letting it simmer, so that a mounting number of incidents exemplifying it may have a cumulative effect on the judicial mind as well as on public and professional opinion. Moreover, an initial series of inconclusive disposi-tions will often provoke the Justices to reflect out loud, as it were, about approaches to an enduring solution, without as yet assuming responsibility for imposing one (Bickel, 1962:176).

A classic example of the latter tendency occurred in the 1970s in a series of inconclusive and contradictory decisions dealing with the constitutionality of affirmative action quotas (*DeFunis v. Odegaard*, 1974; *Regents v. Bakke*, 1978; *Kaiser v. Weber*, 1979; *Fullilove v. Klutznick*, 1980).

Despite the general judicial imposition of self-restraint, however, the courts cannot always avoid the obvious instances of policy making. *The Law* is hardly singular; rather, it is vague and subject to ever-changing interpretation. This is particularly true of the Constitution. Although its general principles may be constant, its words come from another era and its authors could not have fore-seen the kind of issues that now come before the judiciary. The document is ambiguous in its application; it is too general and too vague to answer all questions. Indeed, judges and justices frequently disagree on its meaning and requirements. Controversial constitutional issues are not resolved by consensus, but rather by divided courts. In the end, constitutional law is what a majority on the Supreme Court says it is (see *Owen v. City of Independence*, 1980:669). Some justices are candid about this. Chief Justice Warren, for instance, once stated that "We have no constituency. We serve no majority. We serve no minority. We serve only the public interest as we see it, guided only by the Constitution and *our own consciences*" [emphasis added] (Simon, 1973:2). In essence, the same idea was put forward more elaborately by Justice Cardozo.

> ... There is in each of us a stream of tendency, whether you choose to call it a philosophy or not, which gives coherence and direction to thought and action. Judges cannot escape that current any more than other mortals. All their lives, forces which they do not recognize and cannot name, have been tugging at them—inherited instincts, traditional beliefs, acquired convictions; and the resultant is an outlook on life, a conception of social needs, a sense in James's phrase of "the total push and pressure of the cosmos," which, when reasons are nicely balanced, must determine where choices shall fall. In this mental background every problem finds its setting. We may try to see things as objectively as we please. None the less, we can never see them with any eyes except our own ... (Murphy and Pritchett, 1961:27).

Similarly, Justice Frankfurter, who was among the most forceful proponents of strict judicial self-restraint, also admitted the inadequacy of legal principles in resolving all cases: "The core of the difficulty is that there is hardly a question of any real difficulty before the Court that does not entail more than one so-called principle" (Murphy and Pritchett, 1961:32). For him, the agony of a judge's duty was deciding among conflicting principles, contradictory truths. Although the law could be a guide, the resolution ultimately belongs to the courts, and different judges come to different conclusions.

The constitutional law of the United States abounds with policy judgments handed down by the federal judiciary. These may be couched in legal terminology and may be rationalized as inherent in the Constitution itself. But the stark reality is that the federal judiciary does use its power of judicial review to make policy in a fashion that is not always bounded by the words of the Constitution, statutes, or past precedents. Raoul Berger has been among the most forceful recent critics of this aspect of judicial power.

> The historical records all but incontrovertibly establish that the framers of the Fourteenth Amendment excluded both suffrage and segregation from its reach; they confined it to protection of carefully enumerated rights against State discrimination, deliberately withholding federal power to supply those rights where they were not granted by the State to anybody, white or black. ...

Given the clarity of the framers' intention, it is on settled principles as good as written into the text. To "interpret" the Amendment in diametrical opposition to that intention is to rewrite the Constitution. Whence does the [Supreme] Court derive authority to revise the Constitution? . . . The Court, it is safe to say, has flouted the will of the framers and substituted an interpretation in flat contradiction of the original design: to leave suffrage, segregation, and other matters to State governance. . . . When Chief Justice Warren asserted that "we cannot turn back the clock to 1868," he in fact rejected the framers' intention as irrelevant. On that premise the entire Constitution merely has such relevance as the Court chooses to give it, and the Court is truly a "continuing constitutional convention," constantly engaged in revising the Constitution, a role clearly withheld from the Court. Such conduct impels one to conclude that the Justices are become a law unto themselves (Berger, 1977:407-408).

Berger's book, *Government by Judiciary,* is largely a reaction to the vast expansion of civil rights and civil liberties by the Warren Court (1953-1969). But while the Warren era was outstanding in its extremity, it was not unique. Indeed, Louis B. Boudin published a two-volume work by the same title in 1932, and former Supreme Court Justice Robert H. Jackson's 1941 book, *The Struggle for Judicial Supremacy* included a chapter on "government by lawsuit."

Judicial policy making within the context of great concern for judicial restraint is the preeminent paradox of the judicial process in the United States. In Robert Dahl's words,

If the Court were assumed to be a "political" institution, no particular problems would arise, for it would be taken for granted that the members of the Court would resolve questions of fact and value by introducing assumptions derived from their own predispositions or those of influential clienteles or constituents. However, since much of the legitimacy of the Court's decisions rests upon the belief that it is not a political institution but exclusively a legal one, to accept the Court as a political institution would solve one set of problems at the price of creating another (Dahl, 1972:201).

The judiciary cannot for any very long period of time either avoid the exercise of self-restraint without losing legitimacy or avoid policy making without abdicating its fundamental powers and historical role. Consequently, in an institutional sense, the judiciary is perplexed by the constant need to strike an acceptable balance between the two. The aphorism that the "courts follow the election returns" is appropriate in this context. The judiciary cannot stray too far from prevailing political opinion without exposing its vulnerabilities to regulation by the legislative branch. Nor, however, can it simply reflect the will of a majority at any one time; the constitutional scheme includes protections for minorities, and these may be effectuated best by a branch of government having secure tenure, being somewhat insulated from politics, and being well versed in the nature of the constitutional scheme. Perhaps this judicial dilemma was most succinctly captured by Bickel: "The [Supreme] Court is a leader of opinion, not a mere register of it, but it must lead opinion, not merely impose its own; and— the short of it is—it labors under the obligation to succeed" (1962:239).

But there is no set formula for success. The performance of the judiciary depends upon the nature of the controversies brought before it and the legal and political skills of its members. The tension between judicial self-restraint and the exercise of judicial powers is ever present. Ignoring either of these aspects of the judicial process is a formula for failure, but integrating or balancing them is always elusive. It is important to bear these complexities in mind. Denouncing judicial review as antimajoritarian or undemocratic misses a crucial point. The U.S. Constitution itself contains some antimajoritarian features. Checks and balances exist not only with regard to the three branches of government, and between the national government and the states, but also between the government and the people. Thus, the system of staggered and fixed terms of office for members of the House of Representatives, senators, and the president was established to prevent a wave of popular political passion from sweeping the government clean. Rather, the government was designed to respond to longer-term popular demands. It takes six years to change the entire membership of the Senate; and, when coupled with the need for extraordinary majorities in matters of constitutional amendment and treaties, this feature could have the impact of enabling a relatively small minority to postpone action by a majority for that period of time. The electoral college was similarly created as a check upon the electorate at large. In addition, the judicial branch was intended to be relatively unresponsive to majoritarian impulses and to provide protection to minority interests. These checks upon the majority were created in part because the Founding Fathers were a minority—a propertied minority, acutely aware of their position of economic advantage (Beard, 1913). But the constitutional system they established was intended to protect political and social minorities as well as economic minorities.

Of all the governmental branches, therefore, the judiciary is most directly caught in the tension between majority rule and minority rights. Following the former is well within the spirit of the Constitution; but protecting the latter may be equally so. What, then, is the proper mix between judicial restraint and judicial review? There is obviously no single answer, but certainly C. Herman Pritchett's response is of great utility:

. . . the distinction between judicial self-restraint and judicial avoidance of controversy may be a subtle one, but it is the difference between a sound and stultifying principle of judicial review. The Supreme Court *should* reach constitutional questions reluctantly. It *should* be chary of disagreeing with the legislatures or executives, whether national or state. But its primary obligation is not to avoid controversy. Its primary obligation is to bring all the judgment its members possess and the best wisdom that the times afford, to the interpretation of the basic rules propounded by our Constitution for the direction of a free society. To be sure, the Court cannot achieve certainty. It constitutional interpretations are "guesses," and it must be respectful of the guesses of other authoritative participants in the political process. But the Supreme Court is in a most advantageous position for making informed guesses. It has leisure to take thought. Its work is characterized by an absence of pressure; it has sharply defined questions to answer, a continual awareness of its responsibility to the universal constituency of reason and justice. The Supreme Court has an obligation to be humble, but not to the point of denying the nation the guidance on basic democratic problems which its unique situation equips it to provide . . . (Murphy and Pritchett, 1961:693).

Judicial Review and Public Administration

The arguments for judicial restraint are complex. At their root, however, is the notion that judicial review is undemocratic and therefore must be used sparingly. This line of thought is strongest when applied in the context of judicial review of elective officials, either federal or state. But what is its efficacy when judicial review is being used against unelected public officials, namely public administrators? Should the judiciary be reluctant to apply its concept of constitutional requirements to the actions of unelected public administrators? Are these officials presumptively more representative of a majority than is the judiciary itself? Is the administrator's authority more legitimate than that of a judge?

It should be apparent that when the context of judicial review shifts to the realm of public administration a separate set of concerns emerges. In large part, the appropriateness of judicial review of public administration depends upon the extent to which public administrators are controlled by and held accountable to the elective branches. If administrative agencies were simply adjuncts of the legislature and the elected executive and if they possessed no independent power of their own, then judicial review of their actions would be tantamount to judicial review of the elective branches themselves. In such a case, the same rules or approaches ought to apply to the review of administrative actions as to that of any other governmental action. However, as discussed in the previous chapter, such a concept of public administration is naive and inaccurate. There is no doubt that the rise of the administrative state places *independent* political power in the hands of unelected public administrators. Legislatures and elected executives influence the actions of public agencies, but the agencies are not controlled or held accountable by them in any simple sense. They have a large measure of autonomy; and, indeed, influence and control is not one directional—it is also exercised by public adminstrators over elected officials. Nor is the administrative role apolitical, confined to mere detailed execution of policies established elsewhere. Agencies make public policy, they may employ politically controversial means of implementing these policies, and they may adjudicate alleged breaches of their policies as part of their enforcement.

In recent decades the American political system has come to recognize candidly the extent to which public administration has become a powerful and largely independent fourth branch of government. Both the population and elected officials agree that in large measure the elective branches of government have failed to control the actions of public agencies. So, too, have members of the judiciary. Thus, by the 1970s the issue of bureaucratic power over individuals was placed squarely before the judiciary. In particular, Supreme Court Justice William O. Douglas made certain that none could ignore the power of public agencies. In *Wyman v. James* (1971:335) he wrote, "The bureaucracy of modern government is not only slow, lumbering, and oppressive; it is omnipresent." Similarly, in *Spady v. Mount Vernon* (1974:985), he asserted that, "today's mounting bureaucracy promises to be suffocating and repressive unless it is put into the harness of procedural due process." Douglas also addressed the nature of public bureaucracy and constitutional government in *U.S. v. Richardson* (1974), a taxpayer suit seeking information on CIA expenditures under Article I, section 9, clause 7 of the Constitution. He stated in dissent that *"The sovereign of this Nation is the people, not the bureaucracy.* The statement of accounts of public expenditures goes to the heart of the problems of sovereignty. If taxpayers may not ask that rudimentary question, their sovereignty becomes an empty symbol and a secret bureaucracy is allowed to run our affairs" (201, emphasis added). Douglas's admonitions were joined by Justice Powell in *Branti v. Finkel* (1980), which dealt with patronage dismissals from the public service. A passage of his dissent, joined by Justice Rehnquist, reads:

> Elected officials depend upon appointees who hold similar views to carry out their policies and administer their programs. Patronage—the right to select key personnel and to reward the party "faithful"—serves the public interest by facilitating the implementation of policies endorsed by the electorate.... [T]he Court [i.e., the majority] does not recognize that the implementation of policy often depends upon the cooperation of public employees who do not hold policymaking posts. As one commentator has written: "What the Court forgets is that, if government is to

work, policy implementation is just as important as policymaking. . . ."
*The growth of the civil service system already has limited the ability of
elected politicians to effect political change (Branti v. Finkel,* 1980:
529–530, emphasis added).

Thus, even if one relies only upon these limited statements, it can be seen that
members of the Supreme Court have expressed great concern with the pervasive-
ness of public bureaucracy, its departure from the standards of procedural due
process, its tendency to debilitate democratic citizenship under the Constitution,
and its ability to frustrate the will of elected political authorities. Whether a
minority view among the judiciary—and there is no reason to believe that it is—
such an outlook on public bureaucracy prompts a special consideration of the
balance between judicial review and judicial restraint that ought to be struck
when the courts confront the activities of public administrators.

If public administrative power is perceived as being exercised largely on an
independent basis, the arguments for restraint in the use of judicial review
against it lose much of their force. Under such circumstances, judicial review is
not necessarily antimajoritarian. Yet, there may be other bases for administrative legitimacy that would also suggest that judicial review should be limited.
One possibility is that even though public administrators are not elected, public
bureaucracies as a whole are highly representative bodies. This possibility is
especially strong in the United States, where public bureaucracies are highly
fragmented, interact continually with private interest groups, and use an
incremental decision-making style. In addition, agencies often have overlapping missions and authorities which cause them to compete with one another
and to develop a political consensus for their policies and programs. The
concept of representative bureaucracy is considered in Krislov and Rosenbloom
(1981).

A second possibility is that administrative agencies possess great expertise
which should be accorded far-reaching deference by the judiciary. Judges are
by nature generalists, whereas administrators are highly specialized. The
administrative state emerged in part to enable the society to benefit from
bureaucratic specialization in dealing with social, economic and political
problems. Consequently, it would be self-defeating and irrational to have
judges constantly substituting their own, presumably less informed judgments
for those of the expert administrators. As Martin Shapiro (1968:102) points
out, there is no inherent reason why one governmental branch ought to remake
the decisions of another. This is especially true when both are faced with the
same information and the second is less expert than the first. There is also the
question of whether the legal process, with its reliance on adversary procedure
and case method, is suitable for dealing with amorphous political, social, and economic issues. In the view of Donald Horowitz (1977: 274–284), for example,

the judiciary is far stronger when dealing with "legal facts," than when it is confronted with "social facts" that is, essentially social scientific information.

Bureaucratic representation and expertise can overlap in the sense that the agency becomes both representative and expert through specialized dealings with a particular clientele or constituency. Together, these factors have encouraged the judiciary to exercise self-restraint in reviewing the actions of public administrators—but only up to a point. Although in the past the judiciary accorded great deference to public adminsitrators, today judicial review is more far-reaching, especially when it appears that administrative expertise and administrative values are responsible for the erosion of individuals' constitutional rights and liberties. The immediate rationale for this is quite straightforward: public administrators do not possess greater expertise in constitutional law than do judges, and where individual rights are being violated, the fact that an agency *may* be representing the will of a majority loses some of its constitutional relevance. A deeper and more complex rationale is that the judiciary cannot maintain its essential coequality with the other constitutional branches of government in the administrative state unless it exercises authority over public administrators.

In fact, the current tendency for the judiciary to exercise greater review of the actions of public administrators has contributed strongly to a shift in the nature of constitutional litigation. This shift has been analyzed by Abram Chayes (1976) who calls the new form of suit "public law litigation." It varies from the more traditional lawsuit in the following respects.

1. *The structure of the public law litigation suit is not bipolar*, that is, it is not ". . . organized as a contest between two individuals or at least two unitary interests, diametrically opposed, to be decided on a winner-takes-all basis" (1282). Rather, it concerns issues involving whole communities, and the interests of the litigants may be somewhat overlapping. For example, in a suit aimed at reform of public mental hospitals, both the plaintiff and the defendant will have a similar interest in having the best mental health care system possible. The same would be true in school desegregation cases—the public interest is clearly in providing the best public education possible at any given cost.

2. *The litigation is prospective*, rather than retrospective, in character: "Instead of a dispute retrospectively oriented toward the consequences of a closed set of events, the court has a controversy about future probabilities" (1292).

3. *Rights and remedies lose some of their interdependence.* Whereas in the traditional lawsuit, remedies are generally clear and specific, in the public law litigation model courts are called upon to fashion equitable relief in which the broader public interest must be taken into account. Chayes writes: ". . . if litigation discloses that the relevant purposes or [constitutional] values have been frustrated, the relief that seems to be called for is often an affirmative

program to implement them. And courts, recognizing the undeniable presence of competing interests, many of them unrepresented by the litigants, are increasingly faced with the difficult problem of shaping relief to give due weight to the concerns of the unrepresented" (1295-1296).

4. *Fact-finding is no longer tied to "specific instances of past conduct"* (1296), but rather is essentially legislative in character. "The whole process begins to look like the traditional description of legislation: Attention is drawn to a 'mischief,' existing or threatened, and the activity of the parties and court is directed to the development of on-going measures designed to cure that mischief" (1297). Where relief is on-going and requires administrators to accomplish affirmative steps, such as reforming a prison, Chayes contends that the public law litigation suit is virtually tantamount to a legislative act.

5. *The public law litigation decree*, the "centerpiece" of the emerging model (1298), differs from the traditional decree in that it ". . . seeks to adjust future behavior, not to compensate for past wrong. It is deliberately fashioned rather than logically deduced from the nature of the legal harm suffered. It provides for a complex, on-going regime of performance rather than a simple, one-shot, one-way transfer. . . . [I]t prolongs and deepens, rather than terminates, the court's involvement with the dispute" (1298).

6. *The public law litigation suit* is not controlled by the parties initiating it, but rather, since it involves broad issues of public policy is less dependent upon them for the development of facts, assessment of injury, and explication of right.

7. *The role of the judge* is altered by different conditions: "The judge is not passive, his function limited to analysis and statement of governing legal rules; he is active, with responsibility not only for credible fact evaluation but for organizing and shaping the litigation to ensure a just and viable outcome" (1302).

In large part, the emergence of the public law litigation model is an outgrowth of the judiciary's response to the rise of the administrative state. It was created, or at least allowed to develop, by the judiciary primarily in an effort to bring the activities of public administrators under the rein of the Constitution, which is another way of saying under the influence of the judiciary itself. The model was not established by act of the legislature, but rather by judicial decisions that developed new constitutional rights vis-à-vis public administrators and created new remedies for breaches of those rights. Although sufficient data are not extant to make the point with certitude, there seems little doubt that the public law litigation model is overwhelmingly employed against public administrators, especially those responsible for the operations of prisons, public facilities for the mentally ill and retarded, public personnel systems, and public schools (Berger, 1977:Appendix II; Chayes, 1976:1313-1316). Thus, the emergence of the administrative state has been related to change in the operation of the judiciary as well as in that of the Congress and presidency. Conversely, the changing nature of judicial review of public administration has created a new relationship between public administration and constitutional law which will perforce alter the character of public administration in the future. That is the primary subject of this book. However, before proceeding with an analysis of this remarkable set of developments, it is desirable for the sake of comprehensiveness to consider briefly two earlier stages of the judicial response to the rise of the administrative state.

Judicial Opposition to the Administrative State

Judicial activity concerning the most pressing political issues of any given historical period sometimes falls into relatively coherent patterns. Judge Learned Hand and Justice Frankfurter referred to these patterns as "moods" which preoccupy and inform judicial thought (Frankfurter, 1957:793). They may also be considered responses to newly emergent or newly defined political pressures. It was precisely such a set of pressures that confronted the judiciary during the New Deal. Administrative agencies had existed since the founding and before, but the issue of the independent and far-reaching power of the full-fledged administrative state first confronted the judiciary in an unavoidable fashion in the 1930s. The major purpose behind the development of administrative power at the time was intervention in the national economy in an effort to recover from the depression. The judiciary stood firmly in opposition, both as a result of its adherence to the concept of a laissez-faire economy and its concern for the maintenance of the constitutional system of separation of powers. These two concerns overlapped and, in the words of former Supreme Court Justice Robert Jackson, led the judiciary to try to "nullify the New Deal" (1941:Chapter 4).

Of most importance to the constitutional issues posed by the rise of the administrative state were the questions of how much legislative power could be delegated to administrative agencies, and under what conditions. Today, public agenices derive much of their actual power by possessing the authority to formulate policy and to make binding rules for its implementation. These are essentially legislative functions. Vesting them in administrative agencies transforms the nature of politics by making the administrative branch the focal point of much of the struggle for the representation of organized interests. It also tends to enable administrative agencies to become the locus of the development of much public policy. In consequence, the role of Congress undergoes a profound change. Instead of initiating and formulating public policy, Congress increasingly tends to *react* to the policy proposals of the executive branch. Instead of administrative power being strictly regulated by congressional enactment, administrators are given broad grants of legislative power that can be exercised independently or subject to congressional *oversight*. Thus, instead of Congress proposing public policy and the executive exercising a potential veto of such proposals, as was intended by the Constitution, the executive branch becomes the proactive branch while the legislature becomes reactive. This development has been institutionalized in the growing use of the *legislative veto* (Moynihan, 1978:30). From the perspectives of democracy, this develop-ment raises the serious problem of the devolution of political power into the hands of unelected, relatively permanent public administrators. In terms of constitutional government, it threatens to upset the separation of powers and the system of checks and balances by vesting far-reaching legislative authority in the executive branch.

By the mid-1930s, the federal judiciary became acutely aware of the pressures on the Constitution caused by the emergent administrative state. The courts were overwhelmingly opposed to New Deal programs vesting legislative authority in administrative agencies. Indeed, as former Justice Jackson noted, " 'hell broke loose' in the lower courts. Sixteen hundred injunctions restraining officers of the Federal Government from carrying out acts of Congress were granted by federal judges" in 1935–1936 (1941:115). However, the two most outstanding decisions, in terms of the administrative state, were handed down by the Supreme Court in 1935. The first was in *Panama Refining Co. v. Ryan*, decided January 7, in which the Court struck down the constitutionality of legislation authorizing the president to develop a code to govern the much troubled petroleum industry. The Court's decision was unusually complicated, but the holding was that the legislature could not delegate its powers concerning the regulation of interstate commerce to the president in the absence of strict guidelines for their use. It was the first time in the nation's history that a federal statute was held unconstitutional on this basis (Jackson, 1941:92) and seemed to contravene the Court's previous decisions sustaining delegations of this nature. In Jackson's view, the decision violated a host of precedents and past practices and was best understood ". . . as a deliberate forewarning of what was to come. . . ."

The decision created a new obstacle to effective democratic government. It added a further perplexity in framing legislation. A rigid and inflexible law was in danger of being held unconstitutional because, as applied to some unforseen situation, it might appear to the Court to be arbitrary or capricious. Now it appeared that if legislators sought to avoid this risk and make for greater equity by delegating discretion, such a law ran another risk equally great. Of course some delegation would be per-mitted if adequate standards for the exercise of discretion were laid down. But the Court that required Congress to define standards to govern delegated power has . . . failed to set forth standards by which to define unconstitutional delegation (Jackson, 1941:94-95).

The Court's invocation of the separation of powers to prevent the rise of administrative power was reiterated even more forcefully in *Schecter Poultry Corporation v. U.S.*, decided May 27, 1935. Much of the New Deal hope for terminating the depression had been pinned on the National Industrial Recovery Act of 1933. The statute was passed in response to Roosevelt's request that Congress provide "for the machinery necessary for a great co-operative movement throughout all industry in order to obtain wide re-employment, to shorten the working week, to pay a decent wage for the shorter week, and to prevent unfair competition and disasterous overproduction" (Jackson, 1941:110-111). The act authorized the president the approve industry codes of fair competition. Based upon this authorization, a Recovery Administration developed in the executive branch. When confronted with a dispute arising out of the government's attempt to enforce the *Live Poultry Code* promulgated under the act, the Supreme Court attempted to erect a major barrier to the growth of independent administrative power. It held that under the Constitution, "Congress is not permitted to abdicate or to transfer to others the essential funcions with which it is . . . vested" (529). Indeed, independent authority of a legislative nature could be granted to administrative agencies only if Congress "has itself established the standards of legal obligation, thus performing its essential legislative function" (530). In the Court's view, the act failed to meet this requirement and, consequently, was an unconstitutional violation of the principle of the separation of powers. Even Justice Cardozo, who dissented in the *Panama* case, found the scheme to be one of "delegation running riot" (553). In a highly unusual fashion, the Court went on to find the act also an unconstitutional violation of Congress's power to regulate commerce.

The *Panama* and *Schecter* cases are unique among Supreme Court decisions. Shortly after they were handed down, the Court, under the pressure of Roosevelt's "packing" plan and as the result of its changing membership, retreated from their logical application. Delegations of legislative power to administrative agencies, even in the absence of any semblance of the standards called for in *Schecter*, were regularly upheld. The 1935 decisions were not formally overturned, but they no longer stood as a barrier to the emergence of the contemporary administrative state. Congress became free to allow administrative agencies to exercise legislative authority in regulating a host of aspects of national life under standards as vague as the promotion of "the public interest." As discussed in the previous chapter, eventually the administrative branch took on a great deal of the government's legislative and representational functions. The Court's willingness to tolerate such delegations marked the inauguration of the period of judicial acquiescence in the rise of the administrative state.

Judicial Acquiescence in the Administrative State

There is no doubt that the federal judiciary was severely injured, in an institutional sense, by its forceful opposition to the New Deal. It was politically weakened and its legitimacy impugned. The court packing plan exposed the vulnerability of the Supreme Court. In addition, the power of district court judges was curtailed by the Judiciary Act of 1937, which required that they sit in panels of three, rather than individually, when hearing cases seeking to enjoin the activities of federal officials on constitutional grounds. The judiciary's vulnerability to influence by the other governmental branches was also manifested in the reconstitution of its membership. Between 1937 and 1943, Roosevelt had the opportunity to appoint a chief justice and eight associate justices to the Supreme Court. Justice Roberts and Chief Justice Stone, who Roosevelt elevated to that position, were the only remaining members from the earlier period. Roosevelt also appointed a large number of lower court judges. Having been stung so badly by the exercise of judicial power during his first administration, he took special care to avoid appointments of people who were unsympathetic to his view of government. In the end, the judiciary was substantially changed, both in terms of personnel and mood. It was no longer ideologically opposed to federal intervention in the nation's economy and, though frequently divided, it was far more supportive of the polity's increasing reliance on government by administrative agency. For the most part during this period, which lasted into the 1960s, the judiciary did not *embrace* the exercise of administrative power. Rather, the courts tolerated it and deferred to the elective branches' efforts to regulate its use through the Administrative Procedure Act of 1946 and related statutes.

The Supreme Court's acquiescence in the growth of administrative power was largely out of political as opposed to legal commitment. Roosevelt's appointees supported the administrative state as a means of governance, but they were unable to develop a strong constitutional rationale for this position. No new legal consensus was developed, save that of judicial deference to administrative expertise. New constitutional doctrines did not emerge. Instead, the courts' adhered rigidly to older ones, such as the *doctrine of privilege* (discussed in the next two chapters). But this approach was accompanied by a certain uneasiness because it failed to address the growing dependence of the citizenry upon administrative agencies and the extent to which this dependency had become a vehicle for the erosion of the individual rights and liberties guaranteed by the Bill of Rights. The period of acquiescence, therefore, was politically dictated, not derived out of an evolving constitutional law. And, in the absence of a constitutional consensus on its appropriateness, it would eventually be abandoned.

C. Herman Pritchett comprehensively studied the Roosevelt Court's initial approach to administrative power. He described its political consensus and legal ambivalence as follows.

Under the New Deal, regulatory boards and commissions multiplied to such an extent that alphabetical agencies came to be regarded as the trademark of the Roosevelt Administration. Review of their decisions and enforcement of their orders has become one of the most important functions of the Supreme Court. During the five terms from 1941 to 1946 the eight most important federal regulatory agencies were parties in no less than 143, or 16 percent of all the Court cases decided by full opinion during that period. The generally favorable attitude of the Roosevelt Court toward administrative regulation is indicated by the fact that these agencies were successful in almost three-fourths of their appearances before the Court. However, there was a remarkable amount of disagreement among the judges in the decision of administrative cases, and conflicting tendencies and doctrines have been much in evidence (Pritchett, 1948:167-169).

In Pritchett's view, the one clear principle to emerge from the Roosevelt Court's experience with administrative agencies was "A controlling philosophy which sees 'court and agency' as co-workers for the attainment of a commom aim [that] requires that the courts limit themselves to those functions which they are better fitted than the agencies to perform" (1948:172). This approach had important ramifications.

It led the judiciary to pay great deference to the administrative expertise of public agencies. As Pritchett notes, "A basic assumption of the Roosevelt Court has been that administrative agenices possess an expertness and a competence in economic and social fields which the Court does not share, and that consequently in areas where this expertness is relevant the Court will not disturb or contradict administrative conclusions" (1948:172). One can find numerous examples of this approach at all levels of the federal judicial system and involving a host of issues ranging in complexity from economic rate setting to the transfer of federal employees (*Board of Trade of Kansas City v. U.S.*, 1942; *Kletschka v. Driver*, 1969).

Expertise, of course, is an extremely important basis of administrative power. Judicial deference to it is not surprising and is part of a far broader cultural pattern. Administrative specialization generates information, knowledge, and technology that is literally unmatched elsewhere in the society. Yet, at the same time, unthinking deference to administrative competence seems to belie reality. Certainly, administrative agencies are not always correct, mistakes are made, and in the process individuals are harmed. Moreover, public administrators often make policy judgments that depend upon political values as well as technical expertise. Any judicial approach that ignored these possibilities altogether would constitute and abdication of the courts' role.

These were problems with which the federal judiciary and the Supreme Court in particular were grappling when the Administrative Procedure Act of 1946* was passed. The act, as subsequently amended, has become the fundamental basis of administrative law in the United States, and its provisions have been the subject of a great deal of litigation and attendant judicial involvement in public administration. Indeed, until the judiciary developed its present response to the administrative state, which came to fruition in the 1970s, the Administrative Procedure Act largely defined the extent of its activities vis- à-vis administrative power. As amended, the act contains four types of provisions of importance here.

First, in order to enhance the public's ability to keep track of the administrative state, it requires federal agencies to make public certain information about their operations, including their organizational arrangements, functions, procedures, and general policies. Second, the act contains a procedure that federal agencies must follow when making rules. In brief, and with some exceptions, they are required to provide general notice of the proposed rule making in the *Federal Register* and to allow interested parties to submit written responses. Agencies may also allow oral presentations, at their discretion. These views are to be considered before the agency propounds its final rules, which must also be published in the *Federal Register*. This procedure is intended to encourage sound policy making by the federal bureaucracy and to enable it to be responsive to diverse and relevant interests. Third, it creates a procedure for administrative adjudication. Among other features, it established the right to notice and reply and to a hearing if the dispute cannot be resolved by consent. The hearing follows a quasijudicial format for the discovery of evidence. It is run by an impartial hearing examiner and provides for the opportunity to present evidence and the right to cross-examination.

A fourth feature of the act pertains to the availability and scope of judicial review. It states plainly that the judiciary should be in a position of oversight of administrative treatment of individuals: "A person suffering legal wrong because of agency action, or adversely affected or aggrieved by agency action within the meaning of a relevant statute, is entitled to judicial review thereof" [Sec. 10 (a)]. The scope of review is equally broad: "The reviewing court shall . . . hold unlawful and set aside agency action, findings, and conclusions found to be . . . arbitrary, capricious, an abuse of discretion, or otherwise not in accordance with law; . . . contrary to constitutionl right, power, privilege, or

*60 Stat. 237.

immunity; . . . in excess of statutory jurisdiction . . . ; without observance of procedure required by law; . . . unsupported by substantial evidence . . . ; or . . . unwarranted by the facts to the extent that the facts are subject to trial de novo by the reviewing court."

There have been a substantial number of treatises and disquisitions on the body of administrative law emerging from the Administrative Procedure Act (Davis, 1975; Barry and Whitecomb, 1981). Further exegesis here is wholly unnecessary except to stress that, despite the broad scope of judicial review created by the act, the mood of the courts continued to favor a very limited approach until recently. Procedurally, until the 1960s for the most part, the courts were reluctant to broaden "the scope of review to include a judicial determination as to whether the administrative findings were capricious, arbitrary or unreasonable, or whether such findings were supported by the record" (*West v. Macy*, 1968:106). Substantively, the judiciary's tendency to acquiesce in the exercise of administrative authority was even more pronounced, as Martin Shaprio suggests.

> Judicial review of administrative decision making is then marginal in the sense that, at least in the current Washington situation [1960s], policy differences are unlikely to arise in most instances in which review is theoretically possible. Thus most of the relations between agencies and courts are relations of acquiescence, consent, or compromise arrived at by anticipation of the other participant's position before even a tremor of conflict arises (Shapiro, 1968:268).

Conclusion

The Administrative Procedure Act and administrative law, as traditionally construed, are extremely important to the practice of public administration and the relationship between agencies and courts. But they no longer are the major point of intersection between public administration and law. The Administrative Procedure Act grew out of the Roosevelt Court's acquiescence in the exercise of administrative power and its unwillingness to take actions which seemed politically reminiscent of the judiciary's activity during the early New Deal. The act codified the availability and scope of judicial review of administrative actions, but it could not force a reluctant and acquiescent judiciary to seek to oversee forcefully the administrative state. That development had to await the development of a new judicial mood—one not constrained and circumscribed by the largely self-inflicted injuries to the judiciary in the early 1930s. This, then, constitutes the third stage of the judicial response to the rise of the administrative state. Its evolution and impacts are the primary concern of this book. It is almost revolutionary—without precedent—in its development of new constitutional rights and new means of vindicating these rights for individuals in the contemporary administrative state. It redefines the relationship between judges and the public administrative state. It redefines the relationship between judges and public administrators and forces the latter to be cognizant of constitutional values and rights in a very direct fashion. It also involves the judiciary directly in the administration of public institutions such as mental hospitals, prisons, and school systems. It has been part and parcel of the development of the public law litigation model and, consequently, has had important implications for the litigation process as well as for public administration. No one can remain current in public administration without grasping these developments.

References

Administrative Procedure Act, 1946. 60 Stat. 237.

Barry, Donald and Howard Whitcomb, 1981. *The Legal Foundations of Public Administration.* St. Paul, Minn.: West Publishing.

Beard, Charles, 1913. *An Economic Interpretation of the Constitution of the United States.* New York: Macmillan.

Berger, Raoul, 1977. *Government by Judiciary.* Cambridge, Mass.: Harvard University Press.

Bickel, Alexander, 1962. *The Least Dangerous Branch.* Indianapolis: Bobbs-Merrill.

Black, Charles, 1974. The national court of appeals: An unwise proposal. *Yale Law Journal* 83: 883.

Board of Trade of Kansas City v. U.S., 1942. 314 U.S. 534.

Boudin, Louis, 1932. *Government by Judiciary.* New York: William Godwin.

Branti v. Finkel, 1980. 445 U.S. 507.

Chayes, Abram, 1976. The role of the judge in public law litigation. *Harvard Law Review* 89: 1281-1316.

Cohens v. Virginia, 1821. 6 Wheaton 264.

Colegrove v. Green, 1946. 328 U.S. 549.

Cramton, Roger, 1976. Judicial lawmaking and administration in the leviathan state. *Public Administrative Review* 36 (September/October), 551-555.

Dahl, Robert, 1972. *Democracy in the United States,* 2nd ed. Chicago: Rand McNally.

Davis, Kenneth C., 1975. *Administrative Law and Government.* St. Paul, Minn.: West Publishing.

DeFunis v. Odegaard, 1974. 416 U.S. 312.

Dred Scott v. Sandford, 1857. 19 Howard 393.

Ex Parte McCardle, 1869. 7 Wallace 506.
Federal Baseball Club of Baltimore v. National League, 1922. 259 U.S. 200.
Flood v. Kuhn, 1972. 407 U.S. 258.
Frankfurter, Felix, 1957. The Supreme Court in the mirror of justices. *University of Pennsylvania Law Review* 105: 781-796.
Fullilove v. Klutznick, 1980. 448 U.S. 448.
Horowitz, Donald, 1977. *The Courts and Social Policy.* Washington, D.C.: Brookings Institution.
Jackson, Robert H., 1941. *The Struggle for Judicial Supremacy.* New York: Knopf.
Kaiser v. Weber (Steelworkers v. Weber), 1979. 443 U.S. 193.
Kletcshka v. Driver, 1969. 411 F2d 436.
Krislov, Samuel and David H. Rosenbloom, 1981. *Representative Bureaucracy and the American Political System.* New York: Praeger.
McCulloch v. Maryland, 1819. 4 Wheaton 316.
Marbury v. Madison, 1803. 1 Cranch 137.
Minersville School District v. Gobitis, 1940. 310 U.S. 586.
Moynihan, Daniel P., 1978. Imperial government. *Commentary* 65 (June), 25-32.
Murphy, Walter and C. Herman Pritchett, 1961. *Courts, Judges, and Politics.* New York: Random House.
Owen v. City of Independence, 1980. 445 U.S. 622.
Panama Refining Co. v. Ryan, 1935. 293 U.S. 389.
Poe v. Ullman, 1961. 367 U.S. 497.
Pritchett, C. Herman, 1948. *The Roosevelt Court.* New York: Macmillan.
Pritchett, C. Herman, 1977. *The American Constitution,* 3rd ed. New York: McGraw-Hill.
Radovich v. National Football League, 1957. 352 U.S. 445.
Regents v. Bakke, 1978. 438 U.S. 265.
Ross, Robert, 1972. *American National Government.* Chicago: Markham.
Rossiter, Clinton, ed., 1961. *The Federalist Papers.* New York: New American Library.
Schecter Poultry Corporation vs. U.S., 1935. 295 U.S 495.
Shapiro, Martin, 1968. *The Supreme Court and Administrative Agencies.* New York: Free Press.
Simon, James, 1973. *In His Own Image.* New York: David McKay.
Solberg, Winton, ed., 1958. *The Federal Convention and the Formation of the Union of the American States.* Indianapolis: Bobbs-Merrill.
Spady v. Mount Vernon, 1974. 419 U.S. 983.
Toolson v. New York Yankees, 1953. 346 U.S. 356.
U.S. v. International Boxing Club, 1955. 348 U.S. 236.
U.S. v. Richardson, 1974. 418 U.S. 166.

West v. Macy, 1968. 248 F. Supp. 105.

West Virginia Board of Education v. Barnett, 1943. 319 U.S. 624.

White, G. Edward, 1976. *The American Judicial Tradition.* New York: Oxford University Press.

Wyman v. James, 1971. 400 U.S. 309.

3

The Citizen as Client of the Administrative State

The rise of the administrative state transforms the nature of citizenship by increasingly placing the citizen* in the role of user of government services and client of public bureaucracies. In democratic nations, the development of a patron-client relationship between the government and its citizenry can pose a major challenge to traditional regime values. This is highly evident in the United States where, according to formal theory, the government is considered to be a creature of the political community and constantly dependent upon it. Moreover, the government is considered to have limited ends. The Preamble to the Constitution makes this conception evident.

> We the People of the United States, in Order to form a more perfect Union, establish Justice, insure domestic Tranquility, provide for the common defence, promote the general Welfare, and secure the Blessings of Liberty to ourselves and our Posterity, do ordain and establish this Constitution. . . .

Yet, expansion of governmenal services not only expands the role and activity of government in the society at large, it also tends to reverse the direction of dependence. Instead of government being dependent upon the citizenry, the citizenry becomes increasingly dependent upon the government. With such dependence comes a greater potential for governmental dominance of the citizenry, which, if democratic values are to be preserved, must in turn bring about a redressing of citizens' rights as clients vis-à-vis the government as

*N.B., throughout this book, the word *citizen* is used in the general sense of *member of the political community*. No effort is made to distinguish between the rights of citizens and those of aliens. In general, the constitutional rights discussed herein pertain to citizens and may also extend to aliens.

provider of services. In the United States, the judiciary has responded to this aspect of the rise of the administrative state in precisely such a manner.

The Citizen as Client

Services

The rise of the administrative state has entailed the expansion of public services. This expansion occurs in both a qualitative and quantitative sense, though as Max Weber observes, "bureaucratization is occasioned more by intensive and qualitative enlargement and internal deployment of the scope of administrative tasks than by their extensive and quantitative increase" (1958:212). In fact, as noted in Chapter 1, it is the growth in the provision of services that marks the era of modern public administration. What distinguishes the modern administrative state from previous political arrangements in the West is that the state is no longer considered to be family, property, or society, but rather is a legal association engaged in the provision of public services (Barker, 1966:4). As the scope of these services expands, the citizen's interaction with the government also undergoes quantitative and qualitative change. Public bureaucracy's penetration of the life of the society brings the citizen into increasing contact with government, makes him or her dependent upon it, and, consequently, may lead to an erosion of the individual's political autonomy.

The implications of the rise of the modern administrative state for the nature of citizenship have been the subject of concern for some time. To some extent, contemporary advocates of capitalism have opposed socialism on the political grounds that governmental control of the economy inevitably reduces the individual's political freedom (Friedman, 1962; Hayek, 1944). The United States, remains basically capitalist and is characterized by less governmental penetration of the life of the political community than is found in many other developed nations. Yet, even here, the provision of government services has been thought to alter fundamentally the distribution and process of obtaining wealth. Charles Reich (1964:733) observes:

> One of the most important developments in the United States during the past decade [1950s] has been the emergence of government as a major source of wealth. Government is a gigantic syphon. It draws in revenue and power, and pours forth wealth: money, benefits, services, contracts, franchises, and licenses. Government has always had this function. But while in early times it was minor, today's distribution of largess is on a vast, imperial scale.
>
> The valuables dispensed by government take many forms, but they all share one characteristic. They are steadily taking the place of traditional

forms of wealth—forms which are held as private property. Social insurance substitutes for savings; a government contract replaces a businessman's customers and goodwill, the wealth of more and more Americans depends upon a relationship to government. Increasingly, Americans live on government largess. . . .

Among the largess to which Reich refers are income, benefits, jobs, occupational licenses (extending well beyond jobs requiring much education or training), franchises, contracts, subsidies, the use of public resources, the use of governmental services generally, and drivers' licenses. Although this list leaves a little doubt as to the citizens' dependence upon governmental largess, the extent of citizens' contact with government agencies serves as an additional indicator of the individual's reliance on bureaucracy.

Daniel Katz et al. (1975) sought to explain the scope and character of citizens' interaction with public bureaucracy in the United States. Based upon a national survey in 1973, they found that almost 60 percent of the respondents reported contacting at least one government *service** agency. About 18 percent of the respondents had contacted two agencies, and approximately 11 percent, were frequent users of government services, having contacted three or more such agencies (Katz et al., 1975, table 2.1, p. 20). Extensive though these reported contacts are, they nevertheless dramatically understate the potential for citizens to be clients of the administrative state.

Despite the widespread provision and use of government services, according to Katz and associates (1975:46), "Overall, about a third of the people with a problem do not avail themselves of relevant government services." The authors offered several possible explanations for this, including lack of knowledge of the services provided, the complexity of bureaucratic rules, and the changing nature of eligibility. Although these are largely administrative limitations, the underutilization of public service points to a fundamental political problem inherent in the administrative state.

To the extent that the citizenry becomes dependent upon government largess for its mobility, status maintenance, or survival, it is crucial in democratic regimes that the distribution and utilization of government services not discriminate against groups or individuals in any irrational or invidious fashion. Formal equality of distribution is a matter that can be dealt with by law through the creation of a constitutional or legal right to equal access to government services. This will be discussed later. However, individuals' self-imposed reluctance to use such services, which can be just as debilitating to equality and

---

*Katz et al. draw a distinction between "service" and "constraint" agencies, based on their predominant functions. However, "service" agencies may be deceptive in the extent to which they regulate individuals' behavior. See discussion *Infra*.

is more complex and often less amenable to government control. Several scholars have noted this fact.

Victor Thompson (1961:170) expressed great concern with the psychological makeup of individuals who are reluctant to interact with bureaucratic agencies:

> The bureaucratic culture makes certain demands upon clients as well as upon organization employees. There are many people in our [USA] society who have not been able to adjust to these demands. To them bureaucracy is a curse. They see no good in it whatsoever, but view the demands of modern organization as "red tape." This kind of behavior is external to the organization. . . . Its source will be found within the critic himself, not within the organization.

Thompson called such people "bureautics" and argued that because of their "low powers of abstraction" and "need to personalize the world," the "bureautic can rarely enter successfully into an impersonal, functional, or bureaucratic relationship. The world is peopled only with friends and enemies; it does not have impartial, impersonal functionaries" (1961:172-173). Bureautics feel powerless in relation to bureaucracy and have "no confidence in securing justice through an impersonal, abstract system of norms and routines . . ." (1961:174).

Alvin Gouldner studies the same phenomenon empirically. He found that individuals were likely to consider bureaucratic process to be red tape when

> . . . the individual's ego is challenged on two counts: (1) A claim which he believes legitimate is not taken "at face value." He must either supply proof or allow it to be investigated. He is, as one remarked, "treated as a criminal"—he may feel his worth is questioned, his status impugned.

> (2) Not only are his claims and assertions challenged, but other details of his "private life" are investigated. The individual enters the situation on "official," "technical," or "public" business, and feels that he ends up by being investigated as a person (1952:413).

The extent to which underutilization of bureaucratic services in the United States can be attributed to bureautic behavior is unknown. That it is potentially substantial is suggested not only by the attention Thompson and Gouldner devote to the question, but also by comparative study. For instance, a study of Israel's bureaucratic culture revealed that about 30 percent of the Israeli citizenry could appropriately be called bureautic (Nachmias and Rosenbloom, 1978). As a group, their reactions to the Israeli national bureaucracy differed from those of other citizens. They were much more critical of the bureaucracy's role in nation-building, they felt a lower sense of efficacy in dealing with it, and, overall, they evaluated bureaucratic performance more negatively than did other citizens. They were also substantially less likely than other citizens to use bureaucratic channels to influence the administrative agencies, preferring instead to enlist the support of outside audiences through newspapers and political parties. Importantly, in Israel bureautics were found among all social classes and ethnic groups, although elsewhere this might not be the case.

Underutilization of governmental services may also be especially prevalent among members of the lower class. To the extent that this occurs, the rise of the administrative state may reinforce existing socioeconomic cleavages. Indeed, it has been argued that ". . . bureaucratic systems are the key medium through which the middle class maintains its advantaged position vis-à-vis the lower class" (Rourke, 1978:40). In part, this is because public bureaucracies tend to be overrepresentative of middle-class values and interests. In part, however, it is due to the lower class's difficulty in dealing with bureaucratic structures and norms. Four reasons for this have been identified.

1. "First and foremost, the lower-class person simply lacks knowledge of the rules of the game. Middle-class persons generally learn how to manipulate bureaucratic rules to their advantage and even to acquire special 'favors' by working through the 'private' or 'backstage' (as opposed to the 'public') sector of the bureaucratic organization" (Rourke, 1978:46–47). In some societies the use of such personalized contacts has become virtually institutionalized, as in Israel where it has been labeled *proteksia* and studied at length (Danet and Hartman, 1970:432; Robinson, 1970).

2. "This situation is complicated by the fact that the problems the lower-class person faces are difficult to treat in isolation. The lack of steady employment, of education, and of medical care, for example, interlock in complex ways. . . . [N]o official is able to view the lower-class client as a whole person, and thus he is unable to point up to the client how he might use his strengths to overcome his weaknesses" (Rourke, 1978:47).

3. ". . . [L]ower-class persons typically relate to one another in a personal manner. Middle-class persons are better able to relate to others within an impersonal context" (Rourke, 1978:47). To the extent that this is true in any given culture, members of the lower class may also tend to be more bureautic.

4. Finally, these elements interact with each other making ". . . it more difficult for a lower-class person to acquire knowledge of how the system operates. It is not surprising that under these circumstances members of the lower-class often experience a sense of powerlessness or alienation" (Rourke, 1978:48). Presumably, feelings of powerlessness and alienation would lead to a lower sense of efficacy in using bureaucracy and, therefore, a tendency toward underutilization.

Katz and associates found that patterns of utilization did not strictly follow socioeconomic cleavages. They concluded, however, that in the United States

... the present system of social services does not involve a redistribution of wealth to the poor or uneducated. Rather, services are provided for various constituencies such as the unemployed or retired. The increased sophistication that comes with higher education and its concomitant, higher income, has enabled middle class persons to take advantage of services which are provided. On the other hand, structural considerations have also aided the middle and working classes. For example, only people who have been employed at a regular job are eligible for workmen's compensation, unemployment compensation, or social security retirement benefits (Katz et al., 1975:61).

It is evident, therefore, that the distribution of governmental largess can create problems of equity. It can be used to promote the maintenance of one group's dominance of others and may thereby undermine a regime's formal commitment to equality.

Constraints

The extent of citizens' contact with public bureaucracies goes beyond that reported by Katz and associates with reference to service agencies. They also found that 5 percent of their sample had contact with constraint agencies only and that 10 percent had contact with service and constraint agencies (1975: Appendix D). Among these agencies were those dealing with driver's licenses, traffic violations, income taxes, and general policing. Interestingly, despite their relatively small volume, contacts with constraint agencies seemed to be problematic (1975:24). Bureaucratic constraints can weigh heavily on the mind of the citizen of the contemporary bureaucratic state. The matter is complicated to a far greater extent when it is recognized that even *service* agencies can place substantial constraints upon their clients, just as *constraint* agencies may provide various services. The fact that service and constraint can be so intertwined is of major political importance. Ironically, those agencies that are most directly involved in control functions often use the word *service* in their names, as it is with the Internal Revenue Service, the Immigration and Naturalization Service, and the old military draft agency, the Selective Service System.

Control is infused throughout the individual's interaction as a client of bureaucratic agencies. As Charles Reich has observed, "when government—national, state, or local—hands out something of value, whether a relief check or a television license, government's power grows forthwith; it automatically gains such power as is necessary and proper to supervise its largess. It obtains new rights to investigate, to regulate, and to punish" (Reich, 1964:746). Moreover,

Broad as is the power derived from largess, it is magnified by many administrative factors when it is brought to bear on a recipient. First, the agency granting government largess generally has a wide measure of discretion to interpret its own power. Second, the nature of administrative agencies, the functions they combine, and the sanctions they possess, give them additional power. Third, the circumstances in which the recipients find themselves sometimes make them abettors, rather than resistors of the further growth of power (Reich, 1964:749).

According to Ralph Hummel, bureaucratic language plays a key role here: ". . . the function of bureaucratese is fundamentally to make outsiders powerless. . . . Bureaucratic specialized language is specifically designed to insulate functionaries from clients, to empower them not to have to listen, unless the client first learns the language. For a client who has learned the language is a client who has accepted the bureaucrat's values. Language defines both what the problems we can conceive of and what solutions we can think of. Once a client uses the bureaucracy's language, the bureaucrat may be assured that no solutions contrary to his interests and power will emerge from the dialogue" (1977:147).

However, the intermingling of service and constraint functions does not occur solely to promote the power of bureaucratic agencies. It also can serve more general governmental purposes, including (1) the gathering of information, (2) the restriction of benefits to eligible applicants, (3) the promotion of a general policy, such as equal opportunity or affirmative action, and (4) deterrence of disloyalty to the political system (O'Neil, 1966:445). More subtly, constraints can reduce the costs of providing services by deterring some eligible individuals from using a service (O'Neil, 1966:445). This approach seems especially prevalent in programs having only minimal political support, such as public housing and welfare. Thus, once again, this situation can be inherently discriminatory against certain groups of individuals. As Reinhard Bendix noted,

Access to influence upon the administrative process is a problem of increasing importance. . . . As rights are universalized and governmental activities proliferate, it is less problematic that the uneducated citizen is barred from public employment because he cannot qualify, than that he may not possess the aptitudes and lattitudes needed to obtain reasoned consideration of his case by the public authorities (Bendix, 1964:129).

In the United States, there have been numerous examples of situations in which the distribution of governmental largess has been coupled with constraints upon the ordinary rights of individual citizens and on the behavior of economic enterprises. In some cases the application of these constraints may not be highly controversial. Reich (1964:746) observes:

A government contractor finds that he must comply with wage-hour and child labor requirements. Television and radio licensees learn that their possible violation of the antitrust laws, or allegedly misleading statements to the FCC, are relevant to their right to a license. Doctors find they can lose their licenses for inflating bills that are used as a basis for claims against insurance companies in accident cases, and theaters are threatened with loss of licenses for engaging in illegal ticket practices. The New York State Board of Regents includes in its definition of "unprofessional conduct" by doctors, dentists, and other licensed professions any discrimination against patients or clients on the basis of race, color or creed. Real estate brokers can be suspended for taking advantage of racial tensions by the practice called "blockbusting." California has used its power over the privilege of selling alcoholic beverages in order to compel licensed establishments to cease discriminating.

In this fashion, largess can be used as a lever for promoting public policy. But, it can also be used as a means by which the government can intrude into areas of individual autonomy generally thought to be protected by the Constitution. Again Reich's examples are illuminating:

One of the most significant regulatory by-products of government largess is power over the recipients' "moral character." Some random illustrations will suggest the meaning and application of this phrase. The District of Columbia denied a married man in his forties a permit to operate a taxi partly because when he was a young man in his twenties, he and a woman had been discovered about to have sexual intercourse in his car. Men with criminal records have been denied licenses to work as longshoremen and chenangoes and prevented from holding union office for the same reason. A license to operate a rooming house may be refused for lack of good character. Sonny Liston was barred from receiving a license to box in New York because of his "bad character." Louisiana attempted to deny aid to dependent children if their mothers were of bad character (Reich, 1964:747).

Nor does the list stop at morality, it includes politics as well. Loyalty tests have been imposed upon the receipt of largess ranging from fishing licenses, to unemployment compensation, to drivers' licenses, to the practice of several occupations, including wrestling and piano selling (Brown, 1958:viii, 18, 377).

To the extent that the citizen is dependent upon governmental largess, therefore, the constitutional relationship between individual and government can be turned on its head. The government, which has only limited direct powers over individual morality, political beliefs and activities, and general behavior, gains substantial indirect authority by which it can regulate various aspects of the individual's life. However, although the individual is theoretically free to retain his or her liberty and freedom by rejecting largess, it is clear that in many cases such a course of action would have the effect of banishing one from the mainstream of the society's economic and social life. Consequently, the distribution of largess becomes a major element by which government governs and public policy is implemented. It is not surprising, therefore, that public bureaucrats have expressed a greater desire than the citizenry as a whole to have the goverment pursue an interventionist role in society (Aberbach and Rockman, 1976). Despite its constant denunciations of *bureaucracy*, Congress also benefits from this form of government* (Fiorina, 1977). But what about the citizen?

Citizens' Evaluations of the Bureaucratic State

Understandably, the citizen's view of the contemporary American administrative state is complex. In the abstract, public bureaucracy and its impact on the life of the society are both recognized and opposed. For example, as noted in Chapter 1, surveys undertaken in 1973 showed that a majority of both the population and elected officials believed that public bureaucracy was relatively uncontrolled and that this condition was troublesome.

Thus, the recognition of bureaucratic power is widespread, presumably in part as a result of the individual's dependence on largess. At the same time, however, the citizen's evaluation of the exercise of administrative authority has become drastically more negative over time, as is indicated in Table 3.1. Perhaps this is a direct outgrowth of the citizenry's heightened awareness of its dependence on public bureaucracy. Increasingly, individuals also feel powerlessness in influencing bureaucrats (Nachmias and Rosenbloom, 1980:245–248).

Overall, therefore, the citizen believes that the contemporary American administrative state is largely uncontrolled by elected officials, has a substantial impact on the quality of life, that its impact is negative, and that there is less and less the citizen can do to make bureaucracy work toward his or her desired ends. In their dealings with individual service agencies, however, the citizenry comes to a somewhat different conclusion. For instance, Katz and associates found that about 43 percent of the population was very satisfied in its dealings with these agencies and that another 26 percent were fairly satisfied, as compared to a total of 26 percent who were either dissatisfied or very dissatisfied. Although this minority should not be overlooked, the finding of major significance was that, at least in dealing with service agencies, a substantial majority of the citizenry finds its own personal problems handled in a satisfactory way (Katz et al., 1975:Table 3-1,64). Moreover, "Three out of four [clients of these

---

*See Chapter 1.

Table 3.1   Character of Impact of the Federal Government on the Quality of
Life (Percents)

Direction of Impact	1960	1973
Improved	76	23
Made it worse	3	37
Not changed it much*	19	34
Not sure	2	6
	100%	100%
Total	(821)	(16, 162)

*The response categories in the 1960 survey are not entirely identical with the language of
the 1973 survey. The nearest category in 1960 to "not changed much" is "Sometimes
improves conditions, sometimes does not."
Sources: The 1960 figures are reported in Gabriel A. Almond and Sidney Verba, *The Civic
Culture* (Boston: Little, Brown, 1966), p. 48. The 1973 data come from U.S. Congress,
Confidence and Concern, part 2, p. 147.

agencies] felt that they had been treated fairly, and only one in four felt that
some groups of people received preferential treatment" (Katz et al., 1975:115).

On the other hand, experiences with constraint agencies were evaluated far
less favorably. Although it may be stretching the concept of *client* too far to
include contacts with police and tax agencies within it, the line between service
and constraint is blurred and may depend on the specific circumstances and the
individual's perception of them. For instance, Katz and associates included
motor vehicle licensing departments within the category of constraint agencies
although they clearly provide a service by promoting safety on the highways.
In any event, the public believed its experience with officials in constraint
agencies was handled poorly or very poorly in over half the cases, and very well
or fairly well in 35 percent of their contacts (Katz et al., 1975:Table 3.49,102).

Specifically, "One-fifth of the constraint group stated that they had been
subjected to threats and pressures. . . . On the question of equitable treatment,
a much lower proportion of constraint agency respondents than service agency
respondents felt that they had been treated fairly (45 percent as opposed to 76
percent). In addition, almost two times as many constraint agency clients
perceived constraint bureaucracies as operating on a preferential basis" (Katz
et al., 1975:116).

In sum, the citizenry expresses a disfavorable evaluation of the administrative
state in the abstract, believing it is largely out of control and that it tends to
make the quality of life worse rather than better. Individuals are also critical of
their experiences with constraint agencies; but, given these general outlooks,
they evaluate their experiences with service agencies in a surprisingly favorable

manner. Nevertheless, a sizable minority also remains dissatisfied with these. In sum, then, it appears that there is room for improvement in the citizen-client evaluation of the American administrative state. For as Katz and associates point out, "Even a 75 percent level of satisfaction may be low for some programs in which 90 percent or higher is desirable and feasible. In a population of 200 million, small percentages are large numbers" (1975:115). However, even if such levels of satisfaction were reached, it must be remembered that a substantial political problem would nonetheless remain. Indirect governmental control of the citizenry through the distribution of largess alters the constitutional relationship between citizen and government, no matter how willingly the public accepts this fact. While public administrators have extended such control, the Constitution stands opposed to it. Thus, in this context as in others there is a conflict between administrative values and constitutional values.

Administrative Values and Constitutional Values

As a discipline or intellectual field of study, American public administration places little emphasis on relationships with citizens as clients. Indeed, the vast majority of textbooks in public administration do not even devote a single page to this matter. The word *clients* rarely appears in the index of such works. The few texts that do mention the subject do so in the context of generating support for agency activities, or that of gathering information. Nevertheless, taken as a whole, American public administration is not without an orthodox position concerning relations with clients. That position is related to the classical administrative values of efficiency and economy which received their first modern emphasis in the nineteenth century quest for civil service reform.

The civil service reform movement in the 1870s and 1880s marked a fundamental turning point in the development of American public administration. The reformers' primary objective was to create political change by eradicating the spoils system and thereby undermine the power position of the politicians who benefited from it (Rosenbloom, 1971:Chapter 3). As Carl Schurz, a leading reformer remarked, the task of reform was to

> . . . rescue our political parties, and in great measure the management of our public affairs, from the control of men whose whole statesmanship consists in the low arts of office mongering, and many of whom would never have risen to power had not the spoils system furnished them the means and opportunity for organizing gangs of political followers as mercenary as themselves (Schurz, 1893:614).

Dorman B. Eaton, another leading reformer, observed that under the spoils system, "Politics have tended more and more to become a trade, or separate occupation. High character and capacity have become disassociated from public life in the popular mind" (Eaton, 1880:392). The reformers thought that once spoils was eliminated, people like themselves, that is, middle-class political activists, would be able to play a far greater role in the life of the nation. Even at the height of the reform movement, the reformers agreed then that "the question whether the Departments at Washington are managed well or badly is, in proportion to the whole problem, an insignificant question" (Schurz, 1913: Vol. 2, 123).

However, the reformers' arguments for political change resulting from administrative change were potentially unconvincing. After all, the spoils system did have some important political advantages. It helped sustain political competition organized around mass-based political parties, and it guaranteed that the federal service would be broadly representative of the electorate in several senses. Patronage, it turned out, was far more vulnerable on administrative grounds than on political grounds. Consequently, the reformers developed the well-known and still persistent dichotomy between politics and administration. They adopted the perspective of the latter in their attack on the spoils system. Thus, they maintained that of the great number of "places [in the civil service] very few are political" (Rosenbloom, 1971:75) and that "What civil service reform demands, is simply that the business part of the government shall be carried on in a sound businesslike manner" (Rosenbloom, 1971:75). Such a manner, according to the reformers, meant one that stressed efficient operations. In this fashion efficiency emerged as a primary goal of American pubic administration, and one that stood in stark contrast to the values preceding it in the Jacksonian era. President Jackson, for instance, advanced the views that "I cannot but believe that more is lost by the long continuance of men in office than is generally to be gained by their experience" (Richardson, 1896:Vol. 2, 448–449), and that it should always be borne in mind that "in a free government the demand for moral qualities should be made superior to that of talents" (Jackson, 1926:Vol. 4, 11-12).

In the aftermath of reform, students and practitioners of public administration tended to lose sight of the wider connection of administration to politics and to stress efficiency as the fundamental value of proper administration. This was nowhere more evident than in the Scientific Management movement. Following the approach advanced by Frederick Taylor in *The Principles of Scientific Management* (1911), public management took upon itself the task of determining "the one best way" in which each administrative task could be performed and organized. As a result,

> The "goodness" or "badness" of a particular organizational pattern was a mathematical relationship of "inputs" to "outputs." Where the latter was maximized and the former minimized, a moral "good" resulted. Virtue or "goodness" was therefore equated with the relationship of these two

factors, that is, "efficiency" or "inefficiency." Mathematics was transformed into ethics (Simmons and Dvorin, 1977:217).

In the theory and practice of scientific management, the quest for efficiency
reinforced bureaucratic tendencies toward the dehumanization of workers. The
primary objective was to eliminate from administrative practice "... all purely
personal, irrational, and emotional elements ..." (Weber, 1958:216) that might
interfere with efficiency. The immediate consequences were twofold. First,

> The "efficiency engineer" and the "administrative analyst" were the men
> of the hour and of the age in large and intricate administrative structures.
> Physical layout surveys, resource-allocation studies, product quality con-
> trol, cost control, fiscal audit, work simplification through "flow-process"
> charting and forms (paperwork) management were the stuff of which
> administration was made (Simmons and Dvorin, 1977:216).

Second, the individual worker became a mere appendage to an organizational
machine. The ideal of scientific management was not much different from
Weber's ideal-type bureaucrat who was "... only a single cog in an ever-moving
mechanism which prescribes to him an essentially fixed route of march" (Weber,
1958:228).

But, if administrative processes were to be organized rationally, requiring that
individual administrators be dehumanized, was it not inevitable that such ration-
alization would extend to both nonhuman and human inputs? Certainly, the administrative agency processing the applications, claims, and so forth of individual
clients could rationalize (i.e., make efficient) its procedures by treating them as
standard units rather than as part and parcel of individual human beings with
varying emotional economic, social, and other features. As Ralph Hummel
(1977:24-25) explains:

> Bureaucracy is an efficient means for handling large numbers of people.
> "Efficient" in its own terms. It would be impossible to handle large
> numbers of people in their full depth and complexity. Bureaucracy is a
> tool for ferreting out what is "relevant" to the task for which the
> bureaucracy was established. As a result, only those facts in the complex
> lives of individuals that are relevant to that task need be communicated
> between the individual and the bureaucracy.
>
> To achieve this simplification, the modern bureaucrat has invented the
> "case." At the intake level of the bureaucracy, individual personalities
> are converted into cases. Only if a person can qualify as a case, is he or
> she allowed treatment by the bureaucracy. More accurately, a bureauc-
> racy is never set up to treat or deal with persons: it "processes" only
> "cases."

Thus, there has been a logical progression from the civil service reformers' concern with efficiency to the method by which bureaucratic agencies conceptualize clients as *case-inputs*. This has obvious ramifications for interaction with citizens as clients of the administrative state. However rational from the perspectives of administrative efficiency, interaction with clients is often irrational from other perspectives. In order to become a *processable case* and thereby gain access to the new property of bureaucratic largess, the individual has to conform to the official administrative criteria. However, such dehumanization or impersonal treatment of the client increases the likelihood that by refusing to consider the needs and circumstances of the client as a whole human being, the administrative action taken will be inappropriate. This phenomenon is often subsumed under the label of *catch-22*, or the situation in which what should be a progression of steps becomes circular so that the client is forever unable to become the case necessary to take the first step. For instance, a job may be required to obtain a visa, while a visa is required to obtain a job. So pervasive is red tape of this kind that some administrative systems, such as the bureaucracy of New York State, have engaged in public relations campaigns assuring that they have officials whose sole task is to help businesses cut through it. Similar instances occur when an overly technical application of the criteria for becoming a case are applied, thereby excluding individuals who fall well within the intent of any given program. Overlaps are a different version of the same general phenomenon. Thus, one agency may require a client to perform an activity prohibited by another. For example, one agency may require a corporation seeking a government contract to supply data on the racial composition of its workforce; at the same time, another agency may forbid the identification of all employees by race.

All of the examples mentioned have a commonality in that, as a result of dehumanizing or impersonal bureaucratic routines, the would-be client is deprived of the bureaucratic largess to which he or she is otherwise entitled. While this raises no specific constitutional problem, it does present the issue of whether or not an individual can be denied access to public benefits for the sake of administrative convenience, not to mention arbitrary or capricious administrative action. Although this is an important issue in itself, it is somewhat overshadowed by the larger question of whether relevant or extraneous conditions interfering with the ordinary constitutional rights of clients as citizens can be attached to the application for and receipt of bureaucratic largess.

As Reich (1964) noted, the allotment of bureaucratic largess strengthens government's leverage over citizens as clients. Often this leverage is used in ways that may be rational from the perspectives of a given program or set of administrative values. Perhaps this is true of welfare rules disallowing benefits where an able-bodied man is residing with a woman and her dependent children. Such a rule can reduce the number of individuals eligible for welfare and thereby reduce program costs. However, it can also have harmful social effects, such as the encouragement of single-parent families. This could be construed as undue governmental interference with individual freedom concerning matters of choice pertaining to family life, an individual prerogative that the Supreme Court has recognized in other contexts* (*Cleveland Board of Education v. LaFleur*, 1974; *Cohen v. Chesterfield County School Board*, 1974). Moreover, such a rule, as many others in the area of welfare, requires that the government investigate the living situation of individuals, something it could not ordinarily accomplish constitutionally if the individual were not seeking governmental largess. Thus, such regulations raise a host of questions of constitutional stature, including the relevance of investigations and their effect upon individual liberties.

Even more drastic is the situation in which the conditions attached to the receipt of largess are clearly irrelevant to the use of that largess and, at the same time, place infringements upon the ordinary exercise of constitutional rights. Reich's examples, as just presented, should be reconsidered in this context. To reduce the issue to an ultimate absurdity, but a true case nevertheless, can one be made to swear allegiance to the government in order to obtain a fishing license from it? Such a condition clearly has nothing to do with conservation, environmental preservation, or related state interests. If it serves any purpose, it would be "punish" subversives by denying them the opportunity to fish legally. Such a regulation, of course, has little to do with administrative efficiency, but it nevertheless dehumanizes the "case" by overtly removing any issue of personal political ideology. And it is because administrative values and administrative structures are so well suited to regulation of individual behavior that the state relies upon bureaucratic agencies in attempting to exercise such leverage.

It is evident that administrative values favoring efficiency and, therefore, the dehumanization or impersonalization of clients, consequently stand in some contrast to constitutional values. Neither the Founding Fathers nor the Constitution expresses much concern for efficiency. The government they established is, if anything, highly inefficient by design. The purpose of the separation of powers and the creation of shared and overlapping authorities was to enable the government to be broadly representative of and responsive to a variety of different constituencies. None of these was likely to be able to dominate the course of public policy unless its aims were perceived by others to be clearly in the general interest. A national governmental capability to act quickly and to implement forcefully was precisely what the founders hoped to avoid. The system of government they created, by incorporating a host of opportunities for political minorities to block the adoption of laws and policies, is well suited to protecting individual rights and liberties from official action. There are

*See Chapter 4.

several ways the Constitution, as amended by the Bill of Rights and other provisions, can accomplish this in the administrative realm.

In view of the eventual development of a judicial doctrine of *privilege*, which had the impact of affording little or no constitutional protection to bureaucratic largess, it is interesting to note that Article IV, section 2 reads, "The Citizens of each State shall be entitled to all Privileges and Immunities of Citizens in the several States." Although this clause was hardly intended to regulate the kind of bureaucratic largess with which we are now familiar, it is significant in that the founders recognized that the allotment of privileges was a significant governmental issue and that some protections against their manipulation ought to be afforded. Today, however, such matters as the length of time a state may require newly arrived residents to wait before being eligible for welfare (*Shapiro v. Thompson*, 1969), to vote (*Dunn v. Blumstein*, 1972), or to attend public universities on the same terms as long-time residents (*Vlandis v. Kline*, 1973) are decided on the basis of the Equal Protection Clause.

Several parts of the Bill of Rights, adopted in 1791, also held out some potential for regulating the conditions under which governmental largess could be allotted. For example, the First Amendment reads, in part, "Congress shall make no law respecting the establishment of religion. . . ." Consequently, if the citizen-client's receipt of governmental largess were made contingent upon a declaration of belief in a deity, it could potentially be construed as a violation of this provision. Indeed, it was almost precisely on these grounds that the Supreme Court invalidated a Maryland statute preventing an individual, refusing to declare his belief in God, from becoming a notary public. The Fifth Amendment's prohibition against the denial of property without due process of law also offered some potential protection for the individual in the allotment of federal governmental largess, especially occupational licenses. Although *largess* is not *property* in a traditional sense, as Reich (1964) points out, when government accumulates a high proportion of the wealth of a society, largess may become a kind of *new property*. That is, largess comes to serve many of the purposes of traditional property. Moreover, since individuals have such a strong interest in such largess, it may not be too substantial a conceptual leap to regulate the deprivation of this new property similarly to the deprivation of traditional property. Again, as will be discussed shortly, the courts have moved strongly in this direction. The Fifth Amendment's requirement of due process in the deprivation of liberty by the federal government is also of relevance. If, for example, one has a constitutional right to define one's living arrangements, then the imposition of morality standards as a condition of receiving largess may be limited by that document. The Fourteenth Amendment contains a due process clause that could be used to regulate state administration in similar fashion. Importantly, *due process* can involve the right to a fair hearing which has the effect of personalizing the case at hand by requiring it to be judged on its individual merits.

Finally, the equal protection clause of the Fourteenth Amendment should be mentioned since it can clearly be interpreted as limiting governmental freedom to *distribute* largess unequally, especially in a fashion that denies it to blacks while making it available to whites.

In sum, rather than attempt to turn the citizen into a case, the Constitution seeks to maintain his or her individuality through the protections incorporated in the Bill of Rights and the Fourteenth Amendment. The Founding Fathers believed that individuality, and the diversity of opinion it tends to produce, would protect the republic from being dominated by a majority faction which might tyrannize political and social minorities. In terms of this intent, it would be odd if what government could not accomplish directly, such as the establishment of a religion or the limitation of freedom of speech, it could nevertheless establish indirectly by the manipulation of largess. Yet, for many years, this is precisely what the courts allowed to happen.

Clients in the Court: The Traditional Response

Traditionally, the judiciary was reluctant to hold that the allotment of governmental largess could be regulated by the Constitution. Its primary rationale for this approach was the *doctrine of privilege*, which contained the following premises: (1) the government had no constitutional duty or obligation to supply largess; (2) the client accepted largess voluntarily and without official coercion; (3) therefore, the government was largely free to establish the conditions upon which the client could receive largess; and (4) such largess might even be withheld in a discriminatory fashion under some circumstances. The key to this doctrine was the distinction between privileges and rights; a *privilege* was unregulated by the Constitution and could be obtained solely upon the terms set forth by the government; a *right*, on the other hand, is constitutionally protected and therefore could effectively be asserted by the citizen-client. In large part, under this approach the government's reason for attaching conditions to largess was not subject to more than pro forma judicial scrutiny. This was true whether the purpose was to control indirectly the client's behavior in a way that could not be directly regulated under the Constitution, or whether the conditions were imposed for the sake of administrative convenience. In short, under this traditional approach, the citizen-client was virtually without constitutional protection concerning the allotment of largess. A few examples will serve to illustrate these points.

The U.S. Supreme Court embraced the logic of the doctrine of privilege as it pertained to the citizen-client of the administrative state in *Hamilton v. Regents* (1934). The issue was whether in establishing a state university, California could require students to enroll in a Reserve Officers Training Course (ROTC). The students challenging this requirement claimed it infringed upon their religious freedom as conscientious objectors to war. The Court gave short shrift to this assertion in a passage that well captures the essence of the doctrine of privilege.

California has not drafted or called them to attend the university. They are seeking education offered by the State and at the same time insisting that they be excluded from the prescribed course solely upon grounds of their religious beliefs and conscientious objections to war, preparation for war and military education. . . .
    Viewed in the light of our decisions, that proposition must at once be put aside as untenable (*Hamilton v. Regents*, 1934:262).

In *Barsky v. Board of Regents* (1954), the Court was even more explicit in reaffirming such applications of the doctrine of privilege. The case involved Dr. Barsky, a New York physician, who after refusing to cooperate with an investigation by the U.S. House Committee on Un-American Activites was convicted and jailed under federal law. New York State, acting pursuant to its own regulations, suspended Dr. Barsky's license to practice medicine for a period of six months. Barsky challenged the suspension on the grounds that his conviction was for something not a crime in New York State and did not involve moral turpitude or medical incompetence. In other words, the act for which he was convicted had nothing to do with his medical competence, fitness as a physician, or citizenship in New York. The Court rejected this argument in the following words: "The practice of medicine in New York is lawfully prohibited by the State except upon the conditions it imposes. Such practice is a privilege granted by the State under its substantially plenary power to fix the terms of admission" (451). Significantly, this application of the doctrine of privilege reached a very substantial aspect of largess—the license (and liberty) to practice one's occupation. The breadth and quality of the ruling was attacked by Justice Douglas whose dissent included the following statements: "The right to work, I had assumed, was the most precious liberty that man possesses" (472) and "When a doctor cannot save lives in America because he is opposed to Franco in Spain, it is time to call a halt and look critically at the neurosis that has possessed us" (474).
    Several state court decisions are also of interest. In *Wilkie v. O'Connor* (1941), the Appellate Court of the State of New York was confronted with the odd case of a man who received government largess in the form of an "old age assistance" check. The Commissioner of Public Welfare withheld this benefit on the basis that "despite all efforts to dissuade him, [he] insists upon his right to sleep under an old barn, in a nest of rags to which he has to crawl upon his hands and knees" (618). Since there was no showing that Wilkie's health was endangered, his chief offense seems to have been against the sensibilities of the state. The court showed little regard to Wilkie's argument against the imposition of

conditions upon his "life-style": ". . . he has no right to defy the standards and conventions of civilized society while being supported at public expense. This is true even though some of those conventions may be somewhat artificial" (619). In short, ". . . in accepting charity, the appellant has consented to the provisions of the law under which charity is bestowed" (620).

Two additional cases further convey the essence of the doctrine of privilege and the citizen-client's traditional constitutional position in the administrative state. In *Hornstein v. Illinois Liquor Control Commission* (1952), the Illinois Supreme Court found no constitutional difficulty in an administrative agency's effort to force a citizen-client to choose between his privilege against self-incrimination and his privilege to operate a retail liquor business. It declared that "while Hornstein has a constitutional privilege against self-incrimination, he has no constitutional right to operate a tavern . . ."* (358). The often very limited scope of judicial review in such cases was made evident in *Starkey v. Board of Education* (1963). In assessing the constitutionality of a rule excluding married high school students from participating in some extracurricular activities, but not others, the Supreme Court of Utah reasoned that:

> It is not for the courts to be concerned with the wisdom or propriety of the resolution as to its social desirability, nor whether it best serves the objectives of education, nor with the convenience or inconvenience of its application to the plaintiff in his particular circumstances. So long as the resolution is deemed by the Board of Education to serve the purpose of best promoting the objectives of the school and the standards for eligibility are based upon uniformly applied classifications which bear some reasonable relationship to the objectives, it cannot be said to be capricious, arbitrary or unjustly discriminatory (720).

In view of its widespread application, it is evident that from a constitutional and legal perspective the doctrine of privilege was very appealing. In large part this was due to three factors. First, the doctrine had a logical simplicity. In a well-known statement, a leading law professor explained: "If I have no ground for complaint at being denied a privilege absolutely, it is difficult to see how I acquire such a ground merely because the state, instead of denying me a privilege outright, offers me an alternative, however harsh" (quoted in O'Neil, 1966:445). Second, it enabled the judiciary to avoid comprehensive involvement in public administration. Until recently, as discussed in the previous chapter, this was deemed politically desirable and legally sensible due to the fact that judges' expertise lies largely in law rather than administration or management. To the extent that judges could avoid entering into the administrative thicket, they

---

*This is an echo of a statement by Justice Holmes in 1892. See Chapter 4.

would find themselves on firmer ground, less likely to transgress into the sphere of executive concerns, and more able to manage their caseloads. By holding that the allotment of largess was devoid of constitutional questions, the doctrine of privilege assured minimal judicial involvement in adminstrative affairs. Third, and relatedly, the doctrine of privilege enabled the judiciary to avoid confrontations with the legislature, when the latter was the source of the imposition of conditions upon the receipt of governmental largess. However, despite these characteristics of the doctrine of privilege, it began to break down under several constitutional, legal, and political pressures.

Limitations of the Doctrine of Privilege

The doctrine of privilege enabled the state indirectly to infringe upon constitutional rights in a manner that would be constitutionally unacceptable if accomplished directly. Eventually, as the administrative state expanded and the dependence of the citizen-client upon it became more acute, the judicary began to devise ways of reducing the erosion of rights that resulted from strict adherence to the doctrine of privilege. Eventually, the weight of these countervailing decisions and approaches led to that doctrine's demise and to a much more forceful judicial role in the administrative state.

The doctrine of unconstitutional conditions was an early alternative approach to the doctrine of privilege. It was nowhere better articulated than in *Frost & Frost Trucking Co. v. Railroad Commission* (1926:593–594), where the Supreme Court held:

> It would be a palpable incongruity to strike down an act of state legislation which, by words of express divestment, seeks to strip the citizen of rights guaranteed by the federal Constitution, but to uphold an act by which the same result is accomplished under the guise of a surrender of a right in exchange for a valuable privilege which the state threatens otherwise to withhold. . . . If the state may compel the surrender of one constitutional right as a condition of its favor, it may, in like manner, compel a surrender of all. It is inconceivable that guaranties embedded in the Constitution of the United States may thus be manipulated out of existence.

When forcefully applied, the doctrine of unconstitutional conditions places a heavy burden on the government. As the Supreme Court of California set forth the matter,

... when ... the conditions annexed to the enjoyment of a publicly-
conferred benefit require a waiver of rights secured by the Constitution,
however well-informed and voluntary that waiver, the governmental
entity seeking to impose those conditions must establish: (1) that the
conditions reasonably related to the purposes sought by the legislation
which confers the benefit; (2) that the value accruing to the public from
the imposition of these conditions manifestly outweighs any resulting
impairment of constitutional rights; and (3) that there are available no
alternative means less subversive of constitutional right, narrowly drawn
so as to correlate more closely with the purposes contemplated by con-
ferring the benefit (*Parrish vs. CSC*, 1967:230).

The major limitation on this approach has been that the rights asserted by the
citizen-client must be directly protected by a provison of the Constitution.
As Van Alstyle (1968) observed, "The doctrine of unconstitutional conditions
has usually been applied only to regulations which directly forbid the enjoyment
of an explicit constitutional right. The doctrine has been of little assistance in
situations, however, where the regulation of status in the public sector has had
only an indirect effect on such a right, without directly and wholly forbidding
its exercise" (1449). Nevertheless, a few cases can be found in which conditions
imposed upon largess have been considered unconstitutional as a result of their
indirect effects. One example was an Arkansas statute requiring public school
teachers, as a condition of employment, to provide a list of all the organizations
to which they belonged (*Shelton v. Tucker*, 1960).

A more forceful challenge to the doctrine of privilege has been in the realm of
equal protection. As Van Alstyne explains, "Under that clause, it seemingly
makes no difference that the threatened interest is a privilege rather than a right.
Even a privilege, benefit, opportunity, or public advantage may not be granted
to some but withheld from others where the basis of classification and difference
in treatment is arbitrary" (1968:1454). For example, since the government is
not constitutionally required to make it available, public education is defined as
a privilege, rather than a constitutional right. Nevertheless, the equal protection
clause protects the citizen-client's right to equality of educational opportunity
in public educational systems. Thus, racial exclusion, racial segregation, and
comparable practices are unconstitutional. The same would be true in terms
of other largess, including welfare, occupational licenses, and public services
generally.

The equal protection clause serves as an important check on the distribution
of governmental largess, but it does not compel the equal allotment of benefits
to all citizen-clients of the administrative state. For example, the rich and poor
alike are not entitled to welfare benefits. Distinctions involving such matters as

wealth, age, residency and, at least to date, gender, are acceptable to the courts where there is a clear rational basis for them. Classifications involving such matters as race, ethnicity, and religion require a stricter test: the state must demonstrate that it has a compelling interest in treating different citizen-clients in disparate fashion. Ultimately, of course, it is the judiciary that decides whether the state has shown a rational basis or compelling state interest in drawing distinctions among citizen-clients. This assures it a wider role in the functioning of the administrative state. It is important to remember, however, that at an earlier date some courts did not view the equal protection clause as a limitation on the governmental distribution of privileges. Thus, although the present interpretation of the equal protection clause as a means of protecting the citizen-client's rights grew largely out of a broader concern with civil rights and equality, it nevertheless expands the judiciary's role in the administrative state.

Another important limitation on the application of the doctrine of privilege has emerged out of recent judicial interpretations of procedural due process. The premise that a governmental benefit is a privilege does not necessarily support the conclusion that, therefore, it can be denied to a particular citizen-client in an arbitrary, capricious, or otherwise unfair fashion. For instance, under the doctrine of privilege the fact that welfare benefits are a privilege may allow the government to withhold them from those who are disloyal, but it would not necessarily enable the government to adjudge a citizen-client disloyal without affording the individual a fair procedure to challenge this determination. Or, in the context of public employment, as Justice Jackson expressed it, "The fact that one may not have a legal right to get or keep a government post does not mean that he can be adjudged ineligible illegally" (*Joint Anti-Fascist Refugee Committee v. McGrath*, 1951:185). As Van Alstyne (1968) points out, procedural due process can also be invoked in connection with the concept of unconstitutional conditions. Suppose, for example, there is a strong prima facie case that a welfare check has been withheld because a citizen-client delivered a political speech. The imposition of a condition that welfare recipients not engage in political speech might run afoul of the unconstitutional conditions approach. Consequently, a fair procedure could be required to determine whether in fact the benefit was denied as a result of the speech, and, if so, subsequently whether the denial was actually unconstitutional. The procedural aspect in such circumstances is useful in preventing the imposition of unconstitutional conditions. In either context, however, procedural due process places substantial limitations upon the administrative state because it raises the costs of imposing conditions upon the receipt of largess and raises the costs of withdrawing such benefits. This is clearly evident, for example, in the realm of welfare, where a hearing of some type is now constitutionally required before some benefits can be cut off.

Taken together, these various limitations on the application of the doctrine of privilege have amounted to a complete nullification of its importance in defining the constitutional relationship of the citizen-client to the administrative state. They have also compelled the judiciary to play a far greater role in public admin-istration. In the process, the courts have tended to substitute constitutional values stressing individuality and liberty for values stressing efficiency through dehumanization. By "constitutionalizing" largess, the judiciary has refashioned the citizen-client's rights vis-à-vis the administrative state. Four Supreme Court cases serve to elucidate the radical transformations that have occurred.

The Supreme Court and the Citizen-Client

The issue of unconstitutional conditions in the allotment of governmental largess was clearly confronted by the Supreme Court in *Sherbert v. Verner* (1963). Sherbert, a Seventh-day Adventist, lost her private-sector employment when she refused to work on Saturday. Not being able to find other suitable work, she filed a claim for benefits under the South Carolina Unemployment Compensa-tion Act. However, the ". . . Employment Security Commission . . . found that [Sherbert's] restriction upon her availability for Saturday work brought her within the provision disqualifying for benefits insured workers who fail, without good cause, to accept 'suitable work when offered.' . . ." (1963:401). This administrative ruling was upheld by the South Carolina Supreme Court, which ". . . held specifically that [her] ineligibility infringed no consitutional liberties because such a construction of the statute 'places no restriction upon [Sherbert's] freedom of religion nor does it in any way prevent her in the exercise of her right and freedom to observe her religious beliefs in accordance with the dictates of her conscience' " (401).

The U.S. Supreme Court disagreed on two grounds. First, it reasoned that this application of the statute did in fact infringe upon her free exercise of religion.

> The ruling forces her to choose between following the precepts of her religion and forfeiting benefits, on the one hand, and abandoning one of the precepts of her religion in order to accept work, on the other. Govern-mental imposition of such a choice puts the same kind of burden upon the free exercise of religion as would a fine imposed against appellant for her Saturday worship (404).

This language was in itself significant, for as has been shown, in earlier cases the judiciary was reluctant to recognize that conditions imposed upon the receipt of governmental largess could be construed to infringe upon the recipient's constitutional rights.

More significant, however, was the Court's outright rejection of the notion that the distinction between *rights* and *privileges* had any bearing on the matter.

> Nor may the South Carolina court's construction of the statute be saved from constitutional infirmity on the ground that unemployment compensation benefits are not appellant's "right" but merely a "privilege." It is too late in the day to doubt that the liberties of religion and expression may be infringed by the denial or placing of conditions upon a benefit or privilege. . . . [T]o condition the availability of benefits upon [Sherbert's] willingness to violate a cardinal principle of her religious faith effectively penalizes the free exercise of her constitutional liberties . . . (404–406).

Such an abridgment could withstand constitutional scrutiny only if the state could demonstrate a "compelling state interest" (406), which it was unable to do here.

In retrospect, *Sherbert v. Verner* may seem unremarkable. However, it was a substantial departure from the traditional law concerning citizen-clients of the administrative state. Indeed, in dissent Justice Harlan maintained "today's decision is disturbing both in its rejection of existing precedent and in its implications for the future" (418). The Supreme Court had once and for all served unequivocal notice that the allotment of governmental largess could no longer be used readily to manipulate the behavior of citizen-clients in areas afforded explicit protections by the Constitution. Importantly, as Harlan's dissent pointed out, the Court chose this interpretation over the traditional one despite the fact that by creating an exemption, based on religious belief, from the general requirement that applicants for benefits be willing to accept work, the Court's decision could be construed as fostering the establishment of religion, which is also prohibited by the First and Fourteenth Amendments.

It should be borne in mind that neither *Sherbert v. Verner* nor any other case has held that every condition, invading constitutionally protected areas, imposed upon the receipt of governmental largess will be unconstitutional. The government always has the opportunity to demonstrate a compelling interest in attaching the condition to the benefit. The current presumption, however, is against such conditions, and it is highly unlikely that their constitutionality will be upheld when they are imposed primarily for the sake of administrative convenience or protecting the public fisc. In this sense, constitutional values, as enforced by the judiciary, are clearly considered superior to administrative values.

The same is true in the realm of equal protection. Although any number of cases could be chosen to demonstrate the Supreme Court's limitation of the impact of doctrine of privilege where equal protection is at stake, *Missouri ex rel. Gaines v. Canada* (1938) presents an early example in an area of considerable and continuing judicial involvement in the administrative state. Pursuant to Missouri statute and solely on the basis of his race, Lloyd Gaines, a black, was refused admission to the School of Law at the State University of Missouri. The state did not operate a law school to which he or any other black could be admitted. However, it did offer to send him to the public law school of an adjacent state where blacks were admitted. Gaines brought suit, claiming that his equal protection rights had been violated. In its defense, the state argued that the public law schools in adjacent states taught an identical curriculum to that of the University of Missouri and did so with equal quality. The Supreme Court gave short-shrift to this approach in establishing the constitutional principle that privileges fall squarely within the individual citizen-client's right to equal protection under the Fourteenth Amendment.

The basic consideration is not as to what sort of opportunities other States provide, or whether they are as good as those in Missouri, but as to what opportunities Missouri itself furnishes to white students and denies to negroes (sic) solely upon the ground of color. The admissibility of laws separating the races in the enjoyment of privileges afforded by the State rests wholly upon the equality of the privileges which the laws give to the separated groups within the State. The question here is not of a duty of the State to supply legal training, or of the quality of the training which it does supply, but of its duty when it provides such training to furnish it to the residents of the State upon the basis of an equality of right. By the operation of the laws of Missouri a privilege has been created for white law students which is denied to negroes by reason of their race. The white resident is afforded legal education within the State; the negro resident having the same qualifications is refused it there and must go outside the State to obtain it. That is a denial of the equality of legal right to the enjoyment of the privilege which the State has set up, and the provision for the payment of tuition fees in another State does not remove the discrimination (349-350).

Thus, the constitutional requirement of equal protection cannot be diminished through the allotment of governmental largess to the citizen-clients of the administrative state. If privileges are made available to some groups, they must be made available to others, unless the state can demonstrate a compelling interest or rational basis for the restrictions it imposes. While the government's difficulty in so doing will vary with the nature of the classifications or discriminations imposed, the important point is that all distinctions are subject to judicial scrutiny and the administrative carte blanche favored by the doctrine of privilege has been substantially reduced in this fashion. Nor, as subsequent cases indicate, can privileges be allotted on a racially segregated basis.

In addition, two Supreme Court decisions illustrate the extent to which the doctrine of privilege was weakened by the requirements that standards of procedural due process under the Fifth and Fourteenth Amendments be met in the allocation of governmental largess. These cases also demonstrate the degree of judicial recognition of the individual's dependence upon the largess of the administrative state and of the need to afford citizen-clients' constitutional rights vis-à-vis such benefits. In *Goldberg v. Kelly* (1970) the Court was confronted with the question of whether New York City's termination of welfare payments to an individual without affording him the opportunity for a *prior* evidentiary hearing violated due process. The Court's decision was notable both for the precedent it established and for its direct recognition of the citizen's dependence on governmental privileges. In the course of holding that Kelly was entitled to a prior hearing, the Court stated: "The extent to which procedural due process must be afforded the recipient is influenced by the extent to which he may be 'condemned to suffer grievous loss,' . . . and depends upon whether the recipient's interest in avoiding that loss outweighs the governmental interest in summary adjudication" (262-263). Under the circumstances, in which Kelly might be deprived of "the very means by which to live while he waits" (264) for the opportunity for a posttermination hearing, the Court considered his interests in a prior hearing to outweigh the government's potential interests in not affording one. Indeed, the Court was reluctant to grant any credence to the administrative values opposing a pretermination hearing.

> Moreover, important governmental interests are promoted by affording recipients a pre-termination evidentiary hearing. From its founding the Nation's basic commitment has been to foster the dignity and well-being of all persons within its borders.
>
> Appellant [i.e., the government] does not challenge the force of these considerations but argues that they are outweighed by countervailing governmental interests in conserving fiscal and administrative resources. . . .
>   We agree with the District Court, however, that these governmental interests are not overriding in the welfare context (264-266).

Thus, the Court rejected the administrative rationale offered in defense of the posttermination process, and it also read the administrators a lesson in its version of basic American political values.

Goldberg v. Kelly was remarkable in that only a few decades earlier such a result would have been unthinkable. This facet of the judicial response to the rise of the administrative state was not lost on Justice Black, whose dissent reflected a different and more traditional view of public administration and law.

In the last half century the United States, along with many, perhaps most, other nations of the world, has moved far toward becoming a welfare state, that is, a nation that for one reason or another taxes its most affluent people to help support, feed, clothe, and shelter its less fortunate citizens. The result is that today more than nine million men, women, and children in the United States receive some kind of state or federally financed public assistance in the form of allowances or gratuities. . . . Since these gratuities are paid on the basis of need, the list of recipients is not static, and some people go off the lists and others are added from time to time. These ever-changing lists put a constant administrative burden on government and it certainly could not have responsibly antici- pated that this burden would include the additional procedural expense imposed by the Court today (271-272).

Thus, for Black, who was appointed by Franklin Roosevelt during the tumultous New Deal period, the administrative state was "a new experiment for our Nation" (279) that should not be incumbered by overburdening judicial regula- tion. More significantly perhaps, in his view, largess should not have been constitutionalized.

The Court . . . relies upon the Fourteenth Amendment and in effect says that the failure of the government to pay a promised charitable instalment to an individual deprives that individual of *his own property*, in violation of the Due Process Clause of the Fourteenth Amendment. It somewhat strains credulity to say that the government's promise of charity to an individual is property belonging to that individual when the government denies that the individual is honestly entitled to receive such a payment (275).

Similar views—that is, the traditional and the contemporary judicial approaches—were also contrasted in *Goss v. Lopez* (1975), a case involving the suspension of a student from a public high school. The issue was whether a one-day suspension could be levied against a student without first affording him a hearing of some type. The Court required ". . . that there be at least an informal give-and-take between student and disciplinarian, preferably prior to the suspension . . ." (584). In so doing, it articulated the logic of applying due process to administrative largess.

. . . [A]ppellants contend that because there is no constitutional right to an education at public expense, the Due Process Clause does not protect against expulsions from the public system. This position misconceives the nature of the issue and is refuted by prior decisions (572).

Having chosen to extend the right to an education to people of appellee's class generally, Ohio may not withdraw the right on grounds of misconduct, absent fundamentally fair procedures to determine whether the misconduct has occurred (574).

Requiring that appropriate standards of due process be met in such instances represents an extension of the principle of *Goldberg v. Kelly* into an area of relatively minimal harm.* Thus, Justice Powell argued in dissent that the suspension represented only a fraction of the school year and did not inflict substantial harm upon the student. Yet, it is precisely such an extension that is indicative of the comprehensive character of the judicial response to the rise of the administrative state. Part of that response is *imperialistic* in nature: it represents the exportation of judicial concepts and adjudicatory procedures into areas in which they were previously absent. Hence, the question of the appropriateness of the judicial regulation of aspects of the administrative state often rises to the fore. This was evident in Justice Powell's dissent in *Goss v. Lopez* (1975), which was joined by Justices Blackmun, Rehnquist, and Chief Justice Burger.

One of the more disturbing aspects of today's decision is its indiscriminate reliance upon the judiciary, and the adversary process, as the means of resolving many of the most routine problems arising in the classroom. In mandating due process procedures the Court misapprehends the reality of the normal teacher-pupil relationship. There is an ongoing relationship, one in which the teacher must occupy many roles—educator, adviser, friend, and, at times, parent-substitute. It is rarely adversary in nature except with respect to the chronically disruptive or insubordinate pupil whom the teacher must be free to discipline without frustrating formalities (594).

Nor is the issue of the appropriateness of the adversary process necessarily limited to student-teacher relationships. Certainly, the relationships of social worker and client and public manager and public employee may be better conceptualized in other terms.

Justice Powell was even more explicit about the nature of judicial imperialism and the Court's tendency to promote jurocracy. As a result of the Court's ruling, he feared,

---

*In *Mathews v. Eldridge* (1976), the Supreme Court chose not to extend the *Goldberg* principle to benefits to disabled workers because, in part, disability benefits are not based on financial need.

The discretion and judgment of federal courts across the land often will be substituted for that of the 50 state legislatures, the 14,000 school boards, and the 2,000,000 teachers who heretofore have been responsible for the administration of the American public school system (599).

Finally Justice Powell expressed his opposition to the Court's expansion of the citizen-client's procedural due process protections vis-à-vis the administrative state.

Not so long ago, state deprivations of the most significant forms of state largesse were not thought to require due process protection on the ground that the deprivation resulted only in the loss of a state-provided "benefit." . . . In recent years the Court, wisely in my view, has rejected the "wooden distinction between 'rights' and 'privileges,' " . . . and looked instead to the significance of the state-created or state-enforced right and to the substantiality of the alleged deprivation. Today's opinion appears to abandon this reasonable approach by holding in effect that government infringement of any interest to which a person is entitled, no matter what the interest or how inconsequential the infringement, requires *constitutional* protection. As it is difficult to think of any less consequential infringement than suspension of a junior high school student for a single day, it is equally difficult to perceive any principled limit to the new reach of procedural due process (599–600).

In sum, the judicial response to the claims of the citizen-client of the administrative state has been to eviscerate the doctrine of privilege by creating constitutional constraints on the allotment of governmental largess. The government can no longer attach any conditions it sees fit to the receipt of benefits or privileges. Nor can it distribute them without regard to the requirements of equal protection. Moreover, even though there is no right to any given privilege, it now appears that there is frequently a right not to be denied the benefits of governmental largess in the absence of a fair procedure incorporating the flexible requirements of due process. In this fashion, the new property of which Reich (1964) wrote has in large part been created by the judiciary. Largess has been constitutionalized in such a fashion that it resembles property in the traditional sense. This constitutionalization was a major aspect of the judiciary's response to the rise of the administrative state. No longer would the judiciary grant overriding deference to administrative values and administrative convenience. Instead, to a far greater extent the administrative state was made to operate in concert with the constitutional values of the judiciary. Although the language of various decisions often concerns other matters, such as the free exercise of religion, this facet of the judicial response has been deliberate. Dissents such as that of Justice Black in *Goldberg v. Kelly* and Justices Powell, Blackmun, Rehnquist, and Burger in *Goss v. Lopez* leave no doubt that the Supreme Court is aware of the changes in government wrought by the rise of the administrative state and that it is seeking to respond to them through constitutional law. However, the imposition of judicial values in this context has not been limited to regulating the procedures under which largess is allotted or to review of constitutionality of the conditions under which it is distributed. Employing the public law litigation model, some courts have become deeply and proactively involved in the administration of governmental benefits. This is nowhere better demonstrated than in the realm of public education.

Bench v. Bureau: The Case of Boston's Public Schools

Missouri ex rel. Gaines v. Canada (1938) firmly established the principle that citizen-clients of the administrative state have the constitutional right to equal protection in the distribution of governmental largess, specifically education. Subsequently, in *Sweatt v. Painter* (1950) the Supreme Court held that the equal protection clause requires that educational opportunities for blacks and whites be substantially equal in terms of tangible factors, and where this could not be accomplished on a segregated basis, the educational facilities must be integrated. In *McLaurin v. Oklahoma State Regents* (1950), the Court prohibited racial segregation within a single public university. These decisions clearly pointed toward the abolition of racially segregated public schools generally, but it was not until its decision in *Brown v. Board of Education* (1954) that the Court clearly held that such segregation violated the equal protection rights of black school children. Its decision hinged on the following rationale.

> We come then to the question presented: Does segregation of children in public schools solely on the basis of race, even though the physical facilities and other "tangible" factors may be equal, deprive the children of the minority group of equal educational opportunities? We believe it does. . . . To separate them [blacks] from others of similar age and qualifications solely because of their race generates a feeling of inferiority as to their status in the community that may affect their hearts and minds in a way unlikely ever to be undone. . . .
> We conclude that in the field of public education the doctrine of "separate but equal" has no place. Separate educational facilities are inherently unequal (493–495).

The *Brown* decision was elegant in its simplicity, but its aftermath has been exceedingly complex.

Among the questions left unanswered were issues pertaining to segregation as a result of residential patterns within a single school system or among cities and their suburbs. In addition, the issue of remedying segregation which combined elements of residency and official discrimination became a matter of intense national debate. In shorthand fashion, the question concerned busing, but a major facet of the issue was the extent to which the federal judiciary would run the nation's public schools. Indeed, in *Milliken v. Bradley* (1974), the Supreme Court overturned a district court decision seeking to consolidate Detroit's school system with those of its suburbs, partly on the grounds that it would make the district court the "school superintendent" of a system having 750,000 pupils. Chief Justice Burger called for greater judicial restraint: "This is a task which few, if any, judges are qualified to perform and one which would deprive the people of control of the schools through their elected representatives" (744).*
In the City of Boston, however, matters took a different turn.

In *Morgan v. Kerrigan* (1975) Federal District Court Judge Garrity recounted the historical rise and decline of Boston and its public schools. Among other facts, it had been established that in a public school system that was 61 percent white and 32 percent black, 84 percent of the whites attended schools whose student bodies were at least 80 percent white, whereas 62 percent of the black pupils were in schools whose racial composition was at least 70 percent black. It had been further found that this segregation was knowingly and intentionally maintained. In sum, the Boston school system deprived black students of their right to equal protection and some remedy was necessary.

At first, the district court allowed state and local officials to attempt to correct this breach of the citizen-clients' rights to equal protection and to bring the school system up to constitutional standards. A state-imposed integration plan, involving busing, led to violence and failed to integrate the city's schools in a satisfactory way. Another plan was developed by a local school committee but was opposed by three members of the school board, who objected to the forced busing it imposed. In the end, the court rejected the school committee's plan anyway because it was partly based on parental choice as a means of desegregating and seemed unlikely to succeed. At this point, the court began to take matters into its own hands. It appointed two experts and four special masters** to create a desegregation plan and to make recommendations to the

---

*The main issue was whether equal protection required integration among *separate* school systems where the systems were not established as a means of promoting racial segregations. The supreme Court held that the Constitution did not reach city-suburban residential patterns of this nature.
**A special master is a master appointed to act as the representative of a court in some particular act or transaction. See *Black's Law Dictionary* (St. Paul, Minn.: West Publishing, 1979), p. 879.

court. Eventually, the plan they recommended became the core of the judicially imposed resolution of the case.

The court-imposed plan had four objectives: (1) to bar affirmative discrimination, (2) to prevent continuing injury through racial isolation of minority students, (3) to eliminate racially identifiable schools, and (4) to satisfy the competing interests and practicalities of the situation. The particulars of the plan left no doubt that the court had thoroughly refashioned Boston's school system. Among its main features was the creation of eight school districts within which busing would be used to assure that no single school's racial composition would vary by more than 25 percent of the composition of the school system as a whole. Examination schools were also created for students with superior intellectual merit. Entrance to these schools was based on grades and scores on the Secondary School Admission Test. These schools were to have at least a 35 percent black and Hispanic enrollment. In addition, citywide magnet schools were created with special programs specified by the court. The court's plan required the closing of 20 schools and widespread busing. Implementation was to be supervised by a court-appointed three-member panel and monitored by citywide and school district coordinating councils.

However desirable or necessary to protect the equal protection rights of minority pupils, Judge Garrity's action was remarkable. It left no doubt that the schools would be organized and supervised not by state and local officials, but rather by a federal district court. This type of remedy goes far beyond traditional confrontations between judges and public administrators. Traditionally, a judge would dispose of a case by decreeing that the school board perform some specific function or stop taking some specific action. Less traditionally and more drastically, a court might order that the schools be closed until they could be operated in concert with constitutional requirements (Lehne, 1978). Judge Garrity's remedy, however, brought the court directly and proactively into the realm of public administration. In essence, the district court became the governing body for the Boston public schools. This clearly represented a commingling of judicial and administrative functions and placed the court in the middle of a complex and emotion-laden administrative thicket. This is the type of situation in which the contemporary judicial response to the rise of the administrative state most clearly blends into jurocracy and arouses political opposition. Some of the issues posed by such action are discussed in the concluding chapter; others were addressed in the previous chapter. Here, however, it is desirable to point to the extent to which it established judicial supremacy. Thus, when Judge Garrity's plan was challenged by a citizen's group in the court of appeals on the grounds that it would increase "white flight," that court responded that even if it occurred, white flight would not violate the Constitution since all that document mandates is that blacks be treated equally to whites within the *same* school system. But, if white flight were to occur as a result of plans imposed by any branch of government other than the judiciary, it would indeed provide gounds for court-ordered integration across school district lines. Hence, an important element of judicial supremacy is that the courts are sometimes self-exempt from the requirements they place upon others. This is even more evident in the area of official liability and immunity which is discussed in Chapter 6.

Conclusion

The judicial response to the position of the citizen-client of the administrative state is a microcosm of the wider relationship between law and public administration. Initially, largess was viewed as a privilege to which a variety of conditions could be attached. Once the extent individuals' dependence on largess was recognized, the judicairy began to create substantial constitutional rights for citizen-clients. Specifically, conditions attached to largess could not be used to infringe or erode individual's constitutional rights, at least in the absence of a convincing government rationale for such stipulations. Nor could largess be distributed in a fashion that violated equal protection of the laws. Moreover, largess, although still a privilege, was treated as a kind of property, which meant that it could not be denied to citizen-clients without due process of law. In the process of developing these constitutional limitations on the administrative state, the judiciary asserted legal and constitutional values over administrative ones. Furthermore, in seeking to remedy egregious violations of citizen-clients' constitutional rights, as in the case of the Boston schools, the judicary sometimes directly took on administrative functions.

In sum, judicial activity regarding citizen-clients has enabled the judiciary to play a much wider role in the administrative state. Its decisions now enable it to regulate the conditions and procedures under which largess may be allotted. They also enable it to become directly involved in the provision of largess, as in Boston's public schools. In making the Constitution relevant to the distribution of largess, the judiciary has thrust itself into administrative matters and has asserted far greater influence over the administrative state. This development has important ramifications for the polity. However, these are best addressed after examining the judicial response to the rise of the administrative state in other contexts as well.

References

Aberbach, Joel and Bert Rockman, 1976. Clashing beliefs within the executive branch: The Nixon administration bureaucracy. *American Political Science Review* 70(June), 456–468.

Barker, Ernest, 1966. *The Development of Public Services in Western Europe, 1660-1930.* Hamden, Conn.: Archon Books.

Barsky v. Board of Regents, 1954. 347 U.S. 442.

Bendix, Rheinhard, 1964. *Nation Building and Citizenship.* New York: Wiley.

Brown, Ralph, 1958. *Loyalty and Security.* New Haven, Conn.: Yale University Press.

Brown v. Board of Education, 1954. 347 U.S. 483.

Cleveland Board of Education v. LaFleur, 1974. 414 U.S. 632.

Cohen v. Chesterfield County School Board, 1974. 414 U.S. 632.

Danet, Brenda and H. Hartman, 1972. On "proteksia." *Journal of Comparative Administration* 3 (February), 405-434.

Dunn v. Blumstein, 1972. 405 U.S. 330.

Eaton, Dorman B., 1880. *The Civil Service in Great Britain.* New York: Harper and Bros.

Fiorina, Morris, 1977. *Congress: Keystone of the Washington Establishment.* New Haven, Conn.: Yale University Press.

Friedman, Milton, 1962. *Capitalism and Freedom.* Chicago: University of Chicago Press.

Frost & Frost Trucking v. Railroad Commission, 1926. 271 U.S. 583.

Goldberg v. Kelly, 1970. 397 U.S. 254.

Goss v. Lopez, 1975. 419 U.S. 565.

Gouldner, Alvin, 1952. Red tape as a social problem. In Robert K. Merton, Ailsa Gray, Barbara Hockey, and Hanan Selvin (eds.), *Reader in Bureaucracy.* New York: Free Press, pp. 410-418.

Hamilton v. Regents, 1934. 293 U.S. 245.

Hayek, Friedrich, 1944. *The Road to Serfdom.* Chicago: University of Chicago Press.

Hornstein v. Illinois Liquor Control Commission, 1952. 106 NE 2d 354.

Hummel, Ralph, 1977. *The Bureaucratic Experience.* New York: St. Martin's.

Jackson, Andrew, 1926. *The Correspondence of Andrew Jackson,* J. S. Bassett (ed.). Washington, D.C.: Carnegie Institution.

Joint Anti-Fascist Refugee Committee v. McGrath, 1951. 341 U.S. 123.

Katz, Daniel, Barbara Gutek, Robert Kahn, and Eugenia Barton, 1975. *Bureaucratic Encounters.* Ann Arbor: University of Michigan Survey Research Center and Institute for Social Research.

Lehne, Richard, 1978. *The Quest for Justice.* New York: Longman.

McLaurin v. Oklahoma State Regents, 1950. 339 U.S. 637.

Mathews v. Eldridge, 1976. 424 U.S. 319.

Milliken v. Bradley, 1974. 418 U.S. 717.

Missouri ex rel Gaines v. Canada, 1938. 305 U.S. 337.

Morgan v. Kerrigan, 1975. 401 F. Suppl. 216.

Nachmias, David and David H. Rosenbloom, 1978. *Bureaucratic Culture: Citizens and Administrators in Israel.* New York: St. Martin's.

Nachmias, David and David H. Rosenbloom, 1980. *Bureaucratic Government, USA.* New York: St. Martin's.

O'Neil, Robert, 1966. Unconstitutional conditions: Welfare benefits with strings attached. *California Law Review* 54: 443-478.

Parrish v. CSC, 1967. 425 P2d 233.

Reich, Charles, 1964. The new property. *Yale Law Journal* 73: 733-787.

Richardson, James D., ed., 1896. *A Compilation of the Messages and Papers of the Presidents of the United States, 1789-1897,* 10 vols. Washington, D.C.: U.S. Government Printing Office.

Robinson, Donna, 1970. Patrons and saints: A study of career patterns of higher civil servants in Israel. Ph.D. Dissertation, Department of Political Science, Columbia University.

Rosenbloom, David H., 1971. *Federal Service and the Constitution.* Ithaca, N.Y.: Cornell University Press.

Rourke, Francis, ed., 1978. *Bureaucratic Power in National Politics.* Boston: Little, Brown.

Schurz, Carl, 1893. Editorial. *Harper's Weekly* 37(July 1), 614.

Schurz, Carl, 1913. *Speeches, Correspondence, and Political Papers of Carl Schurz,* 6 vols., Frederick Bancroft (ed.). New York: G. P. Putnam's Sons.

Shapiro v. Thompson, 1969. 394 U.S. 618.

Shelton v. Tucker, 1960. 363 U.S. 479.

Sherbert v. Verner, 1963. 374 U.S. 398.

Simmons, Robert and Eugene Dvorin, 1977. *Public Administration.* Port Washington, N.Y.: Alfred Publishing.

Sjoberg, Gideon, Richard Brymer, and Buford Farris, 1966. Bureaucracy and the lower class. *Sociology and Social Research* 50(April) 325-337.

Starkey v. Board of Education, 1963. 381 P2d 718.

Sweatt v. Painter, 1950. 339 U.S. 629.

Taylor, Frederick, 1911. *The Principles of Scientific Management.* New York: Norton (republished, 1967).

Thompson, Victor, 1961. *Modern Organization.* New York: Knopf.

Van Alstyne, William, 1968. The demise of the right-privilege distinction in constitutional law. *Harvard Law Review* 81: 1439-1464.

Vlandis v. Kline, 1973. 412 U.S. 441.

Weber, Max, 1958. *From Max Weber: Essays in Sociology,* translated and edited by H. H. Gerth and C. W. Mills. New York: Oxford University Press.

Wilkie v. O'Connor, 1941. 25 NYS 2d 617.

4

The Citizen as Public Bureaucrat

To a considerable extent, the current judicial response to the rise of the administrative state began to evolve in cases concerning the constitutional rights of public employees. Historically, this area has witnessed protracted and complex confrontations between public administrative values and constitutional values. From the founding period to the 1950s, however, the judiciary was reluctant to become involved in matters of public personnel administration and had relied upon a constitutional doctrine which made it possible to avoid a host of issues presented by the nature of public employment. Only after the number of public employees increased drastically in the third quarter of the present century and infringements upon their ordinary constitutional rights as citizens became widespread and severe did the judiciary seek to formulate a comprehensive response to this crucial facet of the administrative state.

Public Administrative Values and Public Employment

At the broadest level, the conflict between public administrative values and constitutional values in the realm of public employment is one of uniformity versus diversity. Public administrative values tend to stress uniformity, even within the framework of bureaucratic specialization. The quest for uniformity is based on a desire to enhance organizational efficiency, hierarchical control, and responsiveness to political authorities. It is ironic that two major opposing traditions in public administrative thought converge on the matter of public employment in such a fashion so as to stress uniformity.

Administration as Apolitical

One of these traditions is the apolitical organizational or managerial approach. It draws a strict dictinction between politics and public administration and holds that efficiency and economy are the fundamental objectives of the latter. To a considerable extent, as discussed in Chapter 3, this tradition has its origins in the civil service reform movement of the 1870s and 1880s. Its primary approach to public employment is to make it devoid of politics and to a considerable extent comparable to private employment in terms of general working conditions. Woodrow Wilson, who in many respects can be considered the founder of contemporary American public administrative thought, explained,

> The object of administrative study is to rescue executive methods from the confusion and costliness of empirical experiment and set them upon foundations laid deep in stable principle.
>
> It is for this reason that we must regard civil-service reform in its present stages as but a prelude to a fuller administrative reform. We are now rectifying methods of appointment; we must go on to adjust executive functions more fitly and to prescribe better methods of executive organization and action. Civil-service reform is thus but a moral preparation for what is to follow. It is clearing the moral atmosphere of official life by establishing the sanctity of public office as a public trust, and, by making the service unpartisan, it is opening the way for making it businesslike. By sweetening its motives it is rendering it capable of improving its methods of work.
>
> Let me expand a little what I have said of the province of administration. Most important to be observed is the truth already so much and so fortunately insisted upon by our civil-service reformers; namely, that administration lies outside the proper sphere of *politics*. Administrative questions are not political questions. Although politics sets the tasks for administration, it should not be suffered to manipulate its offices (Wilson, 1941:494).

Once public employment is defined as apolitical, it is evident that the "stable principle" upon which personnel administration ought to rest should be efficient, economical operations. In the words of Luther Gulick, whose work is preeminent in this tradition, "Efficiency is thus axiom number one in the value scale of administration. This brings administration into apparent conflict with the value scale of politics, whether we use that term in its scientific or popular sense." Moreover, administration and politics cannot be combined ". . . within the structure of administration without producing inefficiency" (Gulick and Urwick, 1937:192, 10). But how can politics be eliminated from administration? Traditional public administrative theory offers at least two responses.

First, on the level of the individual, public employee politics can be eliminated from administrative behavior through dehumanization or impersonality. According to Max Weber, "dehumanization" was the "special virtue" of bureaucratic organization (1958:216), and a major reason for the ". . . purely technical superiority [of bureaucracy] over any other form of organization" (1958:214). Its value lay primarily in its reduction of interpersonal friction because "the more bureaucracy is 'dehumanized,' the more completely it succeeds in eliminating from official business love, hatred, and all purely personal, irrational, and emotional elements which escape calculation" (1958:216). In sum, in the Weberian view, "bureaucratization offers above all the optimum possibility for carrying through the principle of specializing administrative functions according to purely objective considerations. . . . [A]nd 'without regard for persons' " (1958:215). Thus in this view, dehumanization enhances rationality and rationality enhances efficiency.

Although the American public administrative tradition has never wholly embraced the Weberian model of bureaucracy, it does promote impersonality. In terms of public personnel management, this is most evident in its reliance upon an elaborate system of position classification, whereby rank and specialization are vested in administrative *positions* rather than in individual administrators. Indeed, a federal report on position classification issued in 1920 stressed the still prevalent principle that ". . . the individual characteristics of an employee occupying a position should have no bearing on the classification of the position" (Shafritz et al., 1978:94). Political neutrality, that is, restrictions on public employees' political activity, is another area in which impersonality has been sought, as is discussed further later on. In addition, there are a variety of subtle devices for promoting impersonality in American public bureaucracies, including the absence of subordinates' names or signatures on the letters, reports, and so forth that they produce. Often these appear with a superordinate's name upon them.

A second response to the matter of how politics can be eliminated from public administration is through hierarchical control. This is also related to dehumanization as Weber explains.

> The individual bureaucrat cannot squirm out of the apparatus in which he is harnessed. In contrast to the honorific or avocational "notable," the professional bureaucrat is chained to his activity by his entire material and ideal existence. In the great majority of cases, he is only a single cog in an ever-moving mechanism which prescribes to him an essentially fixed route of march. The official is entrusted with specialized tasks and normally the mechanism cannot be put into motion or arrested by him, but only from the very top. The individual bureaucrat is thus forged to the community of all the functionaries who are integrated into the mechanism. They have a common interest in seeing that the mechanism continues its functions and that the societally exercised authority carries on (1958: 228–229).

Ralph Hummel elaborates upon these points. He addresses the subject of dehumanization, hierarchy, and administrative values as follows.

> Unless the administrative efficiency and the vastly increased probabilities of control, as the central values of bureaucratization, are themselves to be vitiated—and the need for a bureaucracy thereby reduced to zero—then the official must be trained and conditioned to accept the essential precondition of efficiency and control, that is, acceptance of the rules of the office and of orders from above (1977:134-135).

Training and conditioning, however, require the bureaucrat's personality to be "devastated." Their egos must be "fragmented" to the extent that "it is no longer possible to easily speak of the individual's personality as 'belonging' to him." Ultimately, "hierarchy . . . takes over and externalizes the functions of the formerly internalized super-ego. This means externalization of ultimate knowedge of what is right and wrong. . . . The functionary is stripped of his conscience. He becomes more pliable to direction from outside and above" (1977:129-130, 137).

Traditional American public administrative theory stresses hierarchy to a great extent and, indeed, views it as a fundamental means of creating political accountability. Harold Seidman summarizes the traditional approach as follows.

> Orthodox theory is preoccupied with the anatomy of Government organization and concerned primarily with arrangements to assure that (1) each function is assigned to its appropriate niche within the Government structure; (2) component parts of the executive branch are properly related and articulated; and (3) authorities and responsibilities are clearly assigned (1975:5).

Thus, the American public bureaucracies influenced by this approach are infused with hierarchy. Elaborate rankings are established. Those at the top exercise formal authority over those lower down the hierarchy. Proposals for change stemming from those in lower ranks must pass through several levels of the hierarchy before they can be accepted, though they may be blocked at many points. It is expected that orders flowing downward will be obeyed, and insubordination is grounds for disciplinary action. More subtle indicators of hierarchy are found in the distribution of flags, agency seals, carpets, and other symbols of authority in administrators' offices. The distribution of office space itself is used to reinforce hierarchy. While laughable on one level, the use of these symbols is important because they serve as indicators of administrative rank, which conditions interpersonal interaction in bureaucracy. Indeed, so pervasive is hierarchy that it may even come to affect administrators' personalities. Victor

Thompson writes, "The deference accorded a person who performs a hierarchical role gradually modifies his self-characterization and therefore his self-projection. He comes to feel that the deference is due him by right, that he truly is a superior person; and the deference system is further inflated" (1961:73).

Hierarchy, however, is not just a means of coordinating a host of specialized roles and thereby promoting efficiency. It is also a mechanism for political control, and the traditional approach holds that to the extent that unofficial political views and activities can be eliminated from the performance of their jobs, public employees will have the potential of performing efficiently, whatever the policy area or ultimate objective. This approach also rests upon a distinction between politics and public administration. In Woodrow Wilson's words,

Public administration is detailed and systematic execution of public law. Every particular application of general law is an act of administration. The assessment and raising of taxes, for instance, the hanging of a criminal, the transportation and delivery of the mails, and equipment and recruiting of the army and navy, etc., are all obviously acts of administration; but the general laws which direct these things to be done are as obviously outside of and above administration. The broad plans of governmental action are not administrative; the detailed execution of such plans is administrative. Constitutions, therefore, properly concern themselves only with those instrumentalities of government which are to control general law (Wilson 1941:496).

According to traditional theory, under these conditions, hierarchy serves the needs of accountability because

... power emanates from the people and is to be exercised in trust for the people. Within the government each level of executive authority is accountable to the next, running on up to the President or the Cabinet. The executive authority as a whole is accountable to the Congress or Parliament, which is assisted in its surveillance of expenditures by an independent audit agency. Officials are required to submit themselves to periodic elections as a retrospective evaluation of their performances and to receive a new mandate from the people (Smith and Hague, 1971: 26–27).

Since the public bureaucrat has no legitimate independent political role in this formulation, he or she can be held strictly accountable through the hierarchy for the adherence to the policies issued by political executives or created by statute. The administrative role is purely technical and efficiency and economy are its ultimate values.

There are several ways in which this traditional approach to public administration has translated the desire for dehumanization and hierarchy into the imposition of uniformity among employees. The following can serve as convenient examples.

1. *Uniformity through the reduction of individuality.* The clearest example of this common phenomenon in public administration is the effort to regulate the appearance of public officials. Grooming standards are sometimes formulated in the most minute detail. For instance, Suffolk County, New York regulated the appearance of male personnel according to the following standards: "Hair will not touch the ears or the collar," "Sideburns will not extend below the lowest part of the exterior ear opening, will be of even width (not flared), and will end with a clean-shaven horizontal line," "mustaches . . . shall not extend over the top of the upper lip or beyond the corners of the mouth," "beards and goatees are prohibited, except that a Police Surgeon may grant a waiver . . . for medical reasons. . . . When a Surgeon prescribes that a member not shave, . . . all beard hairs will be kept trimmed so that they do not protrude more than one-half inch from the skin surface of the face" (*Kelley v. Johnson*, 1976:note 1). The Supreme Court upheld the constitutionality of these requirements on the basis that they were not irrational since they could be related to the promotion of the safety of persons and property by making police officers more readily identifiable and enhancing their esprit de corps. However, Justice Marshall, joined by Justice Brennan, dissented, and confronted the quest for administrative impersonality head-on.

An individual's personal appearance may reflect, sustain, and nourish his personality and may well be used as a means of expressing his attitude and lifestyle. In taking control over a citizen's personal appearance, the Government forces him to sacrifice substantial elements of his integrity and identity as well (*Kelley v. Johnson*, 1976:250–251).

2. *Uniformity through the elimination of social diversity.* The purpose of dehumanization is to eliminate personal biases and emotions from on-the-job performance. But what if it is thought that such biases are so ingrained and widespread that no amount of bureaucratic socialization can eliminate or even substantially reduce them? Then the response might be to enhance administrative efficiency by eliminating the objects of distain, if possible. An excellent example of the common effort to promote harmony among public employees by promoting social uniformity occurred during the presidency of Woodrow Wilson. Here we meet Wilson in another context.

It is true that the segregation of the colored employees in the several [federal] departments was begun upon the initiative and at the suggestion of several of the heads of departments, but as much in the interest of the Negroes as for any other reason, with the approval of some of the most influential Negroes I know, and with the idea that the *friction*, or rather the discontent and uneasiness, which has prevailed in many of the departments would thereby be removed (Link, 1956:251, emphasis added).

By the end of the 1920s, segregation was insitutionalized in federal personnel administration as the Civil Service Commission sought to avoid certifying ". . . Negroes to Bureaus where they would be turned down or made unhappy" (Rosenbloom, 1977:55). Racial differences, in this view, not only promote disharmony, they could undercut hierarchy where a member of a minority group was placed in charge of other employees.

The same "logic" was once considered a justification for not placing women in positions of hierarchical authority. In the words of Lucille F. McMillan, the first female U.S. Civil Service Commissioner,

Because the public service must by its nature be responsive to public opinion, and because the public does not yet accept with the same readiness a woman in authority, it is not astonishing that the proportion of women executives is small compared with the total number of women in the Federal Service, nor that a department hesitates to give such positions to any but very outstanding women of proven ability (Rosenbloom 1977:58).

The extent to which public bureaucracy seeks social uniformity is further evidenced in the slow pace at which equal employment opportunity programs have contributed to change in the racial composition of the public service. Among the difficulties encountered in seeking further racial integration are public personnel agencies' reluctance to forego the use of selection devices having a pronounced harsh racial bias against minorities. For instance, at the federal level one major merit exam, the Federal Service Entrance Exam, was replaced by another, the Professional and Administrative Careers Entrance Exam, while under attack in court (*Douglas v. Hampton*, 1972;1975). The newer—abandoned in 1982—also had a harsh tendency to exclude blacks from the federal service. One reason for this is that bureaucratic jobs have been partly defined by these exams in terms of the values and experience of the white middle class. In this fashion the quest for social uniformity becomes institutionalized.

3. *Uniformity through residency.* A number of municipalities and counties require their employees to reside within their boundaries. To a large extent, the motivation behind such regulations is economic. These political jurisdictions seek to recoup, directly and indirectly, some of their employees' salaries through taxes on sales, property, or income. However, such regulations are also defended

on the basis that they will promote employees' subjective commitment to the government and community for which they work. This in turn may enhance their efficiency and effectiveness on the job. Residency requirements for uniformed personnel, such as police and firefighters, have also been promoted on the grounds that they will serve to reduce response time in emergency situations because the employees will reside closer to their place of work. Although they may serve all these purposes, it is undeniable that residency requirements also foster uniformity among employees by limiting geographical diversity in the choice of their housing arrangements.

4. *Uniformity through political neutrality*. Politics, like race and other social factors, can be highly divisive. Overt partianship could lead to disharmony among administrators. It might also undercut hierarchical authority. In addition, it could weaken the public's faith in the neutral expertise of public administrators. Consequently, at several times in U.S. history, and from the early 1900s to the present particularly, there have been efforts to assure the political neutrality of public employees (Rosenbloom, 1971:Chapter 4). Generally, these have taken the form of prohibiting their participation in partisan and electoral activities. As early as 1801, for instance, President Jefferson expressed the belief that electioneering by the federal employee was ". . . inconsistent with the spirit of the Constitution and his duties to it" (Rosenbloom, 1971:40). In 1877, President Hayes restricted federal employees' political activities to participation that, in his view, did ". . . not interfere with the discharge of their official duties" (Rosenbloom, 1971:96). President Cleveland added a new dimension by trying to prevent employees from "offending by a display of obtrusive partisanship" (Rosenbloom, 1971:97). Contemporary regulations at the federal level can be traced back to Theodore Roosevelt's administration. He sought to prevent the federal employee "from turning his official position to the benefit of one of the parties into which the whole public is divided . . ." (Rosenbloom, 1971:98). Accordingly he eventually issued an order specifying that classified (i.e., merit appointed) federal employees "shall take no active part in political management or in political campaigns" (Rosenbloom, 1971:99). In 1939, the Hatch Act extended this requirement to most federal employees who were not in the classified service. However, part of the purpose behind the act was to prevent the political coercion of employees into the formation of a giant national political machine. Thus, regulations for political neutrality promote uniformity in nonpartisanship, but also prevent overt partisan uniformity.

Public Administration as Politics

The American public administrative tradition stressing a dichotomy between politics and administration has been opposed by a more recent emphasis on the extent to which politics takes place within administration. For instance, Paul Appleby (1949), a founder of this approach, considered public administration to be "the eighth political process." Others, including Dwight Waldo (1948), have disputed the rationality of a discipline valuing efficiency and economy as its ultimate objectives. A contemporary expression of this approach has been put forward by Wallace Sayre.

> . . . [T]he staffs of the executive branch agencies have come to exercise an important share of the initiative, the formulation, the bargaining, and in the deciding process by which governmental decisions are taken. They are widely acknowledged to be leading "experts" as to the facts upon which issues are to be settled; they are often permitted to identify authoritatively the broad alternatives available as solutions; and they frequently are allowed to fix the vocabulary of the formal decision. These powers are shared and used by the career staffs in an environment of struggle and competition for influence, but the relatively new fact to be noted with emphasis is that others who share the powers of decision . . . now rarely question the legitimacy of the career staff spokesmen as major participants in the competition.
>
> Great power also belongs naturally to those who carry out decisions of public policy. In this stage, the career staffs have had a paramount role. The choices of means, the pace and tone of governmental performance, reside largely in the hands of the federal government service. Constraints are present, and most of these uses of discretion by the career staffs are subject to bargaining with other participants, but the civil servants have a position of distinct advantage in determining how public policies are executed (Sayre, 1965:2).

Despite the extent to which this view conflicts with the traditional approach to American public administration, it too has often sought uniformity among public employees, though generally for the purpose of political control rather than efficiency and economy.

It is important to note that those stressing the politicality of the public service do not seek to impose uniformity for the sake of impersonality and harmony of operations. Indeed, they stress the extent to which public employees are influenced by personal factors. For instance, Samuel Krislov maintains that "Who writes the [bureaucratic] directive—his or her style, values, concept of role—is as significant as who gets to be president, congressman, senator, member of parliament, or cabinet minister" (1974:7). Nor do proponents of this approach expect hierarchy to yield political accountability: "Government would come to a standstill if our 'closet statesmen' in the civil service suddenly started doing only what they were told" (Storing, 1964:152). And they recognize that inevitably, "accountability gets lost in the shuffle somewhere in the middle ranges of the bureaucracy" (Smith and Hague, 1971:27).

The view that public employees have an important independent political role raises several perplexing issues for democratic government. Frederick Mosher, for instance, asks: "The accretion of specialization and of technological and social complexity seems to be an irreversible trend, one that leads to increasing dependence upon the protected, appointive public service, thrice removed from direct democracy. . . . [H]ow can a public service so constituted be made to operate in a manner compatible with democracy? How can we be assured that a highly differentiated body of public employees will act in the interests of all the people, will be an instrument of all the people?" (Mosher, 1968:3-4). Several responses have been offered. Historically there have been numerous efforts to create political or ideological uniformity among public employees as a means of assuring that their political influence would not be used to subvert the party in power or the nation as a whole. Two examples are illustrative of this approach.

1. *Partisan policy uniformity.* Although the creation of spoils systems and political machines has often constituted an effort to assure the dominance of a particular political party, the extent to which political officials fear subversion of their programs by public administrators should not be underestimated. Indeed, as early as 1795, before political parties were well organized, President Washington wrote:

I shall not, whilst I have the honor to administer the government, bring a man into any office, of consequence knowingly whose political tenets are adverse to the measures which the general government are pursuing; for this, in my opinion, would be a sort of political suicide (Rosenbloom, 1971:36).

Even so, Washington was criticized by his successor, President John Adams, for being lax in promoting political uniformity among public administrators: "Washington appointed a multitude of democrats and jacobins of the deepest die. I have been more cautious in this respect" (Rosenbloom, 1971:36-37). Adams also made the first clearly partisan dismissal from the federal service. President Jefferson was even more politically oriented in his appointment and removal policy (Rosenbloom, 1971: 34-40). After the inauguration of President Jackson in 1829, of course, patronage practices expanded drastically, eventually encompassing a majority of federal positions. Moreover, mere partisan affiliation or belief were no longer sufficient criteria for holding a federal job; an employee also had to support the dominant party financially and work for its electoral victory (Rosenbloom, 1971:Chapter 2).

The Civil Service Act of 1883 set in motion a process that all but eliminated patronage practices. It substituted political neutrality for partisanship as the ideal for the public service. Nevertheless, the desire of political officials to assure the policy support of public administrators has remained strongly evident.

When President Eisenhower succeeded 20 years of Democratic rule, *Schedule C* was created to enable him to make political appointments to some administrative posts which were previously under the merit system. President Nixon's administrations used a variety of legal and illegal means to place the personnel of their choice in a wide range of positions in the federal service (Shafritz et al., 1978: 27-28). Much of what Nixon sought covertly, President Carter was able to achieve overtly. The Civil Service Reform Act of 1978 created a Senior Executive Service in an effort to make the top levels of the federal service more responsive to political executives. Members of the Senior Executive Service can be more readily transferred or reassigned than most other federal employees. They can also be purged from the Senior Executive Service without a formal hearing. In addition, 10 percent of their total ranks can be pure political appointments, with no check on their merit by a personnel agency.

2. *Loyalty and Security.* Throughout the history of the United States there have been several efforts to assure that public employees would not use their official positions to subvert the nation's government. The most recent of these, the loyalty-security program of the late 1940s and early 1950s, placed a heavy stress upon securing ideological uniformity among federal employees. The initial assumption behind the program was that "maximum protection must be afforded the United States against infiltration of disloyal persons into the ranks of its employees . . ." (Rosenbloom, 1971:152). Later, protection against *security risks*—a category which might include those peculiarly subject to blackmail or just careless with their briefcases—was sought as well. Yet, as the program was implemented, it became clear that loyalty and security encompassed a very broad range of thoughts and activites. Whatever the original intentions, the program promoted a high degree of ideological uniformity.

Henry Steele Commager observed:

What is the new loyalty? It is, above all, conformity. It is the uncritical and unquestioning acceptance of America as it is—the political institutions, the social relationships, the economic practices. It rejects inquiry into the race question or socialized medicine, or public housing, or into the wisdom or validity of our foreign policy. It regards as particularly heinous any challenge to what is called "the system of private enterprise," identifying that system with Americanism. It abandons evolution, repudiates the once popular concept of progress, and regards America as a finished product, perfect and complete (Commager, 1947:1975).

That his assessment was correct is revealed in the kinds of questions federal employees were asked in loyalty-security proceedings. Among these were:

What were your feelings at the time concerning race equality?
Were you a regular reader of *The New York Times*?

Do you and your wife regularly attend any organized church services[?]
Have you provided any sort of religious training for your children, sir?
What do you think of female chastity?
In your library at home, could you give me an idea of the type of literature
   or the books that you enjoy accumulating?
Was your father native born?
Have you ever had Negroes in your home?
There is a suspicion in the record that you are in sympathy with the under-
   privileged. Is this true?
Are your friends and associates intelligent, clever?
Do you read Howard Fast? Tom Paine? Upton Sinclair?
(Rosenbloom, 1971:163-164).

Eventually the loyalty-security program eliminated overt ideological disunity
among federal employees on a wide range of issues. Upon empirical investigation,
Marie Jahoda found that a code of behavior had developed among bureaucrats in
Washington under which it was deemed by some, that among other things:

> . . . you should not discuss the admission of Red China to the U.N.; you
> should not advocate interracial equality; you should not mix with people
> unless you know them very well; if you want to read the *Nation*, you
> should not take it to the office; . . . you should take certain books off
> your private bookshelves (Jahoda, 1955:111).

In more recent years, federal employees have sometimes been required to attend
meetings on various topics, such as racial integration and the United Nations, in
an effort to assure that they have the "proper" attitudes, however irrelevant to
their jobs (Rosenbloom, 1971:211-218). In addition, as the loyalty-security
issue faded into the political background in the 1960s, investigations of employee "suitability" often probed the most personal aspects of one's sexual
activity in what could at best be considered a quest for a kind of "moral unity"
(Rosenbloom, 1971:211-212).

Constitutional Values and Public Employment

Public administrative values promoting uniformity in the public service are often
opposed by competing constitutional values. The Constitution, as noted earlier,
clearly seeks to promote diversity within the political community and its government. Indeed, James Madison presumably represented the founders in rejecting
the possibility of ". . . giving to every citizen the same opinions, the same
passions, and the same interests" as "impracticable" (*Federalist 10*; Rossiter,

1961:78). In his view, and that of the founders generally, the purpose of government was to protect diversity.

> As long as the reason of man continues fallible, and he is at liberty to exercise it, different opinions will be formed. As long as the connection subsists between his reason and his self-love, his opinions and his passions will have a reciprocal influence on each other; and the former will be objects to which the latter will attach themselves. The diversity in the faculties of men, from which the rights of property originate, is not less an insuperable obstacle to a uniformity of interests. *The protection of these faculties is the first object of government.* From the protection of different and unequal faculties of acquiring property, the possession of different degrees and kinds of property immediately results; and from the influence of these on the sentiments and views of the respective proprietors ensues a division of the society into different interests and parties [emphasis added] (*Federalist 10*; Rossiter, 1961:78).

There are several constitutional provisions directly aimed at protecting and promoting diversity within the government. The system of shared and separated power was intended to bring different perspectives to bear on political issues and matters of government. This is evident in the area of federal personnel administration, as elsewhere. Thus, the "executive power" is vested in the president, who is charged with taking "Care that the Laws be faithfully executed." But Congress is responsible for establishing administrative positions and for determining whether the power to make appointments to them will be vested in "the President alone, in the Courts of Law, or in the Heads of Departments." Appointments to the latter positions require the advice and consent of the Senate. This clause also provides a basis for congressional involvement in personnel actions. In addition, federal employees are dependent upon Congress for the appropriation of their salaries. Furthermore, bicameralism has sometimes placed the two houses of the legislature at odds with one another in matters concerning public personnel administration.

The Constitution's quest for diversity is also embodied in the Bill of Rights, and these provisions have often seemed to be in conflict with public personnel administration. For instance, political diversity is viewed as the essence of constitutional democracy for citizens generally, but has often been opposed as inappropriate for public employees. The same is true for political speech, as one court pointed out.

> While a free society values robust, vigorous and essentially uninhibited public speech by citizens, when such uninhibited public speech by Government employees produces intolerable disharmony, inefficiency, dissension

and even chaos, it may be subject to reasonable limitations, at least concerning matters relating to the duties, discretion and judgment entrusted
to the employee involved (*Meehan v. Macy*, 1968:835).

Public employees' associational rights have also been viewed differently from
those of other citizens. This is especially true in terms of labor unions and
membership in subversive groups. To the extent that there is a clear constitutional right to privacy (*Griswold v. Connecticut*, 1965), that of public employees
has sometimes been sacrificed to the desire to prevent conflicts of interest and
deviant or subversive behavior in positions of public trust. In addition, over the
years, federal employees have been subjected to various kinds of coercion that,
if applied to other citizens, would be a clear violation of constitutional liberties
(Rosenbloom, 1971).

The conflict between constitutional values and administrative values, as they
intersect in the area of public employment, has been evident from the earliest
days of the republic. However, before reviewing the judiciary's approaches to
this conflict, it is desirable to address briefly the issue of whether the Constitution should serve as a constraint on public personnel administration at all.

The Constitution and Public Employment

Over the years, the position that the Constitution should not be considered a
constraint on public personnel administration has been forcefully put forward.
As noted earlier, Woodrow Wilson argued that "Constitutions . . . properly concern themselves only with those instrumentalities of government which are to
control general law" (Wilson, 1941:496), which in his view included neither
public administration generally nor public personnel administration in particular.
The main rationale for this view is that if the government could not deal with its
employees differently from other citizens, it probably could not be an employer.
It would be unable to require some forms of behavior common to employment
situations generally. For example, the government would be unable to limit
employees' speech on the job, to require certain types of dress, and perhaps even
to require arrival at the work place at a certain time. Perhaps it would also be
unable to require employees to perform certain duties. This is true because the
government cannot ordinarily place such limitations on the liberties and
freedoms of citizens who are not its employees. Nor might the fact that public
employment is voluntarily held create a viable constitutional distinction since
members of the political community cannot voluntarily forfeit their constitutional rights except through the amendment process. From this perspective,
then, the employment relationship must give the government additional authority over those citizens who are also its employess; and making the Constitution

applicable to public employment would serve to reduce that authority and lead to inefficient administration.

The view that the Constitution should not serve as a constraint on public personal administration is opposed by those who are concerned with the rights of public employees and the political and administrative consequences of denying them the same constitutional protections as are afforded to other citizens. Those who take this approach stress the belief that constititional and administrative values must be in balance. For example, Senator Ervin, who supported a *Bill of Rights for Federal Employees* during the 1960s, argued that the variety of restrictions on the rights of federal employees would "result in an intimidated, lack-luster, unimaginative and fearful civil service" (Rosenbloom, 1971: 217). This opinion was also put forth by Robert Ramspeck, a former Civil Service Commission Chairman.

> . . . today, the federal government affects the lives [sic] of every human
> being in the United States. Therefore we need better qualified people,
> more dedicated people, in the Federal Service than we ever needed before.
> And we cannot get them if you are going to deal with them on the basis
> of suspicion, and delve into their private lives, because if there is anything
> the average American cherishes it is his right of freedom of action, and his
> right to privacy (Rosenbloom, 1971:200–201).

Ervin also argued that "practices which affect ten million citizens [in public employment] . . . affect an entire society" (Rosenbloom, 1971:217) and can be detrimental to the exercise of liberty and exchange of information generally.

This general debate as to the role of the Constitution in public personnel administration can be analyzed further. Underlying the perspectives of those who believe that the Constitution should not act as a constraint on public employment is the view that the private employment model should be transferred to the public service. This approach was most evident in the writing of the nineteenth century civil service reformers. As one reformer wrote,

> . . . imagine a merchant discharging his sales men and bookkeepers, a
> manufacturer discharging his foreman and artisans, a railroad corporation
> discharging its engineers and switchmen, a bank discharging its cashiers
> and tellers every four years on the ground that they have been in their
> places long enough and somebody else ought to have them now (Rosen-
> bloom, 1971:75).

As they saw it, the objective was to assure that the "business" functions of government were managed and executed in a "businesslike" manner (Rosenbloom, 1971:75).

Conversely, those who believe that the Constitution should affect public personnel administration find the private employment relationship inappropriate. In their view, the private employment model cannot act as a sufficient constraint on governmental restrictions of employees' rights because private and public employment are fundamentally different. In part, the difference lies in the fact that ". . . bureaus are economically one-faced rather than two-faced. They face input markets where they buy the scarce resources they need to produce their outputs. But they face no economic markets whatever on the output side. Therefore, they have no direct way of evaluating their outputs in relation to the costs of the inputs used to make them. This inability is of profound importance in all aspects of bureaucratic behavior" (Downs, 1967:29–30). In terms of public employment, the lack of free, competitive, external markets makes it possible for public bureaucracies to obtain funding even though they may suffer from gross inefficiencies. In short, they will not generally be driven out of existence by markets or economic competitors. Consequently, market considerations on the output side do not act as a limit upon the ways that public bureaucracies treat their employees. For instance, patronage dismissals in the public sector are not necessarily as economically damaging to the employer as the civil service reformers maintained.

This brings us to a second difference between public and private employment. While private employers' major concerns are typically economic, public employment has always been infused with political considerations. Thus, as the civil service reformers argued, in all but the most peculiar circumstances, it would be ridiculous for a private employer to institute a system of firing all its employees every four years. But unlike public officials, a private employer would have little interest in trying to forge a national political party. Moreover, as Samuel Krislov has argued, there is a " 'multiplier' importance of public service—great changes in a wide arena are instigated by small alterations in governmental personnel policy" (1967:5). Therefore, government may often have a political or policy incentive to limit the civil liberties and rights of its employees. This has been most pronounced in the areas of patronage, political neutrality, and loyalty-security, as already noted.

It is evident from this discussion that if the Constitution cannot act wholly to constrain the government in its dealing with its employees, neither can the private employment model effectively do so. Thus, the task for the judiciary has been to construct a public employment relationship based upon both constitutional and administrative considerations.

Judicial Doctrines

Historically, the judiciary has developed four major doctrines or approaches to deal with the constitutional questions raised by the nature of public employment. Although the courts' focus has generally been on the rights of public employees, the judiciary has also expressed concern with the broad issues posed by the rise of the administrative state. Several of its decisions in this area manifest a strong concern with redressing the balance of power between the individual and the government in a bureaucratic age.

The Doctrine of Privilege

Historically, the judiciary was content to allow administrative values to take precedence over constitutional values in the realm of public employment. This was accomplished by relying upon a judicial doctrine that did not require the Constitution to be considered a constraint on the government's interaction with its employees. Thus, the public employment relationship was defined as outside the scope of the Constitution and, therefore, subject to regulation in accordance with prevailing administrative or political values. The judicial approach that was dominant until the 1960s is generally known as the *doctrine of privilege*, which, as discussed in the previous chapter, also affected the rights of clients of the administrative state. As discussed earlier, its demise has been a central aspect of the judiciary's efforts to exercise greater influence over public administration.

In the area of public employment, the doctrine of privilege relied upon the presumption that because holding a government job is a voluntarily accepted privilege rather than a right or a coerced obligation, the government could place any restrictions it saw fit upon its workers, including those infringing upon their ordinarily held constitutional rights as citizens. As such, it allowed administrative and political values stressing uniformity among public employees to remain relatively unchecked by constitutional values promoting diversity. Arch Dotson (1955:77) provided one of the first analyses of the nature of this approach.

> Its central tenet is that office is held at the pleasure of the government. Its general effect is that the government may impose upon the public employee any requirement it sees fit as conditional to employment. From the point of view of the state, public employment is maintained as an indulgence; from the position of the citizen, his job is a grant concerning which he has no independent rights.

The rationale behind the doctrine of privilege is still best conveyed by Justice Oliver Wendell Holmes's oft-quoted statement that "The petitioner may have a constitutional right to talk politics, but he has no constitutional right to be a policeman" (*McAuliffe v. New Bedford*, 1892:220). In *Bailey v. Richardson* (1950:58-59), a case involving virtually all the constitutional questions raised by the loyalty-security program, it was further explained, and subsequently affirmed by an equally divided Supreme Court in 1951, that "due process of law is not applicable unless one is being deprived of something to which he has a right" and that, consequently, "the plain hard fact is that so far as the Constitution is concerned there is no prohibition against the dismissal of Government employees because of their political beliefs, activities or affiliations."

The doctrine of privilege obviously had far-reaching importance for the nature of public employment. Since there was no right to a government job, under this approach, public employees had little or no constitutional protection of their rights while in public employment. Consequently, several fundamental restrictions could be placed upon the constitutional rights of the citizen as public employee. One of these came in the form of political neutrality, which was first justified by the Supreme Court on the basis that "for regulation of [public] employees it is not necessary that the act regulated be anything more than an act reasonably deemed by Congress to interfere with the efficiency of the public service" (*United Public Workers v. Mitchell*, 1947:101). Another was through the loyalty-security program (*Bailey v. Richardson*, 1950). Employees could also be fired merely for their political affiliation (*Ex Parte Hennen*, 1839). They might also be adversely treated for the exercise of any number of personal liberties including voting, exercise of sexual preferences, and even becoming pregnant (Rosenbloom, 1971; Rosenbloom and Gille, 1975). In addition, public employees were afforded no constitutional protection against coercion and intimidation which ranged from political behavior to buying ". . . everything from savings bonds to electric light bulbs for playgrounds" (Rosenbloom, 1971: 215).

The doctrine of privilege had several important drawbacks. Although it allowed administrative values and some political ones to outweigh constitutional values, and may have promoted administrative efficiency, it also hampered recruitment and performance in some contexts, as noted previously. More important from the judiciary's perspectives, once the full-fledged administrative state emerged, the doctrine had the effect of allowing the erosion of individual rights and liberties on a widespread basis. This occurred in at least three areas of fundamental importance to the judiciary during the 1950s and 1960s.

First, a major constitutional problem with the doctrine of privilege was that it could be construed to allow the government to discriminate against individuals on racial, gender, or other arbitrary grounds. In other words, it might render the Fourteenth Amendment's equal protection clause irrelevant to public employment. If public employment were a privilege, its denial to blacks, for example, might not be unconstitutional because they never had a right to it in the first place. As the Illinois Supreme Court put it in *Fursman v. Chicago* (1917),

> The [school] board has the absolute right to decline to employ or re-employ any applicant for any reason whatever, or for no reason at all.
> . . . It is no infringement upon the constitutional rights of anyone for

the board to decline to employ him . . . and it is immaterial whether the
reason for the refusal . . . is because the applicant is married or unmarried,
is of fair complexion or dark, is or is not a member of a trades union, or
whether no reason is given for such refusal.

As the Supreme Court became more concerned with equal protection—witness
its decision in *Missouri ex rel. Gaines v. Canada* (1938), discussed in Chapter 3—
this result became intolerable. Indeed, in 1947 the Supreme Court expressed its
concern with this potential consequence of the doctrine of privilege and sought
to eliminate it. In the process of upholding the constitutionality of the Hatch
Act in *United Public Workers v. Mitchell* (1947:100), the Court's majority had
occasion to observe that

> Appellants urge that federal employees are protected by the Bill of Rights
> and that Congress may not "enact a regulation providing that no Republi-
> can, Jew or Negro shall be appointed to federal office, or that no federal
> employee shall attend Mass or take any active part in missionary work."
> None would deny such limitations on congressional power.

Yet, as this statement suggests, if the equal protection clause places a constraint
upon the government in its dealings with public employees and applicants, why
should not the same be true of the Bill of Rights generally?

This raises a second point. The rise of the administrative state necessarily
entails the growth of public employment. In the United States, between 1929
and 1966 public employees at all governmental levels increased from 6.2 percent
of the nation's work force to 17 percent (Rosenbloom, 1971:3). Thus, by the
1960s, infringements upon the rights of citizen-public employees no longer pertained to relatively few individuals, but rather applied to a substantial segment
of the nation's population. The judiciary was clearly cognizant of the possibility
that the quantitative growth in public employment required a qualitative change
in constitutional doctrines. As Justice Douglas remarked in a dissent joined by
Justices Brennan and Marshall in *U.S. Civil Service Commission v. National
Association of Letter Carriers* (1973:600),

> I would strike this provision of the law down as unconstitutional so that
> a new start may be made on this old problem that confuses and restricts
> nearly five million federal, state, and local public employees today that
> live under the present [Hatch] Act.

Third, restrictions upon the constitutional rights of public employees may have
a substantial impact on the political community as a whole. This is the *multiplier* effect of which Krislov (1967) speaks. It pertains not simply to the quality

of performance by civil servants, or the government's ability to recruit the kinds of talents it seeks, it also extends to such questions as the representativeness of the public service and the nature of public political discourse. For instance, although speculative and not based upon research findings, the U.S. Commission on Civil Rights maintains that

> If in 1883 the Federal Government had implemented this concept [of merit selection without regard to other personal considerations], the Nation would have discovered during the 20th Century the values inherent in building a government whose personnel is reflective of the population as a whole, in terms of race, ethnicity, sex, economic background, and other factors. The Nation would have discovered that a civil service, operating in a manner consistent with the equal opportunity guarantees embedded in the Constitution would more likely have the broad range of experience and skills necessary to address society's problems. Moreover, it would more likely generate support for government programs by all groups in society (1974:6).

Whether the social composition of a public bureaucracy has a substanial impact on its administrative performance remains undemonstrated (Krislov and Rosenbloom, 1981). However, there is no doubt that the inclusion of members of disadvantaged groups in public bureaucracies can have an important impact on the groups' statuses and positions in the society as a whole and in this fashion may be of great consequence to the political community generally. As Samuel Krislov (1974:129) has expressed this point: "What government does is what fixes social policy. The treatment of its constituent individuals and constituent groups in political form is a tip-off and a harbinger of social action in other guises."

Perhaps more central to the judiciary's concerns has been the extent to which limitations on public employees' freedom of speech can serve to undermine democratic processes. One of the major consequences of the rise of the administrative state is that as political power and knowledge about governmental operations accrue in the hands of public employees, the importance of elections is reduced (Nachmias and Rosenbloom, 1980). This situation can be alleviated somewhat if public employees are free to inform the public about matters under their administration. Often, this can be accomplished with a unique perspective; as Herbert Storing observed, "In our mobile democracy, the civil service is one of the few institutions we have for bringing the accumulated wisdom of the past to bear upon political decisions" (1964:155).

A good example of public employees seeking to inform the public about matters of political and electoral choice occurred in March 1968 during the presidential primary season when 1400 federal employees in the Washington, D.C. area signed the following open petition to the president.

From our position we have seen how the purpose and energy of government are drained by preoccupation with the making of war. We have seen how progress in foreign policy has been obstructed. We have seen how massive national resources are absorbed by a disastrous war while critical domestic needs are inadequately met. And seeing this we fear the political and moral consequences for the future of our country.

All this, together with the tragic and unnecessary suffering of the Vietnamese people, has troubled our conscience and now compels us to speak out to our colleagues and fellow citizens.

We call then for the war's end . . . (Rosenbloom, 1971:214).

Such statements can serve to overcome the effects of news management by elected officials. In addition, the exposure of waste, fraud, abuse, and corruption by public employees engaging in whistle-blowing can provide valuable information to members of the public attempting to make knowledgeable electoral decisions. Under the doctrine of privilege, however, public employees could engage in public speech of this nature only at the peril of dismissal from the civil service.

The Supreme Court recognized both the importance of public employees' freedom to inform the public about matters of political concern and the limitations of the doctrine of privilege in this context in the case of *Pickering v. Board of Education* (1968). Pickering was a public school teacher who was dismissed for writing a letter to a local newspaper in connection with a proposed tax increase in which he criticized the local school authorities' handling of past revenue-raising proposals. In the course of its decision that the dismissal was an unconstitutional violation of Pickering's First and Fourteenth Amendment rights, the Court observed:

. . . free and open debate is vital to informed decision-making by the electorate. Teachers are, as a class, the members of a community most likely to have informed and definite opinions as to how funds allotted to the operation of the schools should be spent. Accordingly, it is essential that they be able to speak out freely on such questions without fear of retaliatory dismissal (571–572).

By implication, the same logic would also apply to other categories of public employees in their areas of expertise.

In sum, by the 1950s and 1960s it became evident that the doctrine of privilege could protect neither the rights of the growing numbers of citizen-public employees nor the needs of constitutional government in the contemporary administrative age. That doctrine was also detrimental to citizens in the role of client of the administrative state, as has already been discussed. However, abandoning the doctrine of privilege in the area of public employment has proved easier than finding a lasting replacement for it.

The Doctrine of Substantial Interest

The approach immediately replacing the doctrine of privilege can be called the *doctrine of substantial interest*. It rejected the notion that a distinction between privileges and rights is of relevance to the constitutional protections afforded to public employees. It begins "with the premise that a state [or the federal government] cannot condition an individual's privilege of public employment on his nonparticipation in conduct which, under the Constitution, is protected from direct interference by the state" (*Gilmore v. James*, 1967:91). Moreover, "whenever there is a *substantial interest*, other than employment by the state, involved in the discharge of a public employee, he can be removed neither on arbitrary grounds nor without a procedure calculated to determine whether legitimate grounds do exist" (*Birnbaum v. Trussell*, 1966:678, emphasis added). Although this approach emerged largely out of lower court decisions, the Supreme Court embraced it on several occasions. For example, in *Board of Regents v. Roth* (1972:571), the Court stated that it has "fully and finally rejected the wooden distinction between 'rights' and 'privileges' that once seemed to govern the applicability of procedural due process rights." In *Sugarman v. Dougall* (1973:644) it reiterated that "this Court now has rejected the concept that constitutional rights turn upon whether a governmental benefit is characterized as a 'right' or as a 'privilege.' "

The demise of the doctrine of privilege and the development of the substantial interest approach enabled the judiciary to make constitutional values stressing diversity dominant over administrative and political values seeking uniformity among public employees. Indeed, for the first time in the nation's history, the constitutional rights of public employees and those of ordinary citizens became similar, although not identical. For instance, in *Kiiskila v. Nichols* (1970:749) it was reasoned that

> A citizen's right to engage in protected expression or debate is substantially unaffected by the fact that he is also an employee of the government and, as a general rule, he cannot be deprived of his employment merely because he exercises those rights. This is so because dismissal from government employment, like criminal sanctions or damages, may inhibit the propensity of a citizen to exercise his right to freedom of speech and association.

This development had important consequences for the nature of the American public service, and, not surprisingly, once limitations were imposed on the extent to which uniformity could be required, public employees began to express themselves in diverse ways. Ultimately, a serious question emerged as to whether the doctrine of substantial interest went too far in weakening administrative discipline.

The public service of the 1960s underwent remarkable change and public employees engaged in activities that only a decade earlier would have been unthinkable. For example, they began to speak out on the major issues of the day, including those with which they had special familiarity as a result of their jobs. Thus, in the federal service there were several antiwar petitions and statements issued by employees of the various departments, including those in the State Department and the Department of Defense. Civil servants in the Department of Justice and others spoke out in the area of civil rights policy. Sometimes these activities took the form of protests, and on at least one occasion a department head was literally chased by some 300 employees seeking to present him with a petition concerning their grievances and demands for the furtherance of racial equality (*Washington Post*, 1970:B1). Such activities gave rise to a variety of more or less formal employee organizations dedicated to changing the nature of both public employment and the society at large. One such group, Federal Employees for a Democratic Society (FEDS), stressed the desirability of participatory bureaucracy in which hierarchy would be reduced to a minimum, rank and file employees would participate in the making of public policy to a greater extent, and employees would be free to refuse to perform work that violated their consciences (Hershey, 1973:51-63). Although less well documented, similar activities took place at the state and local levels as well, and if anything, the "new militancy" (Posey, 1968) of public employees in the 1960s was most important in urban settings. As protest, disruption, and dissent in the public service became more pronounced, some efforts were made by political authorities and public managers to stem its tide. However under the doctrine of substantial interest, most of these activities were protected, and dismissal became highly impracticable *when an employee was willing to take his or her case to court.*

The Case-by-Case Approach

Ultimately, the doctrine of substantial interest began to lose its forcefulness as a result of the lack of discipline that it encouraged in the public service. President Nixon and other political authorities began to complain bitterly of the uncontrollable nature of public bureaucracy. A taped conversation between Nixon and George Schultz, Director of the Office of Management and Budget, in 1971 is highly revealing.

> You've got to get us some discipline, George. You've got to get it, and the only way you get it, is when a bureaucrat thumbs his nose, we're going to get him. . . . They've got to know, that if they do it, something's

going to happen to them. Where anything can happen. I know the Civil
Service pressure. But, you can do a lot there, too. There are many
unpleasant places where Civil Service people can be sent. We just don't
have any discipline in government. That's our trouble (*New York Times*,
1974:A14).

Nixon's concerns with the federal bureaucracy were also manifested in his effort
to establish an "administrative presidency" (Nathan, 1975) and to circumvent
the merit system in various ways (U.S. Civil Service Commission, 1976).

Nixon's outlook on the federal bureaucracy was part of a wider approach to
political life that tended to stress governmental authority over individual civil
rights and liberties. He was quite candid in seeking Supreme Court appointments who shared this view (Miller and Samuels, 1973:252), and was successful,
at least temporarily, when it came to most constitutional issues involving public
employees. As a result, once all four Nixon appointees were on the Court, it
became clearly divided into three groups: the Nixon appointees, comprising
Chief Justice Burger and Justices Rehnquist, Powell, and Blackmun; the liberal
bloc, composed of Justices Douglas, Brennan, and Marshall; and Justices
Stewart and White who fell in between these two groups. The Nixon appointees
and the liberal bloc had a high degree of internal voting cohesion, but since
neither was a majority, both had to seek the support of the remaining justices,
that is, Justices Stewart and White.

In terms of public employment issues, this resulted in a marked tendency for
the Court to avoid doctrinal, across-the-board judicial pronouncements. Rather,
the Court tended to treat each case individually on its own merits. Majorities
could generally be formed only with reference to a specific set of facts and circumstances, and broad, sweeping generalizations that would determine the direction of the law for years to come were consequently precluded. In addition, such
an approach was inherent in the doctrine of substantial interest, which required
the courts to weigh the nature of the injury to the individual against the claimed
benefit to the state in an effort to determine whether substantive constitutional
rights had been violated and in order to decide what procedural safeguards, if
any, had to be made available when adverse actions were taken against public
employees. Thus, in several cases the Supreme Court and the rest of the federal
judiciary required that, in applying general personnel regulations and principles
to individual employees, public employers address the specific sets of facts and
circumstances involved. For example, under this approach it was possible to ban
aliens from some but not all public service positions; race might be used as a
basis in making specific but not general personnel assignments; and, apart from a
regulation requiring a maternity leave very late in the term of a normal pregnancy, such a leave had to be based on a medical determination of the individual
employee's ability to continue in her job (Rosenbloom, 1975).

The case-by-case approach to the constitutional position of public employees had several important consequences. First and simplest, it led to an ever-increasing amount of litigation in the already besieged courts. Since each case was to be treated separately on its own merits, rather than in accordance with broad, general doctrines, this was inevitable. Second, there were few guidelines on how to resolve questions of constitutional law prior to judicial action. Neither the employer's nor the employee's rights were self-evident or adequately delineated by judicial decisions. Moreover, public personnel administrators found themselves being constanly second-guessed by the courts. Third, and more complicated, the case-by-case approach required public personnel administrators to rethink several of their basic premises. A conflict between administrative values and constitutional values, as defined by the judiciary, was evident in many respects (Rosenbloom, 1975).

The case-by-case approach tended to promote diversity in the extreme. In many areas, across-the-board infringements upon public employees' constitutional rights and liberties could not withstand judicial review. Each public employee might have a right to individualized treatment, as in cases involving mandatory maternity leaves and assignment to positions according to race. In the process of establishing this approach, the judiciary largely ignored the standard public personnel administrative concern with the nature of positions. Thus, with regard to freedom of speech, for example, the judiciary was largely unconcerned with such concepts as *classified, excepted, sensitive*, and *nonsensitive* positions. Rather, it substituted considerations of its own, such as the need for superordinate and subordinate to have a close and personal loyalty or a confidential realtionship. It also considered the question of whether the employee's position was such that his or her statements might be hard to counter due to his or her presumed greater access to factual information. In large part, therefore, the case-by-case approach militated against the position orientation of orthodox public personnel management (Rosenbloom, 1975).

Under the case-by-case approach, the judiciary also confronted the moral values of public personnel administration arising out of the nineteenth century civil service reform movement. The reformers' intense interest in reestablishing sound moral values within the civil service led to regulations allowing removals or exclusions for ". . . infamous, dishonest, immoral, or notoriously disgraceful conduct" (Rosenbloom, 1975:56). But, the Supreme Court rulings in the substantial interest and case-by-case vein would require that a public employee dismissed on any of these grounds be afforded an opportunity for a hearing. Moreover, a lower federal court, reflecting this approach held that ". . . a finding that an employee [of the federal government] has done something immoral or indecent could support a dismissal without further inquiry only if all immoral or indecent acts of an employee have some ascertainable deleterious effect on the efficiency of the service" (*Norton v. Macy*, 1969:1165). Consequently, under this approach a removal for immorality involved determining (1) whether an employee had actually engaged in an alleged act; (2) whether the act could be considered immoral; and (3) whether an immoral act, even if committed, was such that the individual's employment would have a demonstrable adverse affect on legitimate objectives of the public service. Needless to add, perhaps, such requirements made dismissals for immorality expensive and painstaking.

It is evident that like the doctrine of substantial interest, the case-by-case approach tended to increase the scope of judicial review of public personnel actions. In seeking to balance the rights of individuals against the needs of government as an employer, the courts were required to assess the rationality of public personnel regulations and practices. During this period, therefore, the courts broadened the scope of judicial review to determine whether the administrative findings were capricious, arbitrary, unreasonable or unsupported by the record (*West v. Macy*, 1968:105). Moreover, the judiciary was apt to strike a different balance than orthodox personnel administration between the administrative desire for efficiency and uniformity and the Constitution's interest in individual rights and diversity. For a time, therefore, it appeared that public personnel administration would be increasingly constrained by the Constitution and more actively controlled by the judicairy. Indeed, the judicial role in public personnel administration has expanded remarkably since the 1950s, and this is an integral part of the judiciary's response to the rise of the administrative state. However, as caseloads grew and the composition of the Supreme Court changed further, a majority of the Supeme Court generally sought to remove the judiciary from ever-expanding involvement in public personnel administration. Thus, while the Nixon appointees to the Supreme Court did not immediately bring about the desired effect, eventually their point of view became predominant.

Deconstitutionalization

By 1975 the Nixon bloc had emerged as the dominant force on the Supreme Court. Their position was enhanced by the departure of Justice Douglas, the intellectual leader of the liberal bloc, and the appointment of Justice John Paul Stevens. A majority of the Court now seemed reluctant generally to expand the constitutional rights of public employees further, preferring instead to exercise greater restraint in the realm of public personnel policy. In large part, this approach was based upon judicial ideologies and preferences. A majority of the Court clearly believed that public personnel policy could be better dealt with elsewhere in government. However, in part the desire to play a limited role in personnel matters was due to the Court's increasing awareness of the problem of overcrowded dockets. For instance, Chief Justice Burger pointed out that the number of annually docketed cases had grown from 1092 in 1935 to over 4000 in 1975. In his view, consequently, "We must face up to the flinty reality that there is a necessity for a choice: If we wish to maintain the Court's historic function with a quality that will command public confidence, the demands we make on it must be reduced to what they were a generation ago" (*New York Times*, 1975:31).

These two desires meshed well in the development of a deconstitutionalization approach to the public employment relationship. The essence of this approach was expressed in *Bishop v. Wood* (1976:349–350), a case dealing with the dismissal of a policeman. The Surpeme Court, per Justice Stevens reasoned that

> The federal court is not the appropriate forum in which to review the multitude of personnel decisions that are made daily by public agencies. We must accept the harsh fact that numerous individual mistakes are inevitable in the day-to-day administration of our affairs. The United States Constitution cannot reasonably be construed to require federal judicial review for every such error. In the absence of any claim that the public employer was motivated by a desire to curtail or to penalize the exercise of an employee's constitutionally protected rights, we must presume that official action was regular and, if erroneous, can best be corrected in other ways. The Due Process Clause of the Fourteenth Amendment is not a guarantee against incorrect or ill-advised personnel decisions.

Similarly, in *Codd v. Velger* (1977:624) the Court held that the due process clause did not entitle public employees to hearings upon dismissal, even if they were likely to be stigmatized by such action, unless there were some factual dispute involved: ". . . if the hearing mandated by the Due Process Clause is to serve any useful purpose, there must be some factual dispute between an employer and a discharged employee which has some significant bearing on the employee's reputation." A measure of deconstitutionalization has also occurred in the area of equal protection (*Washington v. Davis*, 1976), as discussed in the next section.

Deconstitutionalization is an exercise in judicial restraint concerning public personnel administration. It does not presage a return to the doctrine of privilege. Rather, it calls a halt to increasing judicial review of public personnel management. Constitutional values stressing individual freedom and diversity will continue to take precedence over administrative values stressing organizational efficiency, hierarchy, harmony, and uniformity. However, the Supreme Court has now made it clear that not every adverse action has constitutional ramifications. Consequently, routine public personnel administration is relatively free of constitutional constraints, whereas public personnel policy having a substantial connection to political life, such as employees' freedom of speech or patronage dismissals, is likely to continue to be scrutinized continually and closely by the judiciary.

The Rights of Public Employees Today

Having discussed the evolution of doctrines and approaches concerning the public employment relationship, it is possible to summarize the present scope of civil servants' constitutional rights in relatively brief fashion. This exercise will prove valuable to the student and practitioner of public administration, especially when coupled with the new liabilities of public officials, as is discussed in Chapter 6.

Nonpartisan Speech

Under prevailing constitutional interpretations, the public employee's right of freedom of speech is broadly protected, except where its exercise is in conjunction with a partisan political activity. In *Pickering v. Board of Education* (1968), mentioned previously, the Supreme Court held that the special duties and obligations of public employees notwithstanding, the proper test for the regulation of their speech is whether the government's interest in limiting their "opportunities to contribute to public debate is . . . significantly greater than its interest in limiting a similar contribution by any member of the general public" (573). Its interest would be presumptively greater when:

1. There is a need for maintaining discipline and harmony in the work force.
2. There is a need for confidentiality.
3. The employee's statements would be hard to counter due to his or her presumed greater access to factual information.
4. The employee's statements were so unfounded that his or her competence was called into question.
5. The employee's statements impeded the proper performance of work.
6. The employee's remarks jeopardized a close and personal loyalty or confidence.

In applying *Pickering* and these guidelines, the lower courts have held that the Constitution does not protect public employees' public speech concerning matters not of public concern, bickering and running disputes among employees, intermeddling, disruptive speech, and "extremely disrespectful and grossly offensive remarks" (Rosenbloom and Gille, 1975:260). Public criticism of an employer, on the other hand, is generally constitutionally protected.

By and large, these standards also apply to public employees' private speech. *Givhan v. Western Line Consolidated School District* (1979) concerned the dismissal of a teacher after ". . . a series of private encounters between [the teacher] and the school principal in which [the teacher] allegedly made 'petty and unreasonable demands' in a manner variously described by the principal as 'insulting,' 'hostile,' 'loud,' and 'arrogant' " (412). Although the constitutionality of the dismissal was upheld by the Court of Appeals for the Fifth Circuit, the Supreme Court reversed, stating that "we are unable to agree that private expression of one's views is beyond constitutional protection . . ." and that earlier cases ". . . do not support the conclusion that a public employee forfeits his protection against governmental abridgment of freedom of speech if he decides to express his views privately rather than publicly" (414).

Partisan Speech

As mentioned previously, efforts to assure the overt partisan neutrality of the public service date back to the days of President Jefferson's first administration. The constitutionality of regulations prohibiting public employees from engaging in partisan speech, holding party office, and engaging in campaign management or electioneering activity has been addressed by several courts on several occasions over the past century. Although such regulations have sometimes been found unconstitutional elsewhere, the Supreme Court has steadfastly upheld their legitimacy. This was first accomplished with reference to modern regulations, that is, the Hatch Act of 1939, in *United Public Workers v. Mitchell* (1947). Despite the fundamental and far-reaching doctrinal development that had taken place since that case was decided by a four to three margin, in 1973 the Court once again reaffirmed the act's constitutionality (*U.S. Civil Service Commission v. National Association of Letter Carriers*, 1973). Although a federal district court had held that past decisons "coupled with changes in the size and complexity of public service, place *Mitchell* among other decisions outmoded by passage of time," the Supreme Court found no constitutional infirmity in such regulations.

> We unhesitatingly reaffirm the *Mitchell* holding that Congress had, and has, the power to prevent [federal employees] from holding a party office, working at the polls, and acting as party paymaster for other party workers. An Act of Congress going no farther would in our view unquestionably be valid. So would it be if, in plain and understandable language, the statute forbade activities such as organizing a political party or club; actively participating in fund-raising activities for a partisan candidate or political party; becoming a partisan candidate for, or campaigning for, an elective public office; actively managing the campaign of a partisan candidate for public office; initiating or circulating a partisan nominating petition or soliciting votes for a partisan candidate for public office; or serving as a delegate, alternate, or proxy to a political party convention (*USCSC v. NALC*, 1973:556).

In *Broadrick v. Oklahoma* (1973), a companion case, the Court was even willing to uphold political neutrality regulations which were so amibguously worded that they might inhibit speech unrelated to the objective of maintaining a nonpartisan public service. In handing down these rulings, the Court has adopted the view that it is doing

> . . . no more than confirm[ing] the judgment of history, a judgment made by this country over the last century that it is in the best interest of the country, indeed essential, that federal service should depend upon meritorious performance rather than political service, and that the political influence of federal employees on others and on the electoral process should be limited (*USCSC v. NALC*, 1973:557).

Freedom of Association

Public employees' freedom of association was broadly guaranteed by the Supreme Court's holding in *Shelton v. Tucker* (1960). It extends to membership in labor unions and even to membership in subversive organizations (*Elfbrandt v. Russell*, 1966). The right to associate being well established, the most recent cases of importance deal with the right not to join various groups. This issue has arisen with reference to membership in and support for political parties and labor unions.

Elrod v. Burns (1976) concerned the constitutionality of patronage dismissals in the Cook County, Illinois, Sheriff's Department. The Supreme Court held that such dismissals constituted an unconstitutional infringement upon public employees' freedom of belief and association, but it was unable to develop a majority opinion on the issue. A plurality of the Court reasoned that patronage dismissals placed severe restraints upon the freedoms of belief and association and since they were "not the least restrictive means for fostering" (*Elrod v. Burns*, 1976:372) legitimate governmental ends, such as the promotion of efficiency, harmony, and effectiveness, they could not withstand constitutional scrutiny. This decision, therefore, clearly asserted the constitutional value of diversity over the administrative and political values of uniformity.

Justice Stewart, joined by Justice Blackmun, concurred on the narrower ground that ". . . a nonpolicymaking, nonconfidential government employee" cannot constitutionally "be discharged . . . from a job that he is satisfactorily performing upon the sole ground of his political beliefs" (375). On the other hand, Justice Powell, joined by Chief Justice Burger and Justice Rehnquist, dissented on the grounds that

> History and long-prevailing practice across the country support the view that patronage hiring practices make a sufficiently substantial contribution to the practical functioning of our democratic system to support their relatively modest intrusion on First Amendment interests. The judgment

today unnecessarily constitutionalizes another element of American life—
an element certainly not without its faults but one which generations
have accepted on balance as having merit (388-389).

The holding in *Elrod* was modified and strengthened by the Supreme Court's
ruling in *Branti v. Finkel* (1980). The case involved the patronage dismissal of
two assistant public defenders in Rockland County, New York "upon the sole
grounds of their political beliefs" (508-509). The Court, per Justice Stevens,
reasoned that with regard to such dismissals ". . . the ultimate inquiry is not
whether the label 'policymaker' or 'confidential' fits a particular position; rather,
the question is whether the hiring authority can demonstrate that party affiliation is an appropriate requirement for the effective performance of the public
office involved" (518). Such a demonstration, though possible, would, of
course, ordinarily be extremely difficult. In the instance at hand, the Court
concluded that contrary to what the public defender claimed ". . . it would
undermine, rather than promote, the effective performance of an assistant public
defender's office to make his tenure dependent on his allegiance to the dominant
political party" (519-520). Justice Powell, joined by Justice Rehnquist, dissented once again. This time he sought to remind the majority that patronage
was an important means by which elected officials could influence the performance of public bureaucracies.

For the most part, according to these patronage decisions, public employees
cannot be coerced to associate with political parties on pain of dismissal from
their positions. Nor can they be constitutionally forced to contribute funds to
the party in power.

Public employees' situation regarding labor unions is somewhat more complex. In *Abood v. Detroit Board of Education* (1977), the Supreme Court
upheld the constitutionality of a public sector "agency shop" arrangement
"whereby every employee represented by a union—even though not a union
member—must pay to the union, as a condition of employment a service fee
equal in amount to union dues" (211). The Court reasoned that such arrangements are common in private employment and can be considered a fundamental
aspect of collective bargaining. Although the public sector agency shop inter-
feres with the civil servant's freedom of association, "such interference as exists
is constitutionally justified by the legislative assessment of the important contribution of the union shop to the system of labor relations" (222). The Court
ruled that, nevertheless, employees could not be forced to pay for the union's
spending of funds "for the expression of political views, on behalf of political
candidates, or toward the advancement of other ideological causes not germane
to its duties as collective bargaining representative" (235). The Court was
cognizant of the fact that "there will, of course, be difficult problems in drawing
lines between collective bargaining activities, for which contributions may be

compelled, and ideological activities unrelated to collective bargaining, for which such compulsion is prohibited" (236).

Liberty

The broad issue of public employees' liberty has also been the subject of substantial litigation. During the 1970s, the Supreme Court handed down several important rulings in this area. In *Cleveland Board of Education v. LaFleur* and *Cohen v. Chesterfield County School Board*, argued and decided together in 1974, the Court addressed the issue of mandatory maternity leaves. The policies being challenged were particularly arbitrary and harsh by requiring leaves to commence early in the term of a pregnancy, while at the same time serving no rational purpose. Indeed, Justice Powell expressed the opinion that the policies were aimed at preventing school children from gazing upon pregnant teachers. Teachers were also banned from returning to their jobs until three months after the birth of their children. Not surprisingly, the Court found such policies to be unconstitutional. It did so, however, not on the basis of a violation of equal protection of the laws, but rather on the grounds that "by acting to penalize the pregnant teacher for deciding to bear a child, overly restrictive maternity leave regulations can constitute a heavy burden on the exercise of . . . protected freedoms" (640). The Court held that with the exception of a regulation forcing the employee to go on leave a few weeks prior to the expected date of birth of her child, regulations based on elapsed time rather than on the individual's capability to continue at her job were constitutionally unacceptable.

Municipal residency requirements are another area in which adminsistrative and political values tend to conflict with the Constitution's protection of individuals' liberty. However, the constitutionality of such requirements was upheld by the Supreme Court in *McCarthy v. Philadelphia Civil Service Commission* (1976), at least with regard to firefighters. In a very short opinion, the Court found the ". . . bona fide continuing residence requirement" involved to be constitutionally acceptable (647). It did not discuss the issue in broad terms, though, and, therefore, it is not clear whether there are limits to the constitutionality of residency requirements.

Two other issues bear mention. In *Massachusetts Board of Retirement v. Murgia* (1976), the Supreme Court accepted the constitutionality of a mandatory retirement age of 50 years old for state police officers. In contrast to the maternity leave cases, it did not think that individualized determination of fitness was constitutionally required since the regulation applied at "a stage that each of us will reach if we live out our normal span" (313-314). Finally, as discussed earlier, in *Kelley v. Johnson* (1976) the constitutionality of grooming standards for male police officers was upheld on the basis that a challenge to such regulations must "demonstrate that there is no rational connection between the regulation ... and the promotion of safety of persons and property" (247). The Court thought the standards could not be considered irrational since they might make police officers more identifiable to the public and might promote an esprit de corps.

Equal Protection

Issues concerning public employees' right to equal protection of the laws have been at the forefront of public administrative policy for well over a decade. Equal protection has also been an area of considerable judicial intervention in public personnel administration. The courts have been called upon to decide the constitutionality of merit exams that have a harsh racial impact in excluding a disproportionately large number of minorities from the public service. Typically, this has required the judiciary to judge the validity of such exams as predictors of job performance. Few areas, of course, are more central to contemporary public personnel management than the construction and valida- tion of exams. Where the courts found exams to be discriminatory *and* lacking in validity, they frequently required that a system of quota hiring be instituted to remedy the situation. For a time, therefore, it appeared that the judiciary would eventually reformulate the examing and validation processes (Rosenbloom and Obuchowski, 1977). However, the Supreme Court's decisions in this area have obscured matters somewhat.

Perhaps its most important holding was in *Washington v. Davis* (1976) which sought to deconstitutionalize this area to a substantial extent. The case involved a challenge to the constitutionality of a written qualifying examination given to applicants for positions as police officers in the District of Columbia. The exam had a disproportionately harsh racial impact by disqualifying four times as many blacks as whites. Several lower court decisions held that such a disparity required the governmental employer to demonstrate that the exam in question served a compelling state interest. This generally entailed a demonstration of the test's validity. Since satisfactory validation is extremely difficult and often impossible, in effect this meant that the constitutional value of diversity was asserted over an administrative process that tended to reward cultural uniformity.

The Supreme Court, however, rejected this approach in favor of one requiring that "an invidious discriminatory purpose" (*Washington v. Davis*, 1976:242) be shown in order to overturn a public personnel practice on the grounds that it violates the equal protection clause.

This is not to say that the necessary discriminatory racial purpose must be express or appear on the face of the statute, or that a law's dispropor- tionate impact is irrelevant in cases involving Constitution-based claims of racial discrimination. . . .

Necessarily an invidious discriminatory purpose may often be inferred from the totality of the relevant facts, including the fact, if it is true, that the law bears more heavily on one race than another (241-242).

At the time it was decided, it appeared that the impact of *Washington v. Davis* would be limited because identical issues can be litigated under federal equal employment opportunity statutes which, unlike the Constitution, do not require that a discriminatory purpose be shown in order to strike down a public personnel practice having a harsh racial impact. However, the significance of the *Davis* case was made evident in *Massachusetts v. Feeney* (1979), which involved a challenge to the constitutionality of a Massachusetts veteran preference law on the grounds that it violated the equal protection clause by disproportionately excluding women from public service positions. The Equal Employment Opportunity Act of 1972 specifically forecloses a challenge to such procedures on legal grounds. In deciding the case, the Supreme Court agreed with the challengers that the impact of the veteran preference statute on the "public employment opportunities of women has . . . been severe" (*Massachusetts v. Feeney*, 1979: 271). Nevertheless, it upheld the constitutionality of the "absolute" preferential scheme on the basis that not impact, but rather ". . . purposeful discrimination is the condition that offends the Constitution" (274).

According to *Washington v. Davis*, purposeful discrimination in public employment against minorities is unconstitutional. Purposeful discrimination against aliens, however, has been treated more in keeping with the case-by-case approach. *Sugarman v. Dougall* (1973) concerned New York State's exclusion of aliens from public service. The Supreme Court rejected this across-the-board approach. Instead it held that ". . . a flat ban on the employment of aliens in positions that have little, if any, relation to a State's legitimate interest, cannot withstand scrutiny under the Fourteenth Amendment" (647). At the same time, though, "A restriction on the employment of noncitizens, narrowly confined, could have particular relevance to this important state responsibility, for alienage itself is a factor that reasonably could be employed in defining 'political community' " (649). Thus, aliens could be excluded from some positions, but not others, depending on the relationship of the position to state responsibilities. Thus far, the Supreme Court has held that aliens can be excluded from positions as police officers (*Foley v. Connelie*, 1978) and teachers (*Ambach v. Norwick*, 1979).

Purposeful discrimination against groups such as minorities and aliens might be treated differently by the judiciary than purposeful discrimination in their favor. Despite a decade of concern with affirmtive action, the Supreme Court has yet to hand down a definitive ruling on affirmative racial- or gender-based preferences in a public sector employment case. The closest it came was in *Morton v. Mancari* (1974), which involved a preference system for Indians in the Bureau of Indian Affairs. The Court upheld the constitutionality of the preference, but seemed to do so in keeping with the case-by-case approach, by stressing the unique status of Indians as "quasi-sovereign tribal entities" (554). The celebrated cases of *Regents v. Bakke* (1978) and *Steelworkers v. Weber* (1979) shed little light on the matter. The first concerned admission to a state medical school rather than public employment, and did not result in a majority opinion of the Court. The second ruling upholding affirmative action in the allocation of training was specifically limited by the Court to the private sector: "since the . . . plan does not involve state action, this case does not present an alleged violation of the Equal Protection Clause of the Fourteenth Amendment" (200). Nor does *Fullilove v. Klutznick* (1980), which upheld affirmative action in the disbursal of Federal Public Works funds, resolve the issue.

Due Process

The extent to which the consitutional protection of individuals against governmental denial of "life, liberty, or property, without due process of law" should act as a constraint on adverse actions in public personnel management has also been the subject of much litigation. Although perplexing to define in a technical sense, due process generally refers to fundamental fairness (*Hannah v. Larche*, 1960). In the realm of public employment, it raises the question of whether a particular adverse action constitutionally requires that a hearing be held. If so, the issue of the form that hearing must take also becomes salient. This area, as others, has witnessed the evolution of the four doctrinal approaches discussed previously.

By 1972, the Supreme Court had unequivocally established the potential applicability of the constitutional requirement of due process in adverse actions. In *Board of Regents v. Roth* (1972), it identified four situations in which public employees would have a constitutional right to hearing in dismissal actions:

1. Where the dismissal was in retaliation for the exercise of protected rights, such as freedom of speech.
2. "Where a person's good name, reputation, honor, or integrity is at stake because of what the government is doing to him, notice and an opportunity to be heard are essential" (573).
3. Where a dismissal diminished a public employee's future employability.
4. Where the employee has a property right or interest in a position, such as tenure or a contract.

In *Arnett v. Kennedy* (1974), however, the Court was unable to reach a majority opinion on the issue of whether a federal employee could be dismissed, without a *pretermination* hearing, for publicly accusing his supervisor of seeking to bribe a third party. Although six justices agreed that the Constitution was a relevant constraint in such circumstances, two of these believed that its requirements would be met by a posttermination hearing. On the other hand, the three remaining justices argued that the case should be governed solely by the prevailing statute (the Lloyd-LaFollette Act of 1912), rather than the due process clause of the Fifth Amendment. Consequently, a majority of five justices found no constitutional infirmity in the employee's dismissal.

By 1976, a majority of the Court seemed determined to limit the constitutional requirement of due process even further. In *Bishop v. Wood* (1976), it found that a policeman who was defined as a "permanent employee" by a city ordinance, nevertheless had no constitutionally cognizable property interest in his position and, therefore,

> In the absence of any claim that the public employer was motivated by
> a desire to curtail or to penalize the exercise of an employee's constitu-
> tionally protected rights, we must presume that official action was regular
> and, if erroneous, can best be corrected in other ways. The Due Process
> Clause of the Fourteenth Amendment is not a guarantee against incorrect
> or ill-advised personnel decisions (350).

Thus, the public personnel manager now has greater freedom in the realm of adverse actions without running the risk of violating the Constitution.

Under the deconstitutionalization approach of *Bishop v. Wood*, administrative values stressing hierarchy and discipline will remain relatively unencumbered by constitutional values unless an adverse action is motivated by a desire to deny a public employee his or her constitutional rights; that is, unless it impinges on well-established constitutional values. It should also be borne in mind that under *Codd v. Velger* (1977), discussed above, no hearing need be afforded if an issue of fact is not in dispute.

When a hearing is constitutionally appropriate, on the other hand, the courts may require that it afford elaborate protections for the individual. To date there have been cases requiring that the hearing be open and afford the individual the rights of confrontation, cross-examination, and to be judged by an impartial official (Rosenbloom and Gille, 1975).

Conclusion

Part of the contemporary judicial response to the rise of the administrative state has concerned the constitutional status of citizens in public employment. The issues raised by the peculiar nature of public employment did not become highly salient to the judiciary until the 1950s, after the number of citizens in public employment at all levels of government had expanded dramatically. Once embarking upon formulating a response to this aspect of the administrative state that would enable it to intervene in matters of public personnel administration, the judiciary had some difficulty in formulating lasting doctrines or approaches. Despite this limitation on the overall coherence of judicial intervention in this area, there is no doubt that in general the courts have sought to promote the constitutional value of diversity in the face of administrative and political efforts to promote uniformity among public employees. In so doing, the judiciary has shown considerable sensitivity to two issues. One is the extent to which the rise of the administrative state, coupled with traditional approaches to the constitutional rights of public employees, served to deny a substantial segment—indeed, close to 20 percent of the work force—some very fundamental constitutional ˙ rights. To the extent that these rights were highly valued by the judiciary, such a situation was almost intolerable. Thus, in the era of the Warren Court (1953–1969), it was inevitable that as the scope of constitutional rights expanded generally, the doctrine of privilege would be abandoned as it affected public personnel management, and public employees would be afforded substantial constitutional protections within the public employment relationship.

Second, the judiciary has shown considerable awareness of the extent to which the rise of the administrative state has transformed the nature of American politics. Consequently, in some cases the courts have explicitly sought to redress the rights of public employees in an effort to reinvigorate the political process. This was most evident in the *Pickering* case, in which the Supreme Court seemed as much interested in the teacher's right to speak out as the public's right and need to listen. Despite Justice Powell's forceful dissents, the patronage cases can also be interpreted as an effort by the Supreme Court to protect the polity against partisan capture of the public service and the potential rise of a one-party state. In *Elrod v. Burns* (1976), for example, Justice Brennan noted that in patronage systems, "The free functioning of the electoral process also suffers. . . . Patronage . . . tips the electoral process in favor of the incumbent party . . ." (356). Moreover, in his view, this danger becomes more acute with the growth of the administrative state: ". . . where the practice's scope is substantial relative to the size of the electorate, the impact on the process can be significant" (356).

Although judicial intervention in this area of the administrative state has been diverse and has involved a host of only loosely connected matters, overall the courts' activity has served to create a greater measure of freedom and pluralism in public bureaucracies. The administrative values of hierarchy and uniformity have been weakened. Some public managers might claim these have even been reduced to the point at which public management is itself virtually impossible. Certainly the ability of political executives and elected officials to control public bureaucracy has declined, and judicial intervention in this area has hastened the decline. But at the same time, it must be noted that public bureaucracies in the

United States may now be functioning more in tune with the political system as a whole. They have at least the potential of representing a greater range of values and social types than ever before in the nation's history, and public bureaucrats are now freer to attempt to inform the electorate so that the voters can cast their ballots intelligently. Contemporary American public bureaucracies are a far cry from the Wilsonian ideal, but once they became obviously engaged in the formulation of public policy it became desirable to treat them as political, stressing the diversity sought by the Constitution in other power centers, such as the legislature, and enabling public bureaucrats to engage publicly in political activities short of actual campaigning and electioneering. From this perspective, political neutrality regulations and the prohibition against patronage dismissals also promote diversity by preventing one-party domination of this vital power center.

The immediate remaining question is whether the deconstitutionalization approach will go far enough to substantially reverse the scope of judicial intervention in this aspects of the administrative state. Thus far, it has not done so, being confined to questions of liberty such as personal appearance and residency, due process where there is present neither a question of fact nor the issue of the employer's desire to abridge an employee's constitutional rights, and equal protection where there is no evident discriminatory purpose involved. To date, then, it appears that deconstitutionalization will enable the judiciary to delimit its involvement in public personnel administration to areas which it considers fundamental to individual rights or to the political community generally, such as freedom of speech, belief, or association. In sum, then, in this area as in that concerning the citizen-client, the judiciary has altered traditional doctrines to enable it to play a far greater role in public administration.

References

Abood v. Detroit Board of Education, 1977. 431 U.S. 209.
Ambach v. Norwick, 1979. 441 U.S. 68.
Appleby, Paul H., 1949. *Policy and Administration.* Birmingham: University of Alabama Press.
Arnett v. Kennedy, 1974. 416 U.S. 134.
Bailey v. Richardson, 1950. 182 F2d 46.
Bailey v. Richardson, 1951. 341 U.S. 918.
Birnbaum v. Trussell, 1966. 371 F2d 672.
Bishop v. Wood, 1976. 426 U.S. 341.
Board of Regents v. Roth, 1972. 408 U.S. 564.
Branti v. Finkel, 1980. 445 U.S. 507.
Broadrick v. Oklahoma, 1973. 413 U.S. 601.
Cleveland Board of Education v. LaFleur, 1974. 414 U.S. 632.

Codd v. Velger, 1977. 429 U.S. 624.

Cohen v. Chesterfield County School Board, 1974. 414 U.S. 632.

Commager, Henry S., 1947. Who is loyal to America? *Harper's Magazine* 145 (September), 193-199.

Dotson, Arch, 1955. The emerging doctrine of privilege in public employment. *Public Administration Review* 15 (Spring), 77-87.

Douglas v. Hampton, 1972. 338 F. Supp. 18.

Douglas v. Hampton, 1975. 512 F2d 976.

Downs, Anthony, 1967. *Inside Bureaucracy.* Boston: Little, Brown.

Eifbrandt v. Russell, 1966. 384 U.S. 11.

Elrod v. Burns, 1976. 727 U.S. 347.

Ex Parte Hennen, 1839. 13 Peters 230.

Foley v. Connelie, 1978. 435 U.S. 291.

Fursman v. Chicago, 1917. 278 Ill. 318.

Gilmore v. James, 1967. 274 F. Supp. 75.

Givhan v. Western Line Consolidated School District, 1979. 439 U.S. 410.

Griswold v. Connecticut, 1965. 381 U.S. 479.

Gulick, Luther and L. Urwick, eds., 1937. *Papers on the Science of Administration.* New York: Institute of Public Administration.

Hannah v. Larche, 1960. 363 U.S. 420.

Hershey, Carey, 1973. *Protest in the Public Service.* Lexington, Mass.: Lexington Books.

Hummel, Ralph, 1977. *The Bureaucratic Experience.* New York: St. Martin's.

Jahoda, Marie, 1955. Morale in the federal service. *Annals of the American Academy of Political and Social Science* 300 (July), 110-113.

Kelley v. Johnson, 1976. 425 U.S. 238.

Kiiskila v. Nichols, 1970. 433 F2d 745.

Krislov, Samuel, 1967. *The Negro in Federal Employment.* Minneapolis: University of Minnesota Press.

Krislov, Samuel, 1974. *Representative Bureaucracy.* Englewood Cliffs, N.J.: Prentice-Hall.

Krislov, Samuel and David H. Rosenbloom, 1981. *Representative Bureaucracy and the American Political System.* New York: Praeger.

Link, Arthur, 1956. *Wilson: The New Freedom.* Princeton, N.J.: Princeton University Press.

McAuliffe v. New Bedford, 1892. 155 Mass. 216.

McCarthy v. Philadelphia Civil Service Commission, 1976. 424 U.S. 645.

Massachusetts Board of Retirement v. Murgia, 1976. 427 U.S. 307.

Massachusetts v. Feeney, 1979. 422 U.S. 256.

Meehan v. Macy, 1968. 392 F2d 882.

Miller, K. and N. Samuels, eds., 1973. *Power and the People.* Pacific Palisades, Calif.: Goodyear.

Morton v. Mancari, 1974. 417 U.S. 535.

Mosher, Frederick, 1968. *Democracy and the Public Service.* New York: Oxford University Press.

Nachmias, David and David H. Rosenbloom, 1980. *Bureaucratic Government, USA.* New York: St. Martin's.

Nathan, Richard, 1975. *The Plot That Failed.* New York: Wiley.

New York Times, 1974. July 20.

New York Times, 1976. August 14.

Norton v. Macy. 1969. 417 F2d 1161.

Pickering v. Board of Education, 1968. 391 U.S. 563.

Posey, Rollin B., 1968. The new militancy of public employees. *Public Administration Review* 28(March-April), 111-117.

Regents v. Bakke, 1978. 438 U.S. 265.

Rosenbloom, David H., 1971. *Federal Service and the Constitution.* Ithaca, N.Y.: Cornell University Press.

Rosenbloom, David H., 1975. Public personnel administration and the constitution: An emergent approach. *Public Administration Review* 35(January/February), 52-59.

Rosenbloom, David H., 1977. *Federal Equal Employment Opportunity.* New York: Praeger.

Rosenbloom, David H. and Jennifer Gille, 1975. The current constitutional approach to public employment. *University of Kansas Law Review* 23(Winter), 249-275.

Rosenbloom, David H. and Carole C. Obuchowski, 1977. Public personnel examinations and the Constitution: Emergent trends. *Public Administration Review* 37(January/February), 9-18.

Rossiter, Clinton, ed., 1961. *The Federalist Papers.* New York: New American Library.

Sayre, Wallace, ed., 1965. *The Federal Government Service.* Englewood Cliffs, N.J.: Prentice-Hall.

Seidman, Harold, 1975. *Politics, Position, and Power.* New York: Oxford University Press.

Shafritz, Jay, Walter Balk, Albert Hyde, and David H. Rosenbloom, 1978. *Personnel Management in Government.* New York: Marcel Dekker.

Shelton v. Tucker, 1960. 364 U.S. 479.

Smith, B. and D. Hague, 1971. *The Dilemma of Accountability in Modern Government.* New York: St. Martin's.

Steelworkers v. Weber (Kaiser v. Weber), 1979. 443 U.S. 193.

Storing, Herbert, 1964. Political parties and the bureaucracy. In Robert A. Goldwin (ed.), *Political Parties, USA.* Chicago: Rand McNally.

Sugarman v. Dougall, 1973. 413 U.S. 634.

Thompson, Victor, 1961. *Modern Organization.* New York: Knopf.

United Public Workers v. Mitchell, 1947. 330 U.S. 75.

U.S. Civil Service Commission, 1976. *A Self-Inquiry into Merit Staffing.* Washington, D.C.: U.S. Civil Service Commission.

U.S. States Civil Service Commission v. National Association of Letter Carriers, 1973. 413 U.S. 548.

U.S. Commission on Civil Rights, 1974. *The Federal Civil Rights Enforcement Effort.* Washington, D.C.: U.S. Government Printing Office.

Waldo, Dwight, 1948. *The Administrative State.* New York: Ronald Press.

Washington Post, 1970. October 10.

Washington v. Davis, 1976. 426 U.S. 229.

Weber, Max, 1958. *Essays in Sociology.* Translated and edited by H. H. Gerth and C. W. Mills. New York: Oxford University Press.

West v. Macy, 1968. 248 F. Supp. 105.

Wilson, Woodrow, 1941. The study of administration. *Political Science Quarterly* 56(December), 481-506 (originally copyrighted in 1887).

5
The Citizen as Captive in the Administrative State

Citizens not only interact with the administrative state as clients and employees, some of the less fortunate find themselves involuntarily institutionalized by the government. Whether in prisons, public mental hospitals, or public institutions for the mentally retarded, members of the population coming into contact with the government in this fashion are appropriately referred to as *captives* in the administrative state. Their numbers are not especially large: in 1977 there were approximately 292,000 prisoners, 173,000 parolees, 415,600 persons confined to public mental hospitals, and about 15,000 in public facilities for the mentally retarded (U.S. Department of Commerce, 1979:118,194). Although some of those in mental hospitals and institutions for the retarded may have entered voluntarily in some sense, in practice their captivity is often identical to those involuntarily committed (*Pennhurst State School v. Halderman*, 1981). While limited in numbers, however, captives in the administrative state have provided fertile ground for litigation that has led to far-reaching legal developments and broadened the role of the judiciary in public administration.

At the outset, it is desirable to address the concept of citizen as captive in the administrative state. Indeed, there are several reasons why such an approach may at first appear to be an odd or extreme formulation. One objection is that prisons and mental institutions predate the contemporary administrative state. Yet, few would argue that today these are not administrative organizations sharing many features with other contemporary organizations in the bureaucratic mold. Another reason for resisting the label of captive is that American public administrative theory has tended to stress the *service* functions of the administrative state and, conversely, tended to ignore its *control* functions. Thus, despite the abominable conditions that have often prevailed in public mental hospitals and facilities for the retarded, these institutions have often been considered as providers of health and treatment services. It is only when the actual conditions prevalent in such places and the administrative reasons for them are examined that it becomes clear that they are centers for the control or segregation, rather than the cure, of deviants. Even with respect to prisons, where the fact of captivity should be self-evident, it is often claimed that a rehabilitative service is performed. Again, however, upon examination of the conditions under which many prisoners live, such a claim must often be dismissed. In sum, the key to understanding the legal problems associated with the citizen's captivity in such institutions of the administrative state lies in an examination of the nature of the institutions themselves.

Total Institutions and Public Administrative Values

Public mental hospitals, facilities for the retarded, and prisons are often referred to as *total institutions*. The fundamental nature of these is described aptly by Erving Goffman (1961:5-6).

> A basic social arrangement in modern society is that the individual tends to sleep, play, and work in a different places, with different co-partici-pants, under different authorities, and without an over-all rational plan. The central feature of total institutions can be described as a breakdown of the barriers ordinarily separating these three spheres of life. First, all aspects of life are conducted in the same place and under the same single authority. Second, each phase of the member's daily activity is carried on in the immediate company of a large batch of others, all of whom are treated alike and required to do the same thing together. Third, all phases of the day's activities are tightly scheduled, with one activity leading at a prearranged time into the next, the whole sequence of activities being imposed from above by a system of explicit formal rulings and a body of officials. Finally, the various enforced activities are brought together into a single rational plan purportedly designed to fulfill the official aims of the institution.

The administration of total institutions poses unique challenges. However, these are often met with essentially bureaucratic responses stressing the needs of the organization over those of the population it ostensibly serves.

A fundamental aspect of total institutions is the movement of inmates in groups. Whatever the activities—eating, sleeping, exercising, working, and so forth—it is generally considered administratively impracticable to treat individuals as such, but rather administratively preferable to handle them in groups in order to maximize "efficiency." A common relatively benign example is the general practice of requiring inmates to arise, dress, and stand in line hours before breakfast so that they will be ready to eat when the institution is ready to serve them. Thus, in a sense, the captives are prepared for the food, as much as vice versa. Similarly, in mental hospitals the inability to treat patients individually provides an administrative rationale for various group therapies. However, it should be immediately evident that any given individual's interests may be divergent from those of the group to which he or she is assigned. Moreover, the interests of a whole group may be opposed to those of the total institution. In other words, the organization's need to maximize administrative efficiency or convenience may diminish an individual's ability to maximize his or her own interests within the framework of the total institution. Consequently, a fundamental necessity confronting the administration of total institutions is control of the inmate population. Such control is fostered in several ways.

Perhaps the most pervasive means of controlling inmate populations is to diminish the conflict between individual and total institution through dehumanization or impersonalization of the inmate population. It is no accident that Max Weber (1958) considered dehumanization to be the "special virtue" of bureaucratic organization. Bureaucracy functions more efficiently when it can turn individuals into cases suitable for processing. It thrives on the routine application of impersonal rules. The same is generally true of total institutions, however bureaucratic in their overall organizational structure. Dehumahization extends to both routine administration by the staff and, in facilities offering treatment to the mentally ill or retarded, to the medical activities of health professionals as well. Again, Goffman provides an insightful description.

. . . [A] further set of characteristic problems is found in the constant conflict between humane standards on the one hand and institutional efficiency on the other. . . . The personal possessions of an individual are an important part of the materials out of which he builds a self, but as an inmate the ease with which he can be managed by staff is likely to increase with the degree to which he is dispossessed. The remarkable efficiency with which a mental-hospital ward can adjust to a daily shift in number of resident patients is related to the fact that the comers and leavers do not come or leave with any properties but themselves and do not have any right to choose where they will be located. Further, the efficiency with which the clothes of these patients can be kept clean and fresh is related to the fact that everyone's soiled clothing can be indiscriminately placed in one bundle, and laundered clothing can be redistributed not according to ownership but according to approximate size. Similarly, the quickest assurance that patients going on the grounds will be warmly dressed is to march them past a pile of the ward's allotment of coats, allowing no choice as to whether to wear one or which one to wear, and requiring them for the same purposes of health to give up claim to these collectivized garments on returning to the ward. The very structure of a garment can be determined by the interests of efficiency, not self-enhancement. . . .

Just as personal possessions may interfere with the smooth running of an institutional operation and be removed for this reason, so parts of the body may conflict with efficient management and the conflict may be resolved in favor of efficiency. If the heads of inmates are to be kept clean, and the possessor easily categorized, then a complete head shave is efficacious, despite the damage this does to appearance. On similar grounds, some mental hospitals have found it useful to extract the teeth of "biters," give hysterectomies to promiscuous female patients, and perform lobotomies on chronic fighters (Goffman, 1961:78-79).

Just as impersonality can be imposed as a means of promoting administrative efficiency and convenience, it can also be defined as part of the rehabilitative process.

A common characteristic of total institutions is an effort to strip an individual entrant of his or her former self, or self-identity. Whereas this may facilitate socialization to the total institution, it can also be considered part of a rehabilitative process in the sense that the former self has been officially defined as defective in some way, whether because of mental illness or criminality. Thus, rehabilitative therapies often involve a set of humiliations or mortifications of the self. These involve loss of possessions, as noted previously, various kinds of physical contaminations such as forced feeding or medication, and a host of personal debasements, including loss of control over even the most ordinary aspects of one's daily life, activity, and speech. Such a process may be carried out under the label of *milieu therapy*. Its objective is to dehumanize the individual so that he or she can be endowed with a new personality by the total institution. This new personality will be one more amenable to institutional control as well as to living outside the total institution. Hence, dehumanization not only serves the needs of total institutions to provide food, clothing, and so on, it also enables them to exert greater psychological control over their populations. This control can be further enhanced through the distribution of rewards and punishments as a means of promoting adherence to the institution's rules.

Total institutions can impose severe deprivations upon their inmates; they can also reward their populations with various privileges and degrees of autonomy. Rewards such as preferred living quarters, released time, desirable jobs, and other sought-after elements can be distributed as inducements to accept the institution's norms and rules. Likewise, breaches of norms and rules can be punished with loss of privileges, restricted mobility, isolation, and physical pain. With specific reference to mental hospitals,

Demands must be made, and disappointment is shown when a patient does not live up to what is expected of him. Interest in seeing psychiatric "movement" or "improvement" after an initial stay on the wards leads the staff to encourage "proper" conduct and to express disappointment when a patient backslides into "psychosis." The patient is thus re-established as someone whom others are depending on, someone who ought to know enough to act correctly. Some improprieties, especially ones like muteness and apathy that do not obstruct and even ease ward routines, may continue to be perceived naturalistically as symptoms, but on the whole the hospital operates semi-officially on the assumption that the patient ought to act in a manageable way and be respectful of psychiatry, and that he who does will be rewarded by improvement in life conditions and he who doesn't will be punished by a reduction of amenities (Goffman, 1961:308).

Among the problems associated with the distribution of rewards and punishments is the extent to which such decisions can be made on an arbitrary basis. Ward attendants and prison guards are often in a position to dispense minor rewards or punishments; generally, their statements are taken as convincing evidence of the desirability of allocating greater benefits or deprivations. Although dehumanization tends to militate against the exercise of personal bias by the staff, there is reason to believe that informal organizational factors—or the "underlife" of total institutions, as Goffman (1961) refers to them—promote the exercise of independent and unchecked power by the staff over the inmates. Another difficulty with the levying of punishment under the guise of treatment is the possibility of enforcing the total institution's rules through the use of terror.

Control of prisoners is often partly maintained through formal and informal terror. On a formal basis, the authorities may threaten individual inmates with extreme isolation and deprivation of basic human needs and amenities. In some societies, torture and corporal punishment are meted out to instill terror in prisoners. To the extent that informal organizations of prisoners play a role in the actual administration of prison life, terror in the form of threats of physical beatings, homosexual rapes, and even death may be prevalent. Between the formal organization of prison authority and the informal world of prison organizations is the terror employed by prison guards through various kinds of brutality. Gresham Sykes summarizes the nature of prison order in the following terms.

But what is most important, perhaps, is the fact that the maximum security prison represents a social system in which an attempt is made to create and maintain total or almost total social control.

The detailed regulations extending into every area of the individual's life, the constant surveillance, the concentration of power into the hands of a ruling few, the wide gulf between the rulers and the ruled—all are elements of what we would usually call a totalitarian regime. The threat of force lies close beneath the surface of the custodial institution and it is the invisible fist rather than Adam Smith's invisible hand which regulates much of the prisoner's activity. The prison official is a bureaucrat, but he is a bureaucrat with a gun (Sykes, 1958:xiv-xv).

The use of terror, however, seems to be most strategically employed in mental hospitals. Indeed, it has been maintained that "The most brutal and inhumane punishments in our day are meted out not in prisons, but in mental hospitals" (Szasz, 1963:96). One account of the use of shock therapy in a public mental hospital is illustrative.

This knowledge [of shock therapy] is based on the fact that some of the patients in Ward 30 have assisted the shock team in the administration of therapy to patients, holding them down, and helping to strap them in bed, or watching them after they have quieted. The administration of shock on the ward is often carried out in full sight of a group of interested onlookers. The patient's convulsions often resemble those of an accident victim in death agony and are accompanied by choking gasps and at times by a foaming overflow of saliva from the mouth. The patient slowly recovers without memory of the occurrence, but he has served the others as a frightful spectacle of what may be done to them (quoted in Goffman, 1961:33).

Other applications of terror in the guise of treatment include lobotomies, hysterectomies, and the use of various kinds of restraining devices. Historically, an even wider and more terrifying variety of techniques were practiced.

An additional means by which total institutions, especially mental hospitals, control their inmates is through the use of medication. The tranquilizer, rather than therapy, is used to control aggressive patients. Sleeping pills are routinely administered in order to make a ward quiet enough to enable the hospital to cut costs by using reduced staff at night. Although such medication can have therapeutic value, often its major purpose is to serve the needs of administrative convenience and efficiency.

The problems total institutions face in attempting to control their inmates are complex and difficult. The strategies employed to accomplish this control can be dysfunctional. Rather than enable the institutions effectively to rehabilitate their populations, the need for control often turns them into warehouses in which social deviants are stored for the convenience of society. Efficiency becomes narrowly defined as cost per captive per day. These problems are severely exacerbated by the common underfunding of prisons, public mental hospitals, and facilities for the retarded. As a result, the conditions prevailing in such places are often truly abominable. Though unpleasant, it is crucial to grasp the reality of life in such total institutions in order to understand the judicial response to the plight of the captives in the administrative state.

Conditions in Captivity

By their very essence, total institutions are dehumanizing. The individual captive is turned into a serviceable item, as a *case,* by the administrative bureaucracy. Where dehumanization is so pronounced, it is not surprising that facilities for the captives in the administrative state manifest such inhumane living conditions. Yet, responsibility for these conditions goes well beyond the difficulties inherent in the bureaucratic model of prison and mental health administration.

One of the major difficulties faced by the administrators of prisons and facilities for the mentally ill and retarded is that the concepts behind such institutions are ever-changing. For example, in the past, prisons were designed to function as institutions of retribution, punishment, and sometimes deterrence. As such, conditions within them were purposively harsh—often extremely harsh. If "an eye for an eye" is the theory behind incarceration, torture and maiming may be considered effective means to a desired social end. Where deterrence is the major objective, deprivation and brutality may be considered legitimate administrative techniques. Today, in the United States, reform, that is, *correction*, has been added to these traditional objectives of imprisonment. However, since many prisons and jails were architecturally designed to reflect the desire to punish and deter, they may be not only administratively but structurally inadequate for contemporary purposes. In such instances, what once appeared an appropriate institution is later viewed as thoroughly inappropriate. This is true even if it continues to punish and deter adequately.

The history of "treatment" for the mentally ill presents a similar problem. One historical example should dispel all doubts.

Renaissance men developed a delightful, yet horrible way of dealing with their mad denizens: they were put on a ship and entrusted to mariners because folly, water, and sea, as everyone then "knew," had an affinity for each other. Thus, "Ships of Fools" crisscrossed the seas and canals of Europe with their comic and pathetic cargo of souls. Some of them found pleasure and even a cure in the changing surroundings, in the isolation of being cast off, while others withdrew further, became worse, or died alone and away from their families. The cities and villages which had thus rid themselves of their crazed and crazy, could now take pleasure in watching the exciting sideshow when a ship full of foreign lunatics would dock at their harbors (Foucault, 1973:vi–vii).

Historically, in the United States the purposes of institutions for the mentally ill have undergone several changes (Deutsch, 1949). Although many of these changes can be traced to evolving concepts of treatment, those having the greatest impact on the physical design of existing institutions tend to be based more on political and moral considerations. This, of course, is to be expected as the public care of the mentally ill tends to be a product of political rather than medical or psychological decision making.

The first institutional model leaving an important legacy was the asylum. It was designed to provide a *refuge* for the mentally ill. Even though such facilities may have been seriously underfunded and their conditions accordingly harsh, their fundamental purpose was to protect their residents from the society at large. Consequently, asylums tended to be located in remote places and perhaps surrounded by protective walls. However, the physical restraint of "patients" was neither intended for the protection of the society generally nor for reasons of administrative convenience. The asylum was the institutional product of "moral treatment," as Deutsch, (1949:91–92) indicates.

This consists in removing patients from their residence to some proper asylum; and for this purpose a calm retreat in the country is to be preferred: for it is found that continuance at home aggravates the disease, as the improper association of ideas cannot be destroyed. A system of humane vigilance is adopted.

For the most part, in the United States the asylum rarely achieved its ideals. Such places were all too frequently too poor to be humane. In addition, large numbers of the insane were simply stored in poorhouses. Eventually, exposure to the maltreatment of the mentally ill prompted a movement for state care (Deutsch, 1949). But, this movement more or less coincided with another one having rather ominous consequences for the mentally defective. The Social Darwin movement of the turn of the century spawned a widespread and highly emotionally laden concern with eugenics. Deutsch (1949:360) observes:

A period of social hysteria set in, comparable in many respects to the witch-hunting mania of yore. It was generally agreed that mental defect was "the mother of crime, pauperism and degeneracy." Civilization was in imminent danger of being overrun by defective stocks, who were already eating away like internal parasites.

Such concerns led to the segregation of the mentally ill and the retarded from the rest of the society as a means of protecting the species' gene pool. Accordingly, facilities for the mentally ill remained geographically remote, but the conditions within them changed. Walls and restraints were now used to protect the society at large. "Treatment" became even less humane, and sterilization was commonplace. Since the society had little interest in the future of mental defectives, such people were housed and maintained at minimal costs.

The eugenics approach was widely discredited in the aftermath of World War II. As Deutsch (1949:376-377) notes,

> It was revealed at the war-crime trials of Nuremberg in 1947 that more than 275,000 insane, feebleminded and physically handicapped Germans were put to death under the official Nazi euthanasia program. The danger of placing sterilizing power in the hands of men filled with hatred against individuals and groups on racial, religious, political or merely personal grounds, is too obvious to require further elaboration.

As a result, the political concept behind public institutionalization began to change from segregation and storage to treatment and habilation. But, given the inadequate levels of funding in this area of public policy, architectural design could not possibly remain apace with changing concepts of mental health care. Consequently, institutions built with the eugenics approach in mind could not readily be converted to a newer approach. Nor, short of wholesale deinstitutionalization, can the society readily overcome the problems associated with "geographically remote residential institutional care" (*Halderman v. Pennhurst State School*, 1977), which is a direct legacy of the asylum model. As a result, today, the United States is heavily burdened with outdated facilities for the care of the mentally ill and the retarded—a fact that contributes substantially to recognition of the inhumane conditions under which these captives are held. This directly raises the issue of funding.

In the United States, legislatures have been notorious in underfunding prisons, public mental hospitals, and public facilities for the retarded. Whatever callousness may be involved in this tendency, there is no doubt that legislators are constantly confronted with claimants for scarce funds who are far more powerful and visible than those who are held captive in the adminsitrative state. First, the institutionalized neither form a voting bloc nor are able to present their demands effectively through normal political channels. Conceivably, their relatives and friends could bring political pressure to bear on legislators, but the social stigma attached to imprisonment, mental illmess, and retardation militates strongly against this possibility. Second, a major historical purpose of the institutions of captivity has been to segregate their residents from the remainder of society. Although the reasons for this desire are complex, the adage "out of sight, out of mind," is apropos. In their segregated state, captives become relatively invisible—few outsiders are aware of the conditions under which the confined live, and fewer still find their plight a salient concern.

Politically, the powerlessness and invisibility of captives is often translated into inadequate funding for the institutions in which they are held. Lack of funds, in turn, can be translated into harsh and frequently inhumane living conditions, characterized by inadequate staff, insufficient work and recreation, the absence of meaningful treatment, and overcrowding.

Together, bureaucratic dehumanization, badly dated facilities, and insufficient funding create a situation in which prisons, public mental hospitals, and facilities for the retarded become little or nothing more than *warehouses** where the confined are barely and brutally stored. If this statement sounds extreme, the following descriptions of conditions in such institutions may demonstrate its moderation.

Prisons

Depending upon one's theory of incarceration, life in prison may be intentionally harsh. Yet, it is sometimes so brutal that courts have found it to "shock the conscience" and to be "much more cruel than is necessary" (*Hamilton v. Schiro*, 1970:1019). Why? As one court described the situation in a jail that can by no means be considered atypical, "The average inmate spends most of his time sitting or lying upon his bunk. Indeed, inactivity, in miserable surroundings, was the principal feature of the detainee's existence . . ." (*Hamilton v. Love*, 1971: 1189). These "miserable surroundings" were created largely by egregious overcrowding, poor sanitary conditions, no recreation, no medical or dental care, vermin and poisonous insects, inadequate bedding or no bedding, no laundry facilities and, more generally, ". . . evidence of vicious assaults, homosexual attacks, [and] torture." In another typical case, the court found that "inmates are put in constant fear of and subjected to bodily injury and sexual attacks from other inmates" (*Hamilton v. Schiro*, 1970:1018).

Prisons suffer from serious administrative problems, making it difficult to protect their populations from brutality or to motivate them through a coherent system of positive incentives. Gresham Sykes (1958:58-59) has observed that

> . . . the combination of a bureaucratic staff—that most modern, rational form of mobilizing effort to exercise control—and the use of physical violence—that most ancient device to channel man's conduct—must strike us as an anomaly and with good reason. The use of force is actually

---

*Significantly, this term has been used by Judge David Bazelon. See the *New York Times*, January 5, 1982, p. B10.

grossly inefficient as a means for securing obedience, particularly when those who are to be controlled are called on to perform a task of any complexity. A blow with a club may check an immediate revolt, it is true, but it cannot assure effective performance on a punch-press. A "come-along," a straitjacket or a pair of handcuffs may serve to curb one rebellious prisoner in a crisis, but they will be of little aid in moving more than 1200 inmates through the mess-hall in a routine and orderly fashion.

More generally, the problem is that the guards and prison officials are fundamentally unable to control the prison. They are not only badly outnumbered, but

> ... the lack of a sense of duty among those who are held captive, the obvious fallacies of coercion, the pathetic collection of rewards and punishments to induce compliance, the strong pressures toward the corruption of the guard in the form of friendship, reciprocity, and the transfer of duties into the hands of trusted inmates—all are structural defects in the prison's system of power ... (Sykes, 1958:61).

Combined with inadequate physical structures and an aggressive population, these defects in the control system of a typical prison make it inevitable that, to a very considerable extent, a prison will be run by the prisoners. Brutalities will inevitably occur in such a situation. Better facilities and better administration may be the only remedy.

Public Mental Hospitals

Public mental hospitals suffer from many of the same physical and administrative problems. They are often overcrowded and understaffed. Their populations are not readily controlled, and may be given to violence against themselves or others. Here, however, a special form of brutality may be visited upon the captive in the form of treatment. Grant Morris (1969:784) has elaborated.

> ... [S]ociety embarked on a great segregation program. The mentally ill— sick people—were segregated from the criminals—wicked people. The mentally ill were confined in asylums, later called mental hospitals, for the purpose of treatment. The criminals were confined in prisons for the purpose of punishment....
> To be sure, the early treatment methods were barbaric and the mentally ill often suffered as much as the prisoners who were being punished, but the suffering of the mentally ill was under the guise of treatment. One notable example of this treatment—in the twentieth century holes were

not drilled into the skulls of the mentally ill to permit evil spirits to escape, but lobotomies, a surgical severing of nerve fibers in the brain, were performed as a form of treatment to make patients more manageable.

As the technology of warehousing the mentally ill advanced, lobotomies were replaced by tranquilizing and other psychoactive drugs. But the pain did not cease. Morris reports on the use of a drug trade-named Anectine.

Anectine was injected intravenously to produce respiratory arrest. The patients' intercostal muscles and diaphragms were affected and a period of apnea was produced. For a period of one and one-half to two minutes of muscle paralysis, the patients, though fully conscious, were not able to breathe. During this . . . interval, male technicians made oral statements to the patients, suggesting that they improve their behavior in the future. . . . How severe is the Anectine experience from the point of view of the patient? Sixteen likened the experience to dying. Three of these compared it to actual experiences in the past in which they had almost drowned. The majority described it as a terrible, scary experience (Morris, 1969:799).

While the application of torture under the guise of therapy presents a serious problem, the general conditions in many public mental hospitals have long been equally harsh. In 1948, the Philadelphia State Hospital for Mental Diseases was described in the following terms.

. . . I entered buildings swarming with naked humans herded like cattle and treated with less concern, pervaded by a fetid odor so heavy, so nauseating, that the stench seemed to have almost a physical existence of its own. I saw hundreds of patients living under leaking roofs, surrounded by moldy, decaying walls, and sprawling on rotting floors for want of seats or benches. . . . Many of the attendants, I was told, were vagrants recruited directly from courts and police stations where they were reportedly given the choice of a jail sentence or going on the [hospital] payroll (Murdock, 1972:147).

As late as the 1970s, conditions had not changed appreciably in some public mental hospitals, as will become evident from a consideration of the judicial response to the plight of these captives in the administrative state.

Once again, inadequate funding and the bureaucratic model of control can be seen as the primary contributors to such harsh conditions. Morton Birnbaum, a pioneer in the creation of a right to treatment for the mentally ill, not only condemns the widespread lack of funding for such facilities, but also observes the inefficacy of the bureaucratic model which results in ". . . the least-trained member of the staff, the ward attendant, rather than the psychiatrist, having the greatest control over the care and treatment of the patients" (Birnbaum, 1960:500). Indeed, so poor are the conditions in some public mental hospitals, that "there is considerable evidence that a prolonged commitment in an institution providing only custodial confinement for the 'mentally sick' and nothing more may itself cause serious psychological harm or exacerbate any pre-existing condition" (*U.S. ex rel. Schuster v. Herold*, 1969:1079).

Public Facilities for the Mentally Retarded

Perhaps the plight of mentally retarded captives in the administrative state is the harshest of all. Retardation is not curable, but some degree of habilitation is possible in the majority of cases. Nevertheless, historically the retarded have been lumped in with criminals, drunks, and the insane. They have even been "sold" to persons who offered to take responsibility for them for the lowest amount of public support (*Halderman v. Pennhurst State School*, 1977:1299). Again, a bureaucratic model of custodial care results in dehumanizing treatment, which coupled with inadequate physical structures and insufficient funding, often makes for an extremely inhumane environment. In 1965, the life of the institutionalized retarded generally was described in the following terms.

In each of the dormitories for severely retarded residents there is what is euphemistically called a day room or recreation room. The odor in each of these rooms is over-powering. After a visit to a day room we had to send our clothes to the dry cleaners to have the stench removed. The facilities often contribute to the horror. Floors are sometimes wooden and excretions are rubbed into the cracks, leaving permanent stench. Most day rooms have a series of bleacher benches on which sit unclad residents jammed together without purposeful activity, communication, or any interaction. In each day room is an attendant or two, whose main function seems to be to "stand around" and, on occasion, hose down the floor "driving" excretion into a sewer conveniently located at the center of the room. . . .
. . . The question one might ask is, Is it possible to prevent these conditions? Although we are convinced that to teach severely retarded adults to wear clothes one must invest time and patience, we believe it is possible to do so—given adequate staff. There is one more requirement. The staff has to be convinced that residents can be taught to wear clothes, that they can be engaged in purposeful activities, that they can learn to control their

bladders. The staff has to believe that their "boys" and "girls" are human beings who can learn. Obviously, the money and the additional staff are vitally important. However, even more important is the fundamental belief that each of these residents is a human being (Murdock, 1972: 147-148).

Litigation in the 1970s uncovered almost unspeakable brutalities in public facilities for the retarded. For instance, at the Pennhurst State School and Hospital in Pennsylvania residents were given only an average of 15 minutes per day of beneficial programming, but at the same time were subject to excessive restraints; to beatings by staff and assaults by other residents; at least one rape by a member of the staff; denial of wheelchairs, hearing aids, and physical therapy; excessive drugging; and a generally harsh and hazardous physical environment (*Halderman v. Pennhurst State School*, 1977). Perhaps the most abominable conditions to be uncovered to date were at Alabama's Partlow facility in which

(a) a resident was scalded to death by hydrant water; (b) a resident was restrained in a strait jacket for nine years in order to prevent hand and finger sucking; (c) a resident was inappropriately confined in seclusion for a period of years; and (d) a resident died from the insertion by another resident of a running water hose into his rectum (Murdock, 1972:149; *Wyatt v. Stickney*, 1972:393).

It is hardly surprising that residents may actually regress, that is, decline in social quotient, in such institutions.

There is little more to be said about the conditions under which the captives in the administrative state have often been held. Clearly, the custodial model of care, drawing heavily upon bureaucratic concepts, values, and processes, has contributed to the dehumanization and warehousing of these unfortunates. Although public administrators may bemoan judicial interference in their domain, their own hands are hardly clean. Indeed, Morris argues that the Anectine treatments violated the Nuremburg Code, The Declaration of Helsinki, as well as U.S. Food and Drug Administration regulations (1969:800). Similarly, psychiatrists and other members of the medical profession may complain of judicial involvement in the treatment of patients, but their reliance on shock therapy, drugging, and various brutal treatment weakens their position. Finally, where judicial intervention in the conditions under which captives in the administrative state are held practically forces a legislature to appropriate more funds for prisons, mental hospitals, and facilities for the retarded, legislators may complain of a breach of the separation of powers. However, their stance too is weakened by the budgetary neglect often visited upon such institutions. In sum, in a substantial number of instances, administrators, mental health professionals, and legislatures have all failed to display appropriate concern for the rights of individuals held in confinement. Eventually, the judiciary, expressing its traditional concern for individual constitutional rights, sought to fashion a general remedy.

Judicial Creation of the Rights to Treatment and Habilitation

Commitment

It is clear that to be committed to a typical public mental hospital is to be very unfortunate indeed. Even apart from the physical and psychological conditions extant in the typical institution, to be committed, either voluntarily or involuntarily, is to sacrifice a wide range of otherwise constitutionally protected rights and liberties. For example, Thomas Szasz (1963) points out that mental patients suffer some infringement of Fourth, Fifth, Sixth, Seventh, Eighth, Thirteenth, Fourteenth, and Fifteenth Amendment rights. Thus, in his view, they are not afforded comprehensive protections against unreasonable searches and seizures, double jeopardy, self-incrimination, the right to a judicial trial, and a procedure consonant with that afforded persons accused of crimes not involving insanity. Moreover, in Szasz's view, mental patients sometimes receive cruel and unusual punishment, are de facto held in a form of slavery, and forfeit the right to vote. To this list of abridgments of the constitutional rights of the inmates of public mental hospitals must be added the infringements upon the rights of freedom of speech, association, and religion that inevitably accompany life in a total institution. Similarly, a host of other rights and liberties are abridged, including those pertaining to privacy and personal freedom concerning matters of marriage and procreation.

Under the Constitution, therefore, it might be assumed that involuntary commitment could occur only after elaborate procedural due process protections were afforded to the individual. This, however, has not always been the case, and even today commitment procedures may fall short of the protections afforded those accused of crimes. To make matters worse for the involuntarily committed patient, commitment may be indeterminate, that is, until the patient is cured. Thus, it is possible for an individual who is committed to a public mental hospital under a sexual psychopath law, for indecent exposure, for example, to spend years there for an offense that carries a 90-day jail term when treated as a crime according to the normal criminal justice process.

Historically, individuals could be involuntarily committed to mental hospitals for a variety of reasons. As late at 1961,

An American Bar Foundation study . . . found that in five states involuntary commitment of a mentally ill person was based on dangerousness to himself or others; in twelve the need for care and treatment could be an alternative ground; in seven the need for care and treatment was the only basis; and in seven hospitalization could occur only where the welfare of the individual or of others justified it. Six states furnished no statutory criteria, and Massachusetts permitted confinement in cases of "social nonconformity" (*Yale Law Journal*, 1967:92).

Some have found the latter ground particularly dangerous and have argued that whatever the formal criteria, nonconformity is a fundamental factor running through involuntary commitments generally. As Szasz argues, a ". . . crucial factor in commitment is social role. Our problem may now be formulated by asking: Who annoys whom? It is a fact that the vast majority of committed patients are members of the lower classes. Upper-class persons are virtually immune from this sort of social restraint" (1963:47). He points to case after case of involuntary commitment of individuals for nothing more than nonconformity.

Historically, but to a lesser extent nowadays, individuals were afforded only the most rudimentary procedural protections against involuntary commitment. For instance, in the nineteenth century an Illinois statute allowed involuntary commitment as follows.

. . . [M]arried women and infants who, in the judgment of the medical superintendent of the state asylum at Jacksonville are evidently insane or distracted, may be entered or detained in the hospital at the request of the husband of the woman or the guardian of the infant, without the evidence of insanity required in other cases (Szasz, 1963:58).

Today, partly as a result of judicial rulings, the nature of commitment procedures can be summarized as follows.

Although the procedures vary greatly from state to state, there is a common thread that runs through most of the recent statutes and decisions: courts and legislatures now seem willing to give prospective patients substantially the same procedural rights they would have if charged with a crime (Ennis and Emery, 1978:60).

However, some differences and problems remain since commitment is a civil rather than a criminal procedure. Hearings may be before commissioners rather than judges. There is no general constitutional right to a jury decision on commitment. Perhaps most perplexing are the questions of self-incrimination and the extent to which those going through involuntary commitment procedures can be drugged. In general, statutes and court decisions vary on these matters. Consequently, although the general trend is clearly toward greater procedural protections, it is still possible for these to be relatively weak in a given jurisdiction. Thus, as late as 1973, involuntary commitment procedures in Alabama denied the respondent the rights to notice of charges, aid of counsel, confrontation, presentation of evidence, and a jury trial (*Harvard Law Review*, 1973:1287).

It is evident that involuntary commitment to a typical public mental hospital raises grave constitutional questions. In the past two decades, the judiciary has responded primarily in two ways. First, the judiciary rendered a number of decisions strengthening the procedural protections against involuntary commitment. In so doing, courts were playing what can be considered a traditional judicial role: they were engaged in the definition of the rights of individuals being personally and severely affected by governmental action. In practice, the definition of rights in this context does create administrative burdens, but few would consider such judicial activity a usurpation of administrative or even legislative functions. However, after strengthening the rights of those outside the walls of public mental institutions by enhancing their procedural protections against commitment, the judiciary turned its attention to the rights of those actually held in captivity. This brings us to a second, far more complex matter involving pronounced judicial intervention in the administration of public mental facilities themselves.

Treatment and Habilitation

Although other means of protecting individuals confined to public mental hospitals may exist, during the 1970s the judiciary *created* a constitutional right to treatment in order to accomplish this end. The primary case articulating this right was *Wyatt v. Stickney* (1971). It involved a challenge to the constitutionality of the conditions prevailing in public mental health facilities in Alabama. Oddly, the case grew out of cuts in the Alabama state cigarette tax, which led Dr. Stonewall B. Stickney, Commissioner of Mental Health, to order the firing of 99 employees at one of the public hospitals. In October 1970, patients and discharged staff of the hospital brought suit to have the order rescinded on the grounds that the dismissals would deny some 5000 patients any reasonable expectation of receiving treatment. Subsequently, after a discussion in chambers with Federal District Court Judge Frank Johnson, the suit was modified to ask that the ". . . court declare that patients confined to any state-operated mental health facility are constitutionally entitled to adequate, competent treatment" (*Yale Law Journal*, 1975:1347–1348). The conditions prevailing in the Alabama public mental health facilities were not unlike those in other states. However, they were quite severe and Alabama ranked last among the states in expenditures per patient. In part, the problem was one of physical structure.

[T]he dormitories are barn-like structures with no privacy for the patients.
. . . The toilets in restrooms seldom . . . have partitions between them.
These are dehumanizing factors which degenerate the patient's self-
esteem. . . . [C]ontributing to the poor psychological environment are
the shoddy wearing apparel furnished the patients, the nontherapeutic
work assigned . . . and the degrading and humiliating admissions procedures which creates in the patient an impression of the hospital as a
prison or as a "crazy house" (*Yale Law Journal*, 1975:1349).

Understaffing and poor quality staffing were also problems contributing to the
death of four residents, a general lack of individualized treatment plans, and
unsafe and unsanitary conditions. One resident was kept in a wooden cagelike
device, primarily for reasons of administrative convenience. Brutality was not
uncommon, and patients were generally treated in a dehumanizing fashion.

Although conditions of this nature had long prevailed, they were certain to
be exacerbated by the proposed cut in the size of the staff. Traditionally, a
federal district court would have been extremely reluctant to become directly
involved in the operation of a state mental hospital system. If it responded at
all, the federal bench was likely to issue a decree restricting the reduction of
staff or perhaps turn its attention to the nature of commitment procedures in
the future. However, instead of such a limited approach, Judge Johnson chose
a path certain to engender considerable judicial intervention in this realm of
public administration. The court held that "When patients are so committed
[involuntarily] for treatment purposes they unquestionably have a constitutional right to receive such individual treatment as will give each of them a
realistic opportunity to be cured or to improve his or her mental condition"
(*Wyatt v. Stickney*, 1971:784). This was so because "To deprive any citizen
of his or her liberty upon the altruistic theory that the confinement is for
humane therapeutic reasons and then fail to provide adequate treatment violates
the very fundamentals of due process" (785). In these words, a federally recognized constitutional right to treatment was created for the involuntarily committed mentally ill. Subsequently, a right to habilitation for residents of
facilities for the retarded was created as well (*Halderman v. Pennhurst State
School*, 1977; *Welsch v. Likins*, 1977; *Wyatt v. Stickney*, 1972).

The establishment of the right to treatment and the right to habilitation
touched off a wide-ranging debate among lawyers, public administrators, and
mental health officials. As important and revolutionary as these rights are,
however, it is important to understand the extent to which they are limited.
The judiciary has not ruled that anyone in need of mental health treatment is
entitled to it at the public expense. Nor have the courts legally *required* that
states spend additional funds for the treatment of mental patients. Rather,
the logic of these decisions can be expressed as follows.

No constitutional mandate has been called to our attention which would require a state to provide habilitation for its retarded citizens. However, whenever a state accepts retarded individuals into its facilities, it cannot create or maintain those facilities in a manner which deprives those individuals of the basic necessities of life. In the case of the retarded this constitutes an obligation to provide them with minimally adequate habilitation . . . (*Halderman v. Pennhurst State School*, 1977:1318).*

Thus, a state is not constitutionally obligated to maintain facilities for the mentally ill or retarded. However, once it chooses to do so, a state's claim of lack of funds may be considered a "legally insufficient reason" (*Wyatt v. Stickney*, 1972:394) for not providing adequate treatment or habilitation.

This approach affords several advantages. First, it respects the concept of the separation of powers by leaving the ultimate choice of whether to provide mental health care to the state legislatures. Second, in a similar fashion it comports with contemporary notions of federalism by limiting the involvement of the federal judiciary in matters of state policy making. Third, the establishment of a right to treatment for those housed in state facilities for the mentally ill does not require that the government provide treatment to other citizens. Fourth, to a very large extent in establishing the right to treatment, the courts were adhering to a traditional role of defining and protecting the constitutional rights of individuals. Viewed from these perspectives, many of the arguments of opponents of the right to treatment can be readily dismissed as misguided.

However, enforcing the right to treatment and the right to habilitation inevitably required the judiciary to play a much more direct role in the administration of facilities for the mentally ill and the retarded. In fact, in its response to this aspect of the rise of the administrative state, the judiciary frequently all

---

*The status of this decision is currently uncertain. The district court's decision was modified by the court of appeals for the third circuit, which substantially affirmed, but avoided the constitutional issues and based its decision on a federal statute. Subsequently, the Supreme Court, also basing its decision on the relevant statute, overruled these lower court decisions. Much of the discussion concerned whether there was a statutory right to habilitation "under the least restrictive conditions consistent with the purpose of the commitment," as first articulated by the district court. In the Supreme Court's view, ". . . we find nothing in the Act or its legislative history to suggest that Congress intended to require the States to assume the high cost of providing 'appropriate treatment in the "least restrictive environment" ' to their mentally retarded citizens" (*Pennhurst State School v. Halderman*, 1981:4367). In *Youngberg v. Romeo* (1982), however, the Court held that the Constitution requires ". . . the State . . . provide minimally adequate or reasonable training to ensure safety and freedom from undue restraint" of individuals involuntarily committed to public facilities for the retarded (4684).

but took over the jobs of public administrators. *Wyatt v. Stickney* (1971, 1972) presents an excellent example.

Intially, Judge Johnson was reluctant to impose court-established standards for adequate treatment upon the Alabama mental health care system. The state was given an opportunity to bring its program up to his vision of constitutional standards. Only after it failed to do so to the court's satisfaction did Judge Johnson seek to define and to implement the right to treatment more rigorously. He held that three conditions must be met for adequate and effective treatment: (1) there must be a humane psychological and physical environment, (2) there must be qualified staff in sufficient numbers, and (3) individualized treatment plans must be developed for each of the patients. Establishing the first two conditions brought the court directly into the realm of hospital administration; meeting the third required it to intervene in the realm of psychiatry itself.

The administrative conditions imposed by the court upon the state's mental health facilities included the following:

1. Protection of patients' rights to wear their own clothes, have physical exercise, and freedom of religious worship
2. No more than six patients per room
3. No single room with less than 100 square feet of space
4. At least one toilet for each eight patients
5. At least one shower or tub for each 15 patients
6. Not less than 40 square feet per person in the day room
7. Not less than 10 square feet per patient in the dining room
8. A temperature range between 68 and 83°F
9. Various staffing ratios for professionals, clerical workers, and other staff per patient.

The court also became directly involved in the professional aspects of mental health care by ruling that there be no excessive medication, no use of physical restraints except in emergency situations, no experimental research or lobotomies, and no shock therapies without the patient's consent and an opportunity to consult counsel.

It should be immediately evident that in *Wyatt* the court departed from traditional judicial approaches for remedying violations of constitutional rights and extensively entered into the realm of public administration and mental health care. Although such decrees have been subject to a number of criticisms, several courts have followed the *Wyatt* example. For instance, a federal district court ordered comprehensive relief of an administrative and medical nature.

1. A prohibition against seclusion
2. Immediate hiring of additional ward attendants

3. Immediate hiring of at least 85 more nurses
4. Immediate hiring of 30 more physical therapy personnel
5. Immediate hiring of 15 additional physicians
6. Immediate hiring of sufficient recreation staff
7. Immediate and continuing repair of all inoperable toilets
8. Consummation within a reasonable time of a contract with an accredited hospital for the care of acutely ill
9. Periodic reports to the court concerning the progress in meeting these requirements, implementing other plans described to the court, and any hinderances by other state officials to their efforts (*N.Y. State Association for Retarded Children v. Rockefeller*, 1973:768–769)

Judicial involvement in the administration of facilities for the mentally ill and retarded and the courts' definition of adequate treatment can be seen as part of the more general judicial response to the rise of the administrative state. It promotes individual liberty and diversity over opposing administrative values. Its activities pertaining to the plight of these captives in the administrative state, however, have been far more controversial than its definitions of new rights for public employees and recipients of governmental largess. There are several reasons for this. First, the creation of the constitutional rights to treatment and habilitation rest upon somewhat unsatisfying grounds. In part this was due to the court's opinion in *Wyatt*, where the right to treatment was established but its rationale was hardly explicated at all. Perhaps this was because in that case the right to treatment was not actually a matter of dispute: "*Wyatt* marked the first time an American court not only clearly recognized this right, but also the first time that American public mental hospital personnel have agreed during litigation that their patients have this right" (Birnbaum, 1972:584). Subsequently, in interpreting *Wyatt*, it has been observed that

Although the *Wyatt* court was somewhat obscure in its exposition of the constitutional basis for the right to treatment, the recent cases suggest that the elements underlying the *Wyatt* opinion are as follows: 1) Where an individual's liberty is as drastically curtailed as it is in civil commitment, 2) without the procedural safeguards of the criminal process, 3) and the lack of such safeguards is justified by the benevolent purpose of the state in affording needed treatment to the individual, 4) due process requires that he receive such treatment as will give him a reasonable chance to improve or be cured (*Harvard Law Review*, 1973:1287).

Yet, this constitutional logic has important flaws.

It is evident that to the extent that the right to treatment is connected to the nature of the civil commitment process the right can be diminished or negated by elaborate standards of due process at commitment hearings. Indeed, as noted earlier, the general trend today is to afford the civilly committed procedural rights almost as elaborate as those available to criminal defendants. But, a more elaborate process for those outside the walls of mental facilities will not remedy the situation of those subject to inhumane treatment within. Nor will it justify keeping them in a form of captivity that exacerbates their condition and often leads to regression. In the absence of treatment, one of the traditional bases for civil commitment is erased: "The most frequently asserted ground is society's right, if not duty, to commit for treatment people so mentally disordered as to be unable to decide whether to seek treatment themselves" (*Yale Law Journal*, 1967:87).

However, once the need for treatment is no longer a ground for civil commitment, the primary justification would be preventive detention: ". . . some persons are adjudged so dangerous that they must be restrained to protect society or themselves, even though they have not committed any criminal act with the traditionally required *mens rea*" (*Yale Law Journal*, 1967:87). Preventive detention, therefore, can be justified under the government's police power, rather than as part of a mental health *services* program. In this instance it is not evident why preventive detainees should be constitutionally entitled to treatment. Moreover, overlapping considerations of the right to treatment on both therapeutic and detention grounds is the stark fact that no known treatment exists for some mentally ill persons. The right to treatment cannot create an effective treatment in such cases. Therefore, adhering strictly to the court's decision in *Wyatt*, the government might be obligated to release some of the most mentally ill and dangerous inmates of mental institutions simply because it was unable to satisfy meaningfully their right to treatment.

A final problem with the right to treatment as articulated in *Wyatt* is that it pertains only to those involuntarily committed. The connection of procedural due process in civil commitment hearings to the right to treatment cannot be the basis for securing a right to treatment for those who voluntarily enter public mental institutions. Other courts have sought to deal with these problems.

In *N.Y. State Association for Retarded Children v. Rockefeller* (1973), the court was confronted with typically inhumane and brutal conditions at Willowbrook State School for the mentally retarded. Since the retarded are not curable, the concept of a right to treatment loses some of its force despite the fact that a degree of habilitation is generally possible. Instead of relying on a right to treatment or habilitation, the court raised an argument that is particularly appropriate for redressing the rights of the untreatable and preventive detainees: "Since Willowbrook residents are for the most part confined behind locked gates, and are held without the possibility of a meaningful waiver of their rights to freedom, they must be entitled to at least the same living conditions as prisoners" (1973:764). The court reasoned that this right flows from the Eighth

Amendment's prohibition of cruel and unusual punishment as well as Fourteenth Amendment rights to due process and equal protection. Though not generally relied upon, such an approach provides ample ground for the judiciary to order the improvement of structural and administrative shortcomings in mental health facilities, without forcing judges to become heavily involved in the area of medical treatment itself.

The *Rockefeller* case addresses the nature of commitment, but this issue was more explicitly dealt with in *Halderman v. Pennhurst State School* (1977). Although subsequently overturned on other grounds, the court drew no distinction between voluntary and involuntary patients. Instead, it recognized that both were in fact confined to the facility and even the voluntary patients could not leave for they had no other place to go. Although the court relied heavily on a due process argument, it also found that the segregation of the retarded at Pennhurst was in violation of the equal protection clause, since in the absence of habilitation there was no rational basis for it. Such an argument might be used to equalize the rights of the voluntarily and involuntarily committed generally. Despite these cases and interpretations, however, the judicially created constitutional right to treatment remains much debated and is certain to engender further litigation.

Another reason for the controversiality of the judicially created right to treatment has been the question of whether the courts are competent to intervene in an area requiring medical expertise, especially one as scientifically unsettled as psychiatry. Judge David Bazelon, whose decision in *Rouse v. Cameron* (1966) was a major contribution to the eventual establishment of a constitutional right to treatment for the mentally ill, has noted his own agreement with critics who assert the "Courts are not as competent as hospitals to make treatment decisions" and "the evaluation of standards of adequacy and suitability may be next to impossible in the present state of psychiatry, where 'treatment' means different things to different psychiatrists" (Bazelon, 1969: 676). Among these critics has been the American Psychiatric Association, which responded to the *Rouse* decision with an official statement that "The definition of treatment and the appraisal of its adequacy are matters for medical determination" (Bazelon, 1969a:742).

It is evident that these criticisms of the right to treatment posit a conflict between medical and administrative technique and individual rights. The judiciary is unschooled in the medical aspects of treatment but, nevertheless, finds some treatments so inhumane as to require that they not be administered without offering patients some procedural protections. This is what the court did in *Wyatt* with regard to lobotomies and shock treatment. But matters of this nature can become extremely complicated. Some psychiatrists, for example, claim that the milieu of a mental hospital itself affords treatment. If that is the case, then judicial intervention in the administration of such a facility is in itself an interference with treatment. Moreover, the right to treatment requires that "... the hospital pay individual attention to each patient and make an individualized effort to help him" (Bazelon, 1969:678). Consequently, the establishment of the right to treatment may indeed entail the "... courts choosing between therapies on the basis of their relative adequacy and the patient's particular needs," despite the possibility that "... courts may be ill-suited to choose among competing schools of psychotherapy" (*Yale Law Journal*, 1967:105). Although judges may choose to defer to the expertise of members of the psychiatric community, there is little doubt that enforcement of the right to treatment unavoidably involves them in the making of medical determinations. Whether they will generally do so in a competent fashion remains an open question. What is clear is that this aspect of the judicial response to the rise of the administrative state has led to an extension of judicial authority and activity to a wholly new realm.

A closely related criticism of the right to treatment is that it tends to reinforce an outmoded and undesirable model of mental health care. Judge Bazelon also admitted his agreement with the criticism that "no matter how much compulsory treatment is afforded, compulsory hospitalization is itself generally based on ill-conceived standards and goals and ought to be reformed radically or discontinued altogether" (Bazelon, 1969:676). Thomas Szasz has most forcefully developed this line of thought. In his view, "The idea of a 'right' to mental treatment is both naive and dangerous. It is naive because it accepts the problem of the publicly hospitalized mental patient as medical rather than educational, economic, religious, and social. It is dangerous because the remedy creates another problem: compulsory mental treatment. For in a context of involuntary confinement, the treatment too shall have to be compulsory" (Szasz, 1969:740). Why is compulsory treatment dangerous? Not merely because treatments can be painful or even because they may involve invasions of privacy and infringements upon constitutional rights. Compulsory treatment is dangerous in a democratic political system because it can be used to serve a control function as opposed to simply providing a service. In Szasz's words,

> ... bureaucratic care, as contrasted with its entrepreneurial counterpart, ceases to be a system of healing the sick and instead becomes a system of controlling the deviant. ... However, in every situation where medical care is provided bureaucratically, as in communist societies, the physician's role as agent of the sick patient is necessarily alloyed with and often seriously compromised by, his role as agent of the State. Thus the doctor becomes a kind of medical policeman—at times helping the individual, and at times harming him (1969:749).

Szasz's argument is particularly frightening when it is recalled that the courts have linked the nature of the commitment procedure to the need to treat those committed to mental institutions. By the same logic, if treatment were provided as a matter of course, could not the protections afforded to the individual in commitment procedures be relaxed? Szasz points to the distressing example of Ezra Pound who rather than being tried for treason in connection with some of his World War II activities was confined to a public mental hospital for 13 years, subsequently released, though not cured, and never tried for the crime of which he had originally been accused (1963:200-207). This case exemplifies the very essence of using public mental hospitals as a means of political control. It should also be borne in mind that throughout the ages, deviants have been labeled "crazy" and segregated from society. Thus, "politically, the right to treatment is . . . simply the right to submit to authority . . ." (Szasz, 1969:750) and to learn to conform. As a result of these troubling political concerns, some have urged that the mentally ill be given not treatment but rather a return to asylum— decent, humane, and protected places in which to live.

Another criticism of the constitutional right to treatment is that the courts will be unable to implement it effectively, and that, consequently, it will become rhetoric rather than remedy. Essentially, this criticism raises the issue of whether the judiciary can successfully play the role of superadministrator for public mental hospitals and facilities for the retarded. It is clear that in some cases they could not possibly do much worse than hospital administrators. Nevertheless, judges are not trained in mental health administration and, no matter how much assistance they may get from various experts, ultimately some mistakes will be made. These, in turn, may detract from the judiciary's prestige and legitimacy. More importantly, they may introduce a degree of legal and/or constitutional rigidity that will needlessly become a barrier to the attainment of precisely the objectives the judiciary is seeking. *Wyatt v. Stickney* presents an interesting example of some of the difficulties that may stem from the judicial administration of a public mental health system.

Implementation

Although it is common for courts to appoint masters to oversee and implement decrees ordering widespread institutional reform, in *Wyatt* the court chose to appoint human rights committees of seven members for each of the state's mental health facilities. Their job was to

> . . . review . . . all research proposals and all rehabilitation programs, to ensure that the dignity and the human rights of patients are preserved. The committees also shall advise and assist patients who allege that their legal rights have been infringed or that the Mental Health Board has failed to comply with judicially ordered guidelines. At their discretion, the committees may consult appropriate, independent specialists who shall be compensated by the defendant Board (*Yale Law Journal*, 1975:51).

The activities of the Human Rights Committee for the Partlow facility for the retarded was analyzed in an article in the *Yale Law Journal* (1975). It was composed of lay persons with an interest in the habilitation of retarded. The committee was hampered by the lack of a full-time staff, inadequate authority, and inadequate information. Contrary to the general approach when using a master, the committee lacked the authority to issue subpoenas, swear witnesses, and make recommendations to the court. A lack of expertise in institutional administration and care of the retarded also was a limitation at times.

Despite these restrictions, the committee quickly assumed an aggresssive stance. Consequently, its relations with the Partlow staff became quite strained at times. The committee considered Partlow's progress in implementing the decree to be too slow. It also found itself powerless to deal with Partlow's response to the need to reduce overcrowding—"dumping" patients in the community. Indeed, the release of patients in need of further habilitation was both legal and constitutional. It graphically demonstrated the limitations of the constitutional right to treatment, which pertains only to those confined to institutions, and was a presumably unintended administrative consequence of the court's action. In fact, although great improvements occurred at Partlow, after three years ". . . there still remained a large disparity between the reforms achieved and the judicial mandate" (*Yale Law Journal*, 1975:1360). Among the problems remaining were a persistent odor of urine and excrement, fire hazards, restrictions on the residents' movement, staff attitudes favoring the use of rods capable of delivering electric shocks to the patients, the use of seclusion rooms, and very limited habilitation activities which left many residents with nothing useful to do during most of their waking hours.

Of particular interest is whether the judiciary's distrust of public administrators, which encourages the appointment of masters or human rights committees as in *Wyatt*, is misplaced. The failings of mental hospital administrators can be due to many factors, including insufficient powers and resources. Apparently the superintendent of the Partlow facility felt that the court's decree enhanced his power vis-à-vis politicians and members of the community. However, he also considered the Human Rights Committee an encroachment upon his administrative prerogatives. Particularly distressing was the reaction of many professional and nonprofessional staff to the *Wyatt* decision. They developed an *extinction reaction* or a perceived loss of control over the residents, and

> . . . as a result of this "extinction reaction," there have been reports of some personnel becoming more abusive to the patients since the issuance of the decree; moreover, the already strong solidarity among many staff members has increased, producing a "no-ratting" policy whereby many staff members do not report incidents that reflect poorly on others (*Yale Law Journal*, 1975:1368-1369).

In essence, this was a bureaucratic reaction seeking to promote the interests of the staff over those of the clients and an effort to close ranks in the face of outside interference.

Wyatt was but one case. Yet, it raises virtually all of the major questions that must be confronted in dealing with judicial decrees ordering wide-ranging institutional reforms. It clearly led to some successes, but also had a number of unintended consequences. Some of these, such as deinstitutionalization, failed to serve the inmate population well. One remaining aspect of the judiciary's creation of a right to treatment and approach to implementation should be mentioned.

According to a common view, in the realm of mental health care, "the real problem is one of inadequate resources, which the courts are helpless to remedy—the question posed is one for the legislature and is a basic policy judgment involving overall priorities in the allocation of scarce resources" (Bazelon, 1969:676). This reality has led some to argue that judicial decrees seeking to implement the right to treatment constitute a judicial usurpation of the legislative power that should be prohibited by the concept of the separation of powers. As noted earlier, from a formal perspective such criticism is misplaced since the right to treatment is only applicable where the state chooses to operate and to commit persons to mental health facilities. If there were no public mental health institutions, they would not be required by the courts, and there would be no right to treatment. However, on a practical level such reasoning is less than satisfying. In practice, a state cannot simply close down its mental health care facilities and allow the mentally ill to be charged with their own care or place this burden upon their relatives, if any. The public's hostile reaction to the dumping of Partlow patients in the community illustrates the political impossibility of such an approach. Consequently, in practice, it is safe to assume that states will maintain mental health care facilities. But since judicial decrees cost money to implement, in fact, judicial decisions are often budgetary decisions as well. This may be appropriate as "... mental health problems cannot realistically be regarded as a matter of political or of primary legislative concern, at least as an original matter" (Kenrick, 1972:611). Certainly, as noted earlier the residents of public mental health facilities can hardly be effective in politically promoting their own interests. They do need protection. However, because the judiciary is not responsible for budget making as a whole, it neither has to assign a specific price tag to the reforms it decrees nor does it need to worry about policy priorities generally in the face of scarce resources. There are some guides, such as spending in other states and spending for similar facilities elsewhere. In the end, though, budgeting by judicial decree is inherently politically irresponsible as the judges are not in a position to weigh the claims of other interests and other groups. Politically, budgetary protection for some disadvantaged groups may result in hardships being shifted to other groups that are politically weak. And since not all such groups can obtain judicial protection, some will be left without effective spokesmen.

Prisons: Reinterpreting the Eighth Amendment

American prisons often surpass even public mental hospitals in the extent of their barbarity. Perhaps the most extreme example was the Arkansas penal system prior to judicially imposed reforms in the late 1960s. The state's penal approach emphasized punishment and an effort to use inmate labor to generate revenue for the state. The ultimate goal was to make the prisons self-sufficient or even profit-making for the state. Therefore, a premium was placed on obtaining the most labor from the prisoners for the least investment in their food, housing, medical care, clothing, and supervision. The last element was particularly important. In order to reduce the costs of employing "free-world" prison guards, the system relied heavily upon the use of prisoner-trusties to control the general prison population. One study described the *trusty-guard* system as follows.

> Inmate trusties literally ran the prison system. Commissioner of Correction Robert Sarver testified that ". . . more than 90 percent of prison functions relating to inmates [were] [sic] . . . performed by trusties." There were only 35 free world employees at Cummins [prison] and they had responsibility for approximately 1,000 inmates. Of the 35 employees, only eight were available for guard duty and only two were on duty at night.
>   Trusties primarily guarded other inmates, but they also performed administrative tasks traditionally assigned to free world personnel. Many of the trusties were armed and their authority over other inmates was considered great (Harris and Spiller, 1977:49-50).

It is obvious that in such a system, the selection of trusty-guards would be crucial in determining the nature of prison life. In Arkansas,

> Inmates usually achieved trusty status through promotions that were uncritically based upon the recommendation of other trusties. There were few, if any, objective criteria for selecting trusties. The principal criteria were a willingness to prevent escapes and to support free world personnel in relations with the general inmate population. A willingness to "shoot to kill" was considered a strong recommendation for the job. Accordingly, inmates were not disqualified from trusty status because

they were thought dangerous or because they had a record of serious criminal offenses (Harris and Spiller, 1977:50).

Not surprisingly, under these conditions of control and the prevailing penal approach, Arkansas prison life was extremely harsh. A state police investigation in the 1960s revealed the following.

   1. Torture. "Especially infamous among the various torture instrumentalities described in the report was the 'Tucker telephone,' an instrument that '. . . consisted of an electric generator taken from a ring-type telephone, placed in sequence with two dry cell batteries, and attached to an undressed inmate strapped to the treatment table at the Tucker [Prison] hospital by means of one electrode to a big toe and a second electrode to the penis, at which time a crank was turned sending an electric charge into the body of the inmate . . . [s]everal charges were introduced into the inmate of a duration designed to stop just short of the inmate 'passing out' " (Harris and Spiller, 1977:36-37). Other tortures involved the use of ". . . wire pliers to pinch, pull, and squeeze inmates' fingers, toes, ears, noses and genitals. Other practices were jabbing needles under inmates' fingernails, extinguishing cigarettes on inmates' bodies and beating inmates' fingers with wire pliers" (Harris and Spiller, 1977:37).

   2. Beatings. Inmates were viciously beaten by other inmates, and free-world personnel. Such beatings were often explicitly or implicitly sanctioned by prison officials. Beatings were administered with leather straps, chains, automotive fan belts, knotted ropes, shovels, clubs, blackjacks, and brass knuckles (Harris and Spiller, 1977:37).

   3. Financial exploitation. Various goods and services were sold to prisoners by prison administrators of all levels, including trusties and members of the state penitentiary board. Local businessmen also took part in this "thriving entrepreneurial system" (Harris and Spiller, 1977:37). Among the items bought and sold were prison jobs, early release, laundry services, medical care, protection from beatings and torture, drugs, alcoholic beveages, and the use of rooms or cells for sexual contact with inmates' wives or girlfriends.

   4. Sexual abuse. "Sexual abuse of inmates by other inmates was commonplace. Sometimes such abuse was physically forced (particularly in the case of younger inmates), while in other cases sexual favors were exchanged for food. Sexual misconduct reportedly extended to prison employees, who offered preferential treatment or early release to inmates in exchange for sexual favors from the inmates' wives or female friends" (Harris and Spiller, 1977:38).

   5. Malnutrition and lack of sanitation. Field workers' appearance was termed "dreadful." They averaged between 40 and 60 pounds underweight. Their clothing was torn, filthy, and ill-fitting. They were not issued underwear. Meals contained little protein, were prepared under filthy conditions, and were sometimes swarming with insects. Bedding was filthy; showers and toilets were defective.

To be held captive in the administrative state under such conditions was extremely harsh. But other prisons and jails manifested essentially similar conditions. In most cases, the same administrative rationales were used to justify such conditions. Prison administrators sought to control inmates at the lowest possible cost, that is, with the greatest efficiency. Crowding, dehumanization, and inhumane treatment were direct by-products of this approach. They also comported well with a general belief that harsh prison life serves the general penal purposes of punishment and deterrence.

Initially, the judiciary refused to intervene in the administration of prisons. Their role was limited to ensuring that those sent to prison were given a fair opportunity for a fair trial. Under what has been known as the *hands off doctrine*, judges tended to dismiss issues raised by the conditions of prison life as relatively trivial "housekeeping matters" (*Harvard Civil Rights-Civil Liberties Law Review*, 1977). Under this approach, the judiciary avoided addressing issues of overcrowding, sanitation, malnutrition, and brutality. In the late 1960s and throughout the 1970s, however, the judicial response to prison administration underwent a radical transformation.

Unlike the case with regard to mental patients and the retarded, it was unnecessary to create a new constitutional right to afford prisoners protections against abusive treatment. The Eighth Amendment explicitly prohibits cruel and unusual punishment, though it has been subject to a variety of interpretations over the years. In addition, changing concepts of freedom of speech and free exercise of religion, as well as increasing judicial concern with equal protection of the laws could be considered applicable to prisoners. However, precisely why the judiciary chose to abandon the hands off approach when it did remains a matter of conjecture. Among the frequently mentioned possibilities are: (1) The mounting evidence that American prisons were hellish institutions, coupled with a rapidly rising crime rate, placed judges in a very difficult position when it came to sentencing. Knowing that the imprisoned would be dehumanized, brutalized, raped, malnourished, and not rehabilitated, made some judges reluctant to exercise their authority in the fashion they deemed legally appropriate. (2) The expansion of the concept of equal protection perforce brought the judiciary into the realm of prison administration where racial segregation was practiced. (3) Better legal aid and representation for prisoners raised issues in such a fashion that the judiciary could no longer avoid them. (4) The imprisonment of activists and members of the middle class during the turbulent 1960s brought into prison individuals who were skillful at challenging existing institutions and practices. In any event, by the 1970s, several courts had thrown themselves headlong into prison reform with varying success. Indeed, by 1982, 29 states were operating their prison systems under federal court order of some kind (*New York Times*, 1982:B10).

The primary vehicle for judicial entry into this administrative realm has been the Eighth Amendment. In 1972, Justice Brennan articulated the changing judicial approach.

> If a punishment is unusually severe, if there is a strong probability that it is inflicted arbitrarily, if it is substantially rejected by contemporary society, and if there is no reason to believe that it serves any penal purpose more effectively than some less severe punishment, then the continued infliction of that punishment violates the command of the Clause that the State may not inflict inhuman and uncivilized punishments upon those convicted of crimes (*Furman v. Georgia*, 1972:282, concurring).

A similar approach was adopted by many lower federal courts. In *Hamilton v. Schiro*, (1970:1019) the District Court for the Eastern District of Louisiana reasoned that

> Prison life inevitably involves some deprivation of rights, but the conditions of plaintiffs' confinement . . . so shock the conscience as a matter of elemental decency and are so much more cruel than is necessary to achieve a legitimate penal aim that such confinement constitutes cruel and unusual punishment in violation of the Eighth and Fourteenth Amendments. . . .

It is important to stress that many courts adopted a *totality of conditions approach* which assesses the overall nature of life in a prison, rather than focusing on any particular aspect or practice of confinement (*Harvard Civil Rights-Civil Liberties Law Review*, 1977).

Once the Eighth Amendment was interpreted in this general fashion, it became incumbent upon the judiciary to provide remedies for prisoners whose punishment was considered cruel and unusual. Although a wide range of possible remedies exists, as the totality of conditions approach gained favor, the judiciary was increasingly compelled to become heavily involved in prison administration. Thus, it has been observed that in totality of conditions cases,

> . . . courts have done more than simply declare a specific prison condition or practice unconstitutional; instead, they have held that the overall conditions of confinement are so barbaric that mere confinement in the institution constitutes a cruel and unusual punishment. . . . The broader evil has invited a broader remedy: courts have issued decrees mandating extensive reforms of the overall living conditions in the challenged prisons. Going beyond their traditional role, judges have examined prisons in great

detail, fashioning remedies touching on nearly every aspect of prison life and ordering comprehensive institutional reform (*Harvard Civil Rights-Civil Liberties Law Review*, 1977:369-370).

As in the case of other captives in the administrative state, then, the judicial response to the plight of prisoners has been partly to take on the role of administrators per se.

Again, it is important to note that this approach does not actually require state officials to commit funds to make prisons comport with constitutional standards. In theory, states are free to release prisoners or close prisons entirely. As one court put the matter, "inadequate resources can never be an adequate justification for the state's depriving any person of his constitutional rights. If the state cannot obtain the resources to detain persons awaiting trial in accordance with minimum constitutional standards, then the state simply will not be permitted to detain such persons" (*Hamilton v. Love*, 1971:1194). Realistically, however, the wholesale release of dangerous prisoners is neither a desirable nor a viable option. Consequently, despite the state's theoretical freedom, practically it must often institute the reforms mandated by judges.

Judicially ordered reforms of prisons have ranged from extremely broad concerns to very detailed matters. For instance, in one case, a federal district court ordered that "The management and operation of the prison shall be improved immediately" (*Hamilton v. Landrieu*, 1972:550). In addition, it ordered the hiring of 110 new personnel, the creation of a preservice training program for prison personnel, in-service training, better minority recruitment, and better food, sanitation, recreation, and medical treatment. It also specified *where* guards were to be stationed. In all, the court listed a total of 54 conditions that had to be met in order to bring the prison up to constitutional standards. Courts have also ordered improvements in the physical plant of prisons, including better ventilation systems and better plumbing (*Hamilton v. Love*, 1973). Various punishment practices, such as the use of particularly harsh conditions for those in solitary confinement, have also been outlawed by court decree. So was the Arkansas trusty-guard system. Nor have such remedies been advanced solely under the Eighth Amendment; the courts have used various constitutional clauses to protect the inmate's rights to uncensored mail, communications with attorneys, equal protection, and procedural due process.

It is evident that the judicary has become heavily involved in matters of prison administration. How successful has this involvement been? What problems has it caused? These are questions of central importance to the more general judicial response to the rise of the administrative state. Although information is certainly far from complete, it appears that judicial decrees ordering general prison reform have met with a substantial measure of success but nevertheless have displayed the weaknesses of judicial involvement in widespread institutional reform. A study of judicially ordered prison reform in four states found, that on balance,

> The specific changes achieved in each setting as a result of the judicial intervention were necessary and important. However, assessment of the impact of the intervention varies with the standards used. Although virtually everyone interviewed reported significant positive change in the facility with which they were familiar, this reaction was muted or restrained. Summary comments as to the impact of the litigation on the facilities were to the effect that the facilities and services had been raised only to minimal standards. Life in the facilities was described as still dismal and considerable dissatisfaction with the quality of life remained. Most of the institutions continued to be seriously overcrowded. Inmates were not freed from fear. Conditions in the secure confinement areas were generally poor. Limitations imposed by antiquated and poorly designed physical plants were not overcome. Counselling, education, and other programs were not meaningfully available (Harris and Spiller, 1977:23).

Thus, it is apparent that when the courts become involved in administration, their success is far from automatic. Despite their powers, they are limited by some of the same factors that make effective administration difficult generally. Orders are not followed to the letter, employees lack commitment, funds are inadequate, problems defy solution, institutional and organizational inertia make change difficult.

Nevertheless, several factors related to the relative success of judicial intervention in prison administration have been identified:

1. The political and social climate. Where there is widespread legislative and political recognition that judicially imposed prison reforms are necessary and desirable, they will be easier to achieve. Pressures to comply will be placed upon prison administrators.

2. Attitudes of key participants in the litigation. It is especially important for reform that prison administrators do not engage in outright resistance to judicial decrees. In some cases, decrees mandating reform are welcomed by administrators.

3. Attitudes of the judiciary. The judicial attitude must be compatible with those of the public, legislators, and administrators. In some cases this may mean that judges need to tailor their decrees to promote receptivity among these groups. In others, however, where there is little support for judicially mandated prison reform, judges may find it more effective to take a very hard and antagonistic line.

4. Retention of jurisdiction. Where a court retains jurisdiction in a case, pending the implementation of prison reforms, it is more likely to influence the direction and pace of change. Retention of jurisdiction enables the court to monitor implementation and modify its decrees.

   5. *The use of a special master or similar approach.* The special master acts on behalf of the court and mitigates the extent to which reform is dependent wholly upon the cooperativeness and good will of prison administrators.

   6. *Administrative and governmental structure.* The extent to which prison reforms can be implemented often depends upon the power of administrators and local governmental officials to implement change. Where they are dependent upon other levels of government, change is more difficult.

   7. *Practical constraints.* The lack of funds, inability to hire competent staff, and the physical structure of prisons are often practical constraints on implementing reforms.

   In sum, the courts face a complex set of concerns in attempting to reform prisons to make them comport with constitutional standards. In some cases they are more successful than in others, but to date it appears that from an overall perspective, judicial involvement has been effective in eliminating the worst abuses. Once again, the issue of values is explicit. Judges have sought constitutionality, not efficiency and economy. The fact that the Arkansas prison system turned a profit impressed the judiciary very little. In theory, where funds are unavailable to satisfy constitutional requirements, judges will order the release of prisoners or the closing of prisons. Yet, while judicial intervention has generally been somewhat effective, it continues to raise broad political questions.

Conclusion: Judges, Administrators, and Budgets

The judicial response to the plight of captives in the administrative state dramatically raises fundamental issues concerning public administration and law. It is evident that the activity of the courts has blurred traditional distinctions between judges and administrators. Judges have increasingly taken on administrative roles. In the process they have also had an important impact on budgeting. Decisions concerning matters such as staffing, program activity, treatment, and even general management practices are no longer confined to the purview of public administrators, nor is the allocation of funds for public institutions of captivity now solely a legislative function.

   At the broadest level, at least three major issues arise out of this aspect of the judicial response to the rise of the administrative state. First is the matter of what the role of the judiciary in that state should be. In order to maintain their effectiveness, must judges take on administrative and budgetary roles in the well-developed administrative state? What will happen to the character of administrative organizations when constitutional law and public administration become thoroughly entwined? What will be the general political consequences of these developments? These questions are of extreme importance, but they are more appropriately addressed in the conclusion to this book.

A second and related issue is the effectiveness of judges as administrators and budgeters. To date, as discussed previously, judicial intervention in the administration of mental health facilities and prisons has been moderately successful. Many changes have been brought about. However, some judicially mandated reforms have remained unattainable. Even with their greater powers, when judges face administrative problems they fall victim to the same limitations that plague public administrators generally. Thus, organizations and their personnel often behave differently in practice than is suggested by organizational charts and position descriptions. This seems to be particularly true in public institutions of captivity. Communication is imperfect. Funds are inadequate. Motivation may be a limiting factor. Corruption may be present and even pervasive. The judiciary's inability to attain fully the reforms it seeks may reduce the prestige and legitimacy of the courts. The price of an expanding judicial role in public administration may be the emergence of judges as bureaucrats in black robes. Like other bureaucrats, they may be publicly perceived as bunglers and incompetents. This possibility becomes all the greater when judges stray into areas with which they are wholly unfamiliar, such as medical treatments or the stationing of guards in prisons. Ironically, as judges become more active in the administrative state, their legitimacy and prestige may be tainted as in the case of other public officials.

But even if judges emerge as successful in public administration, what will their intervention in public administration mean for the role of administrators generally? It is evident that the judicial response to the plight of captives in the administrative state has placed public administrators in a position clearly subordinate to judges. The traditional distinction between judicial expertise and administrative expertise, that is, between law and public administration, is being erased. As a practical matter, this requires public administrators to become familiar with the judicial process and with broad aspects of constitutional law. Put differently, those public administrators responsible for mental patients or prisoners must now be familiar with judicial and constitutional values. No longer will the claims of efficiency and economy be sufficient in court.

The judicial involvement in a traditional domain of legislatures also raises important questions. On the one hand, the creation of rights by an unelected body is antithetical to the democratic process. On the other, the protection of disadvantaged minorities, who cannot practically use that process to assert their demands, does not run counter to American constitutional concepts. What is perhaps more problematic is the impact of judicially mandated reforms of the institutions of captivity on public budgets. The difficulty here is that budget-making is de facto parceled up among different branches of government. No single authority can establish a political or policy coherence to public spending. The judiciary has come to speak for some functions and groups; legislators speak for others, as do executives. But who will be responsible for the overall enterprise? The division of authority over government spending may make government less manageable. Groups finding a deaf ear in the legislature may turn to the judiciary; but the judiciary will be unable to weigh the relative merits of their claims vis-à-vis those of all other groups. Politically, this creates a measure of built-in irresponsibility. Of course, in assessing this condition, it should always be borne in mind that the current judicial approach was brought on largely by legislative and administrative neglect of the plight of mental patients and prisoners. In this sense, the judiciary is simply filling a vacuum left by these other branches of government.

It should be evident that the expansion of the judicial role in the contemporary American administrative state places judges in a measure of conflict with public administrators and legislators. From the judiciary's perspectives, this requires mechanisms for making its authority available to the citizenry. This matter is addressed in the next chapter.

References

Bazelon, David, 1969. A symposium: The right to treatment. *Georgetown Law Journal* 57:676-679

Bazelon, David, 1969a. Implementing the right to treatment. *University of Chicago Law Review* 36:742-754.

Birnbaum, Morton, 1960. The right to treatment. *American Bar Association Journal* 46:499-505.

Birnbaum, Morton, 1972. The right to treatment—Some comments on implementation. *Duquesne Law Review* 10:579-608.

Deutsch, Albert, 1949. *The Mentally Ill in America*, 2nd ed. New York: Columbia University Press.

Ennis, Bruce and Richard Emery, 1978. *The Rights of Mental Patients.* New York: Avon Books.

Foucault, Michel, 1965. *Madness and Civilization.* New York: Pantheon Books.

Furman v. Georgia, 1972. 408 U.S. 238.

Goffman, Erving, 1961. *Asylums.* Garden City, N.Y.: Anchor.

Halderman v. Pennhurst State School, 1977. 446 F. Suppl. 1295.

Hamilton v. Landrieu, 1972. 351 F. Supp. 549.

Hamilton v. Love, 1971. 328 F. Supp. 1182.

Hamilton v. Love, 1973. 358 F. Supp. 338.

Hamilton v. Schiro, 1970. 338 F. Supp. 1016.

Harris, M. Kay and Dudley P. Spiller, Jr., 1977. *After Decision: Implementation of Judicial Decrees in Correctional Settings.* Washington, D.C.: National Institute of Law Enforcement and Criminal Justice; Law Enforcement Assistance Administration; Department of Justice. Printed by the U.S. Government Printing Office. Copyright, American Bar Association.

Harvard Civil Rights-Civil Liberties Law Review, 1977. Confronting the conditions of confinement: An expanded role for courts in prison reform. Vol. 12: 367-404.

Harvard Law Review, 1973. Case comment: *Wyatt v. Stickney* and the right of civilly committed mental patients to adequate treatment. Vol. 86: 1282-1306.

Kenrick, Charles, 1972. The right to treatment: Judicial realism—judicial initiative. *Duquesne Law Review* 10:609-625.

Morris, Grant, 1969. "Criminality" and the right to treatment. *University of Chicago Law Review* 36:784-801.

Murdock, Charles, 1972. Civil rights of the mentally retarded: Some critical issues. *Notre Dame Lawyer* 48:133-188.

N.Y. State Association for Retarded Children v. Rockefeller, 1973. 357 F. Supp. 752.

New York Times, 1982. January 5.

Pennhurst State School v. Halderman, 1981. 49 Law Week 4363.

Rouse v. Cameron, 1966. 373 F2d 451.

Sykes, Gresham, 1958. *Society of Captives.* Princeton, N.J.: Princeton University Press.

Szasz, Thomas, 1963. *Law, Liberty, and Psychiatry.* New York: Macmillan.

Szasz, Thomas, 1969. The right to health. *Georgetown Law Journal* 57:734-751.

U.S. Department of Commerce, 1979. *Statistical Abstract.* Washington, D.C.: Bureau of the Census.

U.S. ex rel. Schuster v. Herold, 1969. 410 F2d 1071.

Weber, Max, 1958. *From Max Weber: Essays in Sociology.* Translated and edited by H. H. Gerth and C. W. Mills. New York: Oxford University Press.

Welsch v. Likins, 1977. 550 F2d 1122.

Wyatt v. Stickney, 1971. 325 F. Supp. 781; 334 F. Supp. 1341.

Wyatt v. Stickney, 1972. 344 F. Supp. 373; 344 F. Supp. 387; 503 F2d 1305.

Yale Law Journal, 1967. Notes and comments: Civil restraint, mental illness, and the right to treatment. Vol. 77:87-116.

Yale Law Journal, 1975. The *Wyatt* case: Implementation of a judicial decree ordering institutional change. Vol. 84: 1338-1379.

Youngberg v. Romeo, 1982. 50 Law Week 4681.

6

The Citizen as Antagonist of the Administrative State

The capstone of the judicial response to the rise of the administrative state has been the creation of new rights for individuals seeking to oppose public agencies and public bureaucrats through litigation. The creation of these new rights for the citizen-antagonist of the administrative state follows logically, and more or less chronologically, from the development of new rights for individuals in other forms of interaction with the administrative state. Thus, once the judiciary created new rights and expanded old ones for citizen-clients, citizen-public employees, and citizen-captives in the administrative state, the establishment of some means of enabling individuals to vindicate their rights became paramount. Otherwise, the judiciary's effort to make public administration more compatible with constitutional values could be frustrated.

To be successful, any comprehensive judicial effort to create enforcement mechanisms would have to meet at least five conditions. First, those mechanisms would have to be under judicial control. This requirement was dictated by the fact that the individual's expanded rights vis-à-vis public agencies were created as part of a general judicial response to the rise of the administrative state. In order to control the character of this response and to maintain the ability to condition it according to judicial values, the judiciary had to remain in a position to supervise enforcement. Second, enforcement had to be such that any individual was in a position to initiate the process of vindicating breaches of his or her rights. Reliance upon bureaucratic agencies for enforcement presented obvious shortcomings and would not readily make public administration responsive to constitutional values. Third, enforcement mechanisms had to offer the individual sufficient promise of reward. If victorious, the antagonist had to be made whole in some sense. Fourth, as in the case of other enforcement mechanisms, the approach adopted had to have a deterrent value in serving to diminish the likelihood of future breaches of individual rights.

Finally, any such mechanisms had to strike a balance between the need to protect individual rights and the ability of the administrative state to function. Granting antagonists an ability to harrass public bureaucrats or challenge them in a frivolous manner would be as undesirable as providing no protection for the individual at all. Although at first glance it may appear that meeting all these conditions simultaneously would be extremely difficult, in fact, the judiciary was able to accomplish this end in relatively straightforward fashion.

The Citizen-Antagonist of the Administrative State

The rise of the administrative state reduces the ability of the citizenry to influence the direction and mode of governance. The overall consequences of this development were addressed in Chapter 1. Here, however, it is necessary to focus attention briefly upon the ways in which the administrative state limits the individual's ability to oppose government. At the outset, of course, it must be recognized that public bureaucracy in the United States is unpopular enough to generate considerable opposition. Indeed, as discussed in Chapter 3, a survey of the U.S. population in 1973 showed that 37 percent of the public thought the federal government had made the quality of life worse, whereas only 23 percent subscribed to the view that the government had improved it (U.S. Congress, 1973:Part 2, 147). Opposition to constraint or regulatory agencies has been especially strong. Being dissatisfied, to whom can citizens of the administrative state turn for redress of their grievances against public bureaucrats? The traditional answer to this question would be, "To the elected officials, of course." However, the political ramifications of the rise of the administrative state make such a response increasingly dubious. As discussed in Chapter 1, the rise of the American administrative state has been accompanied by a devolution of power and influence into the hands of the unelected components and the unelected staff of government. These elements, by virtue of their very nature, cannot be directly influenced by the electorate. Nor are they tightly or automatically controlled by their nominal political supervisors, whether these are elected or politically appointed. Although at variance from traditional and more comfortable notions about American constitutional government, these relative new realities are widely recognized by both the public and elected officials. Indeed, as noted earlier, in 1973 some 65 percent of the public and 57 percent of a sample of state and local governmental officials agreed with the statement that "the trouble with government is that elected officials have lost control over the bureaucrats, who really run the country" (U.S. Congress, 197:Part 2, 115; Part 3, 61).

   Elections have become a less effective means of challenging the administrative state for other reasons as well. Not only have members of Congress sought to secure administrative largess such as improved roads, buildings, and waterways for their districts, but bureaucrats sometimes distribute resources in a fashion intended to generate greater support for their agencies among specific congressmen (Fiorina, 1977; Arnold, 1979). The net result has been that the outcome of elections has been affected by the relationship between congressional incumbents and public bureaucrats in a way that favors those candidates who are supportive of the administrative state. Moreover, despite their public hue and cry against the bureaucracy, members of Congress often find their electoral interests intertwined with the citizenry's dependence upon public agencies and the red tape that surrounds their operations. Thus, *case work*, or the cutting of bureaucratic red tape, has emerged as a fundamental aspect of a congressman's job. In fact, an increasing proportion of congressional staff has been assigned to the home districts, as opposed to Washington, in an effort both to generate and complete case work successfully (Fiorina, 1977).

To a lesser extent, what is true for members of Congress also pertains to presidential electoral interests. In recent years presidential candidates have tended to attack the federal bureaucracy and to proclaim their intentions to reduce its size and power and to manage it better. However, once in office they may seek to use bureaucratic largess to enhance their opportunities for reelection. This approach was exceptionally explicit during President Carter's campaign in 1980. He ordered the expedited disbursement of bureaucratic largess to some states in an effort to win primaries, and sought to withhold it from other places as a means of punishing local officials who supported other candidates. Whatever the success of such tactics, the central lesson is clear: where bureaucratic largess is used to influence the outcome of elections, the administrative state is not likely to be checked effectively by elected officials, or even the electorate at large.

Elections are not the only means of political action available to anatagonists of the administrative state. Lobbying, public debate, and protest—not to mention revolution—are also possible. Again, however, by its very nature the administrative state tends to reduce the effectiveness of such channels. There are at least two central reasons for this. First, to the extent that individuals are dependent upon administrative largess, such as welfare payments, social security, or employment, they are less likely to engage in open criticism of public agencies. Even though such individuals may have elaborate due process protections available, the fear of reprisal is often present. Indeed, over the years it has often been alleged that despite every effort to protect them, federal employees are often reluctant to file complaints of racial discrimination for fear of reprisal *even if they win their cases* (Rosenbloom, 1977). The activities of would-be whistle-blowers also seems dampened by such prospects. Dependence upon bureaucratic largess almost inevitably is accompanied by a reduction of the individual's political influence.

Cooptation is also fostered by such dependence. The individual who depends upon bureaucratic largess, or simply enjoys the benefits of it, must interact with public agencies. In the process, the individual is socialized to be a client, employee, or perhaps, captive. He or she comes to think in bureaucratic terms; rules are no longer contested with vehemence, however, irrational their content; bureaucratic concepts color the individual's thinking; and, bureaucratic language becomes a medium of communication (Hummel, 1977:Chapter 4). In addition, of course, individuals who benefit from bureaucratic activities are likely to become more supportive of at least some aspects of the administrative state.

A final political means by which antagonists of the administrative state might oppose government agencies has had more potential than actual effectiveness. Citizen participation in the formulation and implementation of bureaucratic policy has been tried in several contexts. Although sometimes effective, in general such programs tend to suffer from lack of the very participation they seek. This appears to be especially true of those programs hoping to involve lower-class and disadvantaged citizens in the workings of the administrative state. For instance, both the poverty program and the model cities program of the late 1960s failed largely for this reason. In some major cities, participation in poverty program elections consisted of less than 5 percent of all those eligible to vote (Moynihan, 1970:137). However, even where participation is extensive, as in agricultural programs, it may be seriously tainted by cooptation and coercion (Lowi, 1969; McConnell, 1966). Nevertheless, public participation in bureaucratic governance remains a plausible potential check on the administrative state.

Political means of these kinds are not the only channels of opposition available to antagonists of the administrative state. Various administrative processes can be developed to handle protests and challenges. The most common of these is the administrative appeal through the bureaucracy itself. While often offering the antagonist substantial potential for success, such means require individuals to accept bureaucratic authority and to use bureaucratic language and concepts. This tends to promote some degree of cooptation. Moreover, it has been found that some people, often called *bureautics*, are so distrustful of bureaucracy that they are exceptionally reluctant to use such channels in seeking to change the content of administrative decisions (Nachmias and Rosenbloom, 1978).

A second administrative channel sometimes available to antagonists of the administrative state is the office of the ombudsman. Although ombudsmen can be very successful in resolving individual complaints of specific and limited nature, they are less likely to be able to effectuate overall reform or to bring about change in the fundamental nature and direction of bureaucratic government. In the United States, as noted previously, the ombudsman role is increasingly played by congressmen in their case work.

This brings us to another and potentially highly effective means of opposing the activities of public agencies: *litigation*. The potential advantages of litigation as a channel for antagonists are substantial. Litigation can tap the traditional role of the courts as agents for establishing the nation's political agenda. One court decision such as *Wyatt v. Stickney* (1971) can have a nationwide political impact that obviates the need to seek reform through legislation in each of the 50 states or through congressional action. Indeed, such cases can bring the nation under one constitutional standard. Moreover, although the courts are passive in the sense that their decisions and powers depend upon the nature of the cases brought before them, litigation is an ideal channel for antagonists of the administrative state because it does not require the formation of groups or the mobilization of the public. Indeed, litigation resulting in fundamental changes in constitutional interpretations can be brought by a single individual, and often one without substantial resources. In addition, where litigation is used to oppose the administrative state, both the plaintiff and the defendant can share a rough degree of equality in the forum in which the contest is held. Judges can be more or less favorable to the administrative state, but unlike members of Congress, their political futures are not bound up with it.

There is also a broader and more fundamental advantage to litigation as a means of challenging the administrative state. As we have seen throughout this book, constitutional values and administrative values are often incompatible. In general, the Constitution supports values that promote diversity among the citizenry and protect the individual's rights and dignity. Administrative values, on the other hand, tend to support uniformity and often stress dehumanization or impersonality in a quest for efficiency and economy. To the extent that this conflict defines the tension between constitutional democracy and bureaucratic government in the United States, it is evident that litigation offers the greatest opportunity for constitutional values to be expressed. Of all public officials, it is the judiciary that is most likely to be imbued with constitutional values and inclined to disregard administrative and legislative perspectives. This is not simply a result of judges' training, it stems directly from their role in American government. For it is the courts' duty to define and redefine the Constitution and to apply and reapply it to ever-changing political, social, and economic conditions. Their role in the separation of powers is to say what the Constitution and the law is. As keepers of the Constitution, therefore, they are also the keepers of its underlying values. If these are to constrain the administrative state and make public administration more compatible with constitutional principles, the courts must play a substantial role in the making of public policy as it effects interaction between individuals and public agencies. Litigation not only affords a means by which this can be accomplished, but it also allows the judicary to exercise some degree of control over the pace of change. Thus, once a case comes before the courts, they can decide it in a relatively broad or more narrow fashion. Judicially mandated reforms can be required immediately or implemented over a number of years. This is true even where the specific case at hand signals major changes in American life. For instance, in *Brown v. Board of Education* (1954) the Supreme Court ordered public school integration with "all deliberate speed." Racial integration was required, but the pace of change was left unfixed. In other situations, such as prison reform, the judiciary may require its mandated reforms to be implemented on a far more rapid basis.

A related advantage of litigation is that courts are far less restrained by budgets than the other branches of government. Where constitutional rights are at stake, the courts are not likely to be impressed by the cost of affording individuals the requisite protections. In their view, generally, lack of funds is no excuse for the violation of constititutional rights. But unlike legislatures, the courts will not directly face the wrath of the electorate should their decisions require the raising of taxes or the shifting of budgetary priorities from more popular programs to less popular ones. Consequently, they are freer to speak on behalf of the rights of disadvantaged and even despised groups, such as prisoners. Similarly, for the most part, the judiciary is now unimpressed by the claims of administrative economy, efficiency, and convenience where these infringe upon individuals' constitutional rights. But simply put, effective administrative performance is not generally the judiciary's chief concern or major problem. The net result of these characteristics of litigation is that antagonists of the administrative state often, perhaps generally, have a greater chance of success before the courts than before other branches of government. Yet the courts have not always been highly favorable to such litigation.

The Antagonist in Court: Traditional Approaches

Traditionally the courts were unsupportive of the claims of antagonists of the administrative state. Indeed, they strongly favored the interests of public agencies. For instance, as late as 1968, Martin Shapiro concluded that ". . . the federal court system . . . devoted the vast bulk of its energies to simply giving legal approval to agency decisions" (1968:264).

There were several mechanisms through which this pattern was established and maintained. First, as we have seen, the doctrine of privilege had a devastating impact upon the purported constitutional rights of citizens of the administrative state. Not having a right to the largess they claimed, they had few if any rights concerning its distribution or allotment. Second, the concept of standing to sue created a substantial barrier to individual suits against bureaucratic agencies. Third, even where a suit was entertained, the courts were likely to be highly deferential to the expertise of administrators and agencies. Indeed, they

generally limited the scope of their review to a consideration of whether the
proper procedures had been followed by the administrative decision makers.
Only infrequently did the courts ever evaluate the substance of those decisions.
Hence, judicial review of public administration tended to be very narrow. A
classic example of this tendency occurred in *Kletschka v. Driver* (1969) in which
the court found a number of reasons to avoid a review of the substance of a
decision by the Veterans Administration.

> It would not be feasible for the courts to review decisions by the V.A.
> awarding or refusing to award research grants. Each such decision . . .
> requires considerable expertise in the scientific, medical, and technical
> aspects of each application. A reviewing court would have to master
> considerable technical data before it could even attempt to determine
> whether one application . . . was so superior to the others that its rejec-
> tion by the V.A. was an abuse of discretion. Furthermore, even if these
> technical aspects were mastered it would be difficult for the court to
> review the judgments of relative personal competence which necessarily
> play a role in the agency determination . . . (443).

Eventually, however, as the judiciary began to develop a response to the rise
of the administrative state, this approach underwent drastic reversal. New rights
for antagonists were created and old ones were expanded. Importantly, the
development of these rights enabled the individuals to assert and protect their
rights as clients, employees, and captives of the administrative state and enabled
the judiciary to oversee the enforcement of these rights on a continuing basis.
The two areas of greatest importance in this regard are the expansion of public
administrators' liability for their actions and the easing of requirements of
standing to challenge the administrative state in court.

Public Administrators' Liability and Immunity

How can the judiciary force public administrators to place greater priority on
constitutional values and to behave in a fashion that protects the constitutional
rights of the citizenry at large? How can public administrators be weaned from
the all-encompassing values of administrative efficiency, economy, and convenience when these concerns lead to infringements upon individual rights and
liberties? These are central issues of the judicial response to the rise of the
administrative state. During the 1970s, the courts were, for the most part, able
to resolve them in a forceful and practicable manner by drastically expanding
the liability of public administrators for their unconstitutional and/or illegal
actions within the framework of their jobs. Paradoxically, however, the effort

to use litigation to make public administrators directly responsible for the exercise of their authority began a century earlier and had been largely frustrated by the judiciary until after its present response to the rise of the administrative state was well underway.

The concept of enabling private citizens to hold public officials accountable through litigation in the federal courts was placed in statutory form in the Civil Rights Act of 1871. Subsequently codified as 42 U.S. Code, section 1983, it provides in part that

> Every person who, under color of any statute, ordinance, regulation, custom, usage, of any State or Territory, subjects, or causes to be subjected, any citizen of the United States or any other person within the jurisdiction thereof to the deprivation of any rights, privileges, or immunities secured by the Constitution and laws, shall be liable to the party injured in an action at law, suit in equity, or other proper proceeding for redress.

Its purpose was straightforward—to protect the emancipated population in the South. But its ramifications have been substantially more far-reaching.

The post-Civil War period witnessed a fundamental change in the nature of American federalism. Prior to the adoption of the post-Civil War constitutional amendments and civil rights statutes, the federal government played a very limited role in protecting individuals from state governmental actions. For the most part, the Constitution limited the federal government's ability to act upon individuals, but left the states free from federally imposed constraints. Thus, the Bill of Rights was considered applicable to the federal government, but not the states, though the latter were generally limited by their own constitutions. Much of this condition was altered by the adoption of the Thirteenth, Fourteenth, and Fifteenth Amendments to the Constitution. The Thirteenth prohibited slavery ("involuntary servitude"). The Fourteenth accomplished a number of ends including requiring the states to provide equal protection of the laws and to forbid them from depriving any person of life, liberty, or property without due process of law. The Fifteenth provides that "the right of citizens of the United States to vote shall not be denied or abridged by the United States or by any State on account of race, color, or previous condition of servitude." Each of these amendments further provides that "Congress shall have the power to enforce" their provisions through "appropriate legislation." Hence, for the first time in the nation's constitutional history, the national government was authorized to regulate voting within the states and to assure that the states did not abridge the equality, or life, liberty, or property rights of individuals within their jurisdictions.

But how was the federal government actually to enforce these provisions effectively to protect individuals from state activities? Several possibilities existed. First, Reconstruction rested upon control of the states through the military authority of the federal government. Although such military occupation was a temporary process, another form of bureaucratic regulation might possibly have followed it. Today, for example, there are several federal bureaucratic agencies charged with regulating the treatment of individuals by state governments. In the post-Civil War years, however, such an approach was not favored. Civil service reform had not yet been instituted and federal administration was generally considered corrupt and inefficient. Another possibility was the protection of individual rights through the state courts. This approach was rejected on the grounds that state judges were unlikely to contest strenuously the activities of state governments. Third, perhaps the states' police power could be relied upon. But in the context of the times this appeared to be largely a contradiction in terms. Once these approaches were discarded, reliance upon the federal courts was almost inevitable. Federal judges were viewed as relatively neutral in contests between states and their citizens. Moreover, as agents of the federal government they seemed well suited to protect federally created rights. In addition, such an approach offered flexibility in terms of fashioning redress for aggrieved citizens and enabled the individual allegedly harmed to initiate the proceedings. Yet, almost immediately after its passage, the breadth and importance of the Civil Rights Act of 1871 was reduced by a number of federal court decisions.

Despite the intentions of Congress, federal judges were reluctant to alter the balance of federalism by strengthening the roles of the national government and of the federal court system as protectors of individual rights and liberties from state encroachment. The reasons for this general approach are uncertain, but the net result was to construe the terms of the Civil Rights Act of 1871 very narrowly—so narrowly, in fact, that until 1961 it was almost moribund.

One of the most devastating decisions in terms of the protection of individuals from the activities of state governments was issued in the *Slaughterhouse Cases* (1873). The Supreme Court rejected the contention of butchers in Louisiana that action by the state creating a monopoly in slaughtering, and depriving them of their livelihood, violated their Fourteenth Amendment rights under the privileges and immunities and due process clauses. In reviewing the impact of this decision, it has been observed that

Justice Miller limited the interests protected by the amendment to only those rights correlative to the existence of national government, effectively excluding almost all civil rights from its purview. Thus, the fourteenth amendment was interpreted to have no impact on the position of the states in safeguarding fundamental rights . . . (*Harvard Law Review*, 1977:1157–1158).

The debilitating effect of this decision on individual's rights vis-à-vis state governments was especially evident in the Court's listing of the privileges and immunities of national citizenship protected by the Fourteenth Amendment. Among these were the right to come to the seat of government for political or business activity with it; free access to national seaports, subtreasuries, land offices, and courts; protection by the national government in international waters or foreign jurisdictions; the right to assemble and petition the national government; the writ of habeas corpus; the use of navigable waters; rights derived from federal treaties; the right to due process and equal protection; and the rights secured by the Thirteenth and Fifteenth Amendments. In assessing the impact of the *Slaughterhouse Cases* it must be remembered that the concept of due process was extremely limited at the time.

The scope of the "rights, privileges, and immunities" clause in the Civil Rights Act of 1871 was drastically limited by this interpretation of the Fourteenth Amendment. A further diminution of its applicability occurred when the equal protection clause was read to allow the "separate but equal" treatment of blacks—with the emphasis on separate, not equal. Consequently, states could constitutionally and legally enact laws promoting racial segregation generally. The act was further weakened when its phrase, "under color of any statute, ordinance, regulation, custom, usage" came to be interpreted as "pursuant to" such regulations rather than "under the guise or pretense" of them. This limited the possibilities of recovering damages to situations where the letter of a state regulation was carried out, and in the process an individual's rights under the federal Constitution were violated.

The historical consequences of decisions along these lines has been summarized in the following fashion.

The effect of such narrow judicial construction of state action and "privileges and immunities" on section 1983 was devastating. Despite continuing infringements of the civil liberties of the freedmen and their descendants, virtually no actions were brought under the statute. By the turn of the century, federal protection of these rights had declined to the point that the Southern states were able to introduce Jim Crow laws, resembling the Black Codes, which imposed patently exclusionary "literacy" tests on blacks as a requirement of voting. The federal courts, notwithstanding the fact that it was a specific purpose of civil rights legislation to secure the vote for freedmen, were reluctant to intervene even in cases where state officials disenfranchised blacks with the obvious approval of the state government, and outrages grimly reminiscent of those perpetrated by the Klan were held to be beyond the scope of section 1983. Throughout the period between the end of Reconstruction and the Depression, the federal judiciary seemed disposed to allow a relatively wide latitude to state police power, and to place higher priority on the preservation of a tranquil federalism than on the safeguarding of individual civil rights (*Harvard Law Review*, 1977:1161).

Thus, rather than seizing the opportunity to increase its powers and role in the government, the federal judiciary refused to respond to the legislative intent of the Civil Rights Act of 1871. As a result, the act remained largely dormant until the 1970s, when it became a major vehicle for the imposition of judicial and constitutional values upon American public administration.

As debilitating as the initial judicial interpretation of section 1983 was, even greater limitations were placed upon the ability of an individual to recover damages from public officials, despite his or her statement of a valid and judicially cognizable claim. This brings us to the issue of public officials' immunity itself. Although the act reads that *"every person"* who acting under color of state authority abridges another's rights is liable to that person, the federal courts held that many public officials were often covered by a broad immunity from civil suits for damages. Such immunity has its origins in common law, but was more or less given constitutional stature in *Spalding v. Vilas* (1896) which did not involve a section 1983 suit but did provide a judicial rationale for public administrators' immunity. The case involved U.S. Postmaster General Vilas who had sent a communication to several postmasters who were seeking a salary increase and were represented by Spalding. It allegedly placed Spalding ". . . before the country as a common swindler," and brought ". . . him into public scandal, infamy, and disgrace . . . and injure[d] his business. . . ." The communication also made it clear that Spalding's clients were under no legal obligation to pay him. Consequently, Spalding sought damages in court. In its decision, the Supreme Court recognized the principle that

> In exercising the functions of his office, the head of an Executive Department, keeping within the limits of his authority, should not be under an apprehension that the motives that control this official conduct may, at any time, become the subject of inquiry in a civil suit for damages. It would seriously cripple the proper and effective administration of public affairs as entrusted to the executive branch of the government, if he were subjected to any such restraint (*Spalding v. Vilas*, 1896:498).

Consequently, federal department heads were provided with an absolute immunity from civil suits arising out of their actions connected with their official functions, regardless of the motives that may have controlled their behavior.

It would be difficult to imagine a condition more supportive of the growth of the administrative state than that articulated by the Court in the *Spalding* case. It severely limits public administrators' liability to the individuals upon whom they act. The *Spalding* decision does not strike a balance between the needs of public administrators for flexibility and authority to administer and those of the citizenry for protection against administrative infringement upon their constitutional and legal rights. Rather, it provided public administrators with a great deal of protection and the citizenry with almost none at all.

Although this approach could have been confined to department heads, as in *Spalding*, it was extended to other federal administrators in *Barr v. Matteo* (1959). There, a plurality of the Supreme Court provided further analysis of the immunity issue.

We are called upon in this case to weigh in a particular context two considerations which now and again come into sharp conflict—on the one hand, the protection of the individual citizen against pecuniary damage caused by oppressive or malicious action on the part of officials of the Federal Government; and on the other, the protection of the public interest by shielding responsible governmental officers against the harassment and inevitable hazards of vindictive or ill-founded damage suits brought on account of action taken in the exercise of their official responsibilities (1959:564-565).

Again, however, the interests of the administrative state were to prevail over those of the individual citizen.

It has been thought important that officials of the government should be free to exercise their duties unembarrassed by the fear of damage suits in respect of acts done in the course of those duties—suits which would consume time and energies which would otherwise be devoted to governmental service and the threat of which might appreciably inhibit the . . . administration of policies of government.

To be sure, the occasions upon which the acts of the head of an executive department will be protected by the privilege [of immunity] are doubtless far greater than in the case of an officer with less sweeping functions. But that is because the higher the post, the broader the range of responsibilities and duties, and the wider the scope of discretion, it entails. It is not the title of his office but the duties with which the particular officer sought to be made to respond in damages is entrusted—the relation of the act complained of to "matters commited by law to his control or supervision" . . . which must provide the guide in delineating the scope of the rule which clothes the official acts of the executive officer with immunity from civil defamation suits (1959:571, 573-574).

The plurality concluded that the public official in question, the acting director of the Federal Office of Rent Stabilization, was entitled to an absolute immunity for actions within the line of duty.

There were concurring and dissenting opinions in the *Barr* case that suggested the Court was not solidly committed to the extension of immunity to public administrators generally. Moreover, the *Spalding* and *Barr* cases involved federal administrators who are not covered by section 1983, which applies only to those acting under color of *state* law, i.e., state and local employees. Yet, the Supreme Court had held that state legislators were immune from section 1983 actions in *Tenney v. Brandhove* (1951). Their rationale there was somewhat different, relying on the firmly established common law tradition of legislative immunity and reasoning that if, in 1871, Congress had intended the words "every person" to apply to state legislators, they would have explicitly so stated. Subsequent to the *Barr* decision, an immunity from section 1983 suits for judicial officials was recognized by the Court in *Pierson v. Ray* (1967) and for prosecutors in *Imbler v. Pachtman* (1976). Importantly, "Building on these decisions, some lower courts . . . extended absolute immunities to justices of the peace, municipal referees, parole board members, and judicial clerks, as well as to those acting pursuant to presumptively valid court orders" (*Harvard Law Review*, 1977: 1199). Federal administrators exercising judicial functions were given an equivalent immunity from civil suits for damages in *Butz v. Economou* (1978).

In summarizing this aspect of the traditional judicial approach to the claims of the antagonist of the administrative state in court, two observations can be made. First, as was true in other contexts as well, the federal courts were reluctant to assert their power to regulate the administrative activities of government. The Civil Rights Act of 1871 provided them with an excellent vehicle for protecting individual rights against encroachments at the hands of state administrators, but the federal judiciary chose to narrow its own authority under this statute almost to the point of nonexistence. Indeed, section 1983 met with modest success only in voting rights cases. The federal courts were simply not ready to alter the nature of federalism as it then existed or to interfere with the administrative activities of the states as they affected individuals' fundamental rights. Second, the federal judiciary developed or accepted a rationale for providing public administrators with an absolute immunity from civil suits for damages. This position clearly established the superiority of the administrative process over the protection of individual rights. Together, these approaches amounted to judicial support for the development of an administrative state, relatively unregulated by the judiciary and relatively oblivious to constitutional values. But this judicial approach had its origins in a prebureaucratic period. It was only after the development of the administrative state and the formulation of a general judicial response to it that the citizen-antagonist was afforded greater legal rights and protections.

The year 1971 marked the beginning of a fundamental change in judicial doctrines concerning the nature of public administrators' official immunity and liability. In that year, the Supreme Court was presented with an occasion for reassessing the *Spalding* and *Barr* precedents in the case of *Bivens v. Six Unknown Named Federal Narcotics Agents*. Bivens was seeking $15,000 from each of the agents for humiliation, embarrassment, and mental suffering caused when they broke into his apartment, handcuffed him in the presence of his family, threatened the entire family with arrest, searched the apartment, used excessive force, and subjected Bivens to a "visual strip search" after taking him to a federal court house. The use of these heavy-handed methods by the agents of the administrative state was accomplished in the absence of a warrant or probable cause.

Although the case was well framed to evoke a judicial response intended to restrain the administrative state, in principle the issues were similar to those considered earlier in the *Spalding* case. Bivens suffered an invasion of privacy and physical harm, but both he and Spalding were humiliated and Spalding suffered financial damage in addition. Traditionally, under the *Spalding* approach, Bivens' standard recourse would have been to bring an action in tort in the state court, under prevailing state law, rather than to seek assignment of damages for the violation of his constitutional rights in the federal forum. Indeed, since section 1983 does not cover officials acting under color of federal law, there was no established federal legal mechanism through which Bivens could presume to recover the damages he sought. Moreover, even if the suit were entertained by the federal courts, the agents presumably would be covered by an immunity. In short, from a traditional perspective, it would appear that an antagonist of the administrative state such as Bivens had little recourse before the federal courts.

However, traditional legal logic did not prevail. In the interim between the *Barr* decision in 1959 and the *Bivens* suit, the federal judiciary's attitude toward the administrative state had undergone substantial change. The courts had become cognizant of the extent to which the rise of the administrative state had undermined the traditional constitutional rights and liberties associated with citizenship. Consequently, they were far less willing to grant great deference to the claims of administrative expertise, efficiency, economy, and convenience. In fact, they devoted much of their energies during that time period to strengthening the rights of clients, public employees, and captives. Clearly, restraining the administrative state and harmonizing its operations with the needs of constitutional democracy had weighed heavily on the courts.

This was wholly evident in the Supreme Court's treatment of *Bivens*. The Court, per Justice Brennan, directly addressed the imbalance between the status of citizens and that of agents of the administrative state.

Respondents [the agents] seek to treat the relationship between a citizen and a federal agent unconstitutionally exercising his authority as no different from the relationship between two private citizens. In doing so, they ignore the fact that power, once granted, does not disappear like a magic gift when it is wrongfully used. An agent acting—albeit unconstitutionally—in the name of the United States possesses a far greater capacity for harm than an individual trespasser exercising no authority other than his own (*Bivens v. Six Unknown Named Federal Narcotics Agents*, 1971: 391-392).

In order to redress this imbalance and thereby enable the citizen to attempt to protect himself on an equal footing with the agents of the administrative state, the Court went on to hold that Bivens's only realistic remedy was the kind of suit he brought. Thus, the Court created a *constitutional* right to sue federal administrative officials for monetary damages in connections with alleged violations of Fourth Amendment rights. This right was a direct response to the overarching power of the administrative state and it has since been extended to cases involving breaches of the Fifth and Eighth Amendments (*Davis v. Passman*, 1979; *Carlson v. Green*, 1980).

The creation of this new right for antagonists of the administrative state indirectly had very significant ramifications for section 1983 litigation and for the liability of public administrators. First, it suggested the Supreme Court's interest in resurrecting section 1983 and reinterpreting it so as to turn it into a forceful check on public administrators. The creation of a constitutional right, similar to section 1983, to sue federal administrators for violation of individual constitutional rights would seem peculiar unless accompanied by a willingness to enable section 1983 to serve an equivalent purpose in constraining state administrative officials. Unlike a century earlier, in 1971 the main issue in the Court's mind in such cases was not federalism, but rather the erosion of individual rights and liberties at the hands of the administrative state.

The *Bivens* decision also signaled a fundamental shift in the Supreme Court's outlook on the immunity/liability of public administrators. It would seem almost entirely pointless to fashion the new right of antagonists to sue such officials for monetary damages, if the officials nevertheless remained free to assert an absolute immunity from the assessment of personal damages by the courts. Thus, it appeared inevitable that new standards of official immunity and liability would be developed. In retrospect, the Supreme Court established them both soundly and rapidly.

In *Bivens*, the Supreme Court did not examine the issue of whether the narcotics agents possessed immunity under the logic of the *Spalding-Barr* approach. Instead, it remanded the case to the court of appeals for a consideration of this question. Subsequently, that court held that the agents lacked an absolute immunity ". . . because we do not agree that the Agents were alleged to be engaged in the performance of the sort of 'discretionary' acts that require the protection of immunity" and "it would be a sorry state of affairs if an officer had the 'discretion' to enter a dwelling at 6:30 A.M., without a warrant or probable cause, and make an arrest by employing unreasonable force" (*Bivens v. Six Unknown Named Federal Narcotics Agents*, 1972:1343,1346). However, so entrenched was the notion of immunity that the appeals court left the door open for the agents to develop a good-faith defense based on the reasonability of the officials' actions at the time that they occurred.

The Supreme Court returned to the immunity/liability issue in *Scheuer v. Rhodes* (1974). The case grew out of a decade of confrontation between citizens and the government over such fundamental concerns as civil rights and the war in Southeast Asia. During this period, governmental administrators and even high officials in the White House had engaged in illegal activities abridging the constitutional rights of private citizens. Allegedly, some of these activities were carried out by administrative agencies such as the FBI, CIA, and IRS. Consequently, as the Watergate scandal unfolded and these events became known, the issue of individual constitutional rights in the administrative state was very much before the courts and the society generally. It was abundantly clear, as perhaps never before, that within the administrative state lay a tremendous potential for the abuse of individual rights.

Perhaps no legal case could have captured this more than *Scheuer v. Rhodes*. During demonstrations at Kent State University against the U.S. invasion of Cambodia in 1970, the Ohio National Guard opened fire on a group of students and fatally shot three of them. Representatives of the estates of the students were seeking monetary damages from the governor of Ohio (Rhodes) and other officials. They alleged that the officials had "acted either outside the scope of their respective office or, if within the scope, acted in an arbitrary manner, grossly abusing the lawful powers of office" (*Scheuer v. Rhodes*, 1974:235). Certainly, the quelling of such a demonstration through the use of military force was an extreme step that seemed to display the arrogance of government and a blatant disregard for the lives of its citizens. One of the objectives of radical antiwar groups had been achieved: the war had been brought home.

Yet, the next major battle in the Kent State case was fought in the courts. The primary legal vehicle for the *Scheuer* suit was section 1983. Thus, when the case reached the Supreme Court, the issue of immunity/liability was certain to figure heavily in its disposition. If the Court clung to traditional doctrines of immunity, the recovery of damages, even in such extreme circumstances as those that occurred at Kent State, would be precluded. Consequently, even the gravest abuses by political and administrative officials might go unchecked. On the other hand, for the reasons set forth in *Spalding* and *Barr*, public officials' immunity from such suits could not be simply swept away. It appeared, therefore, that a new balance would have to be struck in an effort to protect individuals against administrative infringements of their rights on the one hand, and to enable the administrative state to remain unfettered and unharassed by ill-founded suits for damages on the other.

In addressing the immunity/liability question, a unanimous Supreme Court discarded the notion of absolute immunity in favor of a new standard.

> . . . [I]n varying scope, a qualified immunity is available to officers of the executive branch of government, the variation being dependent upon the scope of discretion and responsibilities of the office and all the circumstances as they reasonably appeared at the time of the action on which liability is sought to be based. It is the existence of reasonable grounds for the belief formed at the time and in light of all the circumstances, coupled with good-faith belief, that affords a basis for qualified immunity of executive officers for acts performed in the course of official conduct (*Scheuer v. Rhodes*, 1974:247-248).

Thus, the immunity of executive branch officials was qualified and depended ultimately upon a judicial (or jury) determination of the reasonability of their actions at the time they were taken and upon the officials' intent. Where the actions were unreasonable or where the officials acted with malicious intent to violate individuals' rights, damages could be assessed. Having developed this new standard, the Court remanded the case to the court of appeals for a further exploration of the liability of the officials in this particular set of circumstances. Eventually, however, the case was settled out of court.

Before addressing the next major case dealing with the immunity/liability of public officials, a few observations are in order. It is crucial to bear in mind that the liability under discussion is *personal* liability. The issue is whether public officials can be held personally liable for monetary damages, the payment of which would be their private responsibility. Although some form of insurance or governmental indemnification might be relied upon to cover their liabilities, the damages are not sought from public agencies or the government per se. Consequently, such suits become a means of regulating the behavior of public administrators as individuals. The ability of antagonists to bring such litigation successfully gives the administrative officials a strong and direct personal incentive not to violate the rights of clients, public employees, captives, or other citizens. *Scheuer v. Rhodes* put such officials on notice that such violations might be at their own personal peril. However, in a somewhat contrary vein, the assigning of personal damages would not necessarily work to the antagonist's personal advantage. This is because it is impossible to recover more in damages than an official can pay. Suits for huge amounts of money against individual officials are likely to fall far short of their mark. Given these two circumstances, it is apparent that a major virtue of the erosion of public administrators' official immunity is to enable the judiciary to regulate the activities of the administrative state and to deter abuses of individual rights by its agents. Thus, under the *Scheuer* approach the courts placed themselves in the position of ultimately determining whether administrative action infringing upon constitutional rights was reasonable. In the future, public administrators would have to ask themselves, "Can I demonstrate to a court that what I am doing or ordering is reasonable under the prevailing circumstances?" The question itself would have a deterrent effect, but within a year, the Supreme Court developed an even more elaborate standard.

In contrast to *Scheuer v. Rhodes, Wood v. Strickland* (1975) grew out of a moment of frivolousness. It arose from a high school prank in which three tenth-grade public school students in Mena, Arkansas spiked the punch at a school gathering. Although, as Justice White put it, "the punch was served at the meeting without apparent effect" (*Wood v. Strickland*, 1975:311), the students were subsequently expelled for their misdeed. They turned to the federal courts for damages, injunctive, and declaratory relief on the grounds that their expulsions, in the absence of a full-fledged hearing, violated their constitutional right to due process of law. The suit was brought under section 1983.

Before examining the Supreme Court's treatment of the immunity issue, it is worth emphasizing the extent to which the *Wood* case demonstrates the agenda-setting role of the courts and litigation. Out of a rather unimaginative high school prank—perhaps repeated hundreds of times each year in various school districts around the nation—emerged a new standard of official immunity that effectively forces the administrative state to adhere to constitutional and judicial values. No constitutional amendment was necessary, no mobilization of the electorate required, no lobbyists hired; rather, antagonists of the administrative state, feeling victimized by its heavy-handed reprisals, filed suit and won a victory of very major constitutional proportions. The advantages of litigation for the antagonists are not always so dramatically displayed, but they are always potentially present.

In addressing the immunity issue in *Wood*, the Supreme Court, per Justice White, reasoned that both an objective and a subjective standard must be applied in such circumstances. The standards arrived at were two-pronged.

[1.] The official himself must be acting sincerely and with a belief that he is doing right, but an act violating a student's constitutional rights can be no more justified by ignorance or disregard of settled, indisputable law on the part of one entrusted with supervision of students' daily lives than by the presence of actual malice.

[2.] ... [A] school board member is not immune from liability for damages . . . *if he knew or reasonably should have known* that the action he took within his sphere of official responsibility would violate the constitutional rights of the student affected, or if he took the action with the malicious intention to cause a deprivation of constitutional rights or other injury to the student (*Wood v. Strickland*, 1975:321–322, emphasis added).

Thus, good faith and the reasonability of the actions at the time they were taken were no longer sufficient to convey immunity to public officials. In addition, in order to be immune, they had to have reasonable knowledge of the constitutional rights of the persons upon whom they were acting and could not knowingly violate these rights.*

The ramifications of the *Wood* standard for public adminsitration would be difficult to overstate. It forces public administrators to be cognizant of constitutional law as it affects their interaction with the public. In order to protect their immunity, they must protect the constitutional rights of clients, public employees, captives, and others affected by their official conduct. Thus, knowledge of constitutional law becomes a positive job requirement for many public administrators. The study of law, therefore, must return to the study of American public administration. Indeed, whereas mistakes in budgeting or accounting may cost a public administrator a job, ignorance about the constitutional rights of the citizenry may cost the administrator dearly in terms of his or her personal property. But the issue goes much deeper than this.

Wood v. Strickland requires public administrators to be knowledgeable about constitutional law. But what is constitutional law? As Justice Powell once remarked, "Constitutional law is what the courts say it is" (*Owen v. City of Independence*, 1980:669). Therefore, public administrators are now required to adhere to judicial values as they are incorporated into the general body of constitutional law. Effectively, this means that traditional administrative values, such as efficiency and economy, can no longer provide the primary direction to administrative action where constitutional rights are at stake. Rather, it is the values of the judiciary and those traditionally embodied in the Constitution that must now guide administrative action. This immediately destroys the legitimacy of many administrative rationales for practices that abridge constitutional rights. Efficiency is not recognized by the courts as legitimate grounds for the deprivation of fundamental rights.

---

*In *Harlow v. Fitzgerald* (1982), the Supreme Court eliminated the issue of intent, thereby obviating the need for jury trial in many instances. Public administrators remained liable if their conduct violated ". . . clearly established statutory or constitutional rights of which a reasonable person would have known." (4820)

Thus, the *Wood* standard goes a long way toward accomplishing two ends inherent in the judicial response to the rise of the administrative state. First, it promotes the harmonizing of constitutional democracy with public administration. Constitutional values must be incorporated into administrative values. An administrator can ignore them only at great personal peril. Second, the *Wood* approach enables the judiciary to play a much wider role in determining the character of the American administrative state. A way has been found to force administrative officials to be observant of judicial values, as expressed in constitutional law. The federal judiciary thereby takes a place alongside the president and Congress in directing the behavior of public bureaucrats. Thus, the new standard of official liability serves as a capstone to the judicial response to the rise of the administrative state. It enables the judiciary to see effectively that its decisions pertaining to the rights of clients, public employees, and captives are enforced, and at the same time it strongly promotes judicial power in a bureaucratized government.

There is another ramification as well. Although this changing standard has promoted increased litigation under section 1983, it nevertheless has an inherent deterrent effect which acts as a general restraint on the administrative state. Not only must public administrators adhere to the law or risk the assignment of personal damages, where the law is uncertain, or where they are uncertain, bureaucrats are encouraged to take the line of action most protective of individual rights. This has been wholly intentional on the part of the Supreme Court. In *Carlson v. Green* (1980), which extended the *Bivens* principle to Eighth Amendment cases, the Court observed, ". . . the Bivens remedy, in addition to compensating victims, serves a deterrent purpose" (21). In *Owen v. City of Independence* (1980), a case which will be discussed shortly, the court reasoned that "The knowledge that a municipality will be liable for all of its injurious conduct, whether committed in good faith or not, should create an incentive for officials who may harbor doubts about the lawfulness of their intended actions to err on the side of protecting citizens' constitutional rights" (652). Consequently, the judiciary has found a way to work its will generally, without having to address each and every instance of breach of constitutioal rights by administrative action. The incentive for public administrators to avoid unconstitutional action is simply too great for them to purposely provoke antagonists to bring suits or to ignore the judiciary's decisions.

It is evident, therefore, that the *Wood* standard is well designed to protect the citizenry against unconstitutional administrative action. But does it afford sufficient protection to public administrators against ill-founded suits and against the possibility of having damages assessed in areas where the constitutional law is unclear? In theory, the standard is rigorous enough to deter ill-founded or harassing suits. Certainly, a public administrator is not liable if not responsible for a breach of an individual's constitutional or legal rights. And even if responsible, a defense is available, especially where the law is unclear as to the rights of the client, public employee, captive, or other person acted upon.* In practice, however, the *reasonably should have known* standard may raise some serious problems. Four justices dissented in *Wood* on the ground that it was unreasonable for the courts to sit in judgment of what school board members "reasonably should have known." Although the majority specifically pointed out that under the standard created in *Wood*, school board members are not "charged with predicting the future course of constitutional law" (*Wood v. Strickland*, 1975:322), the law is, in fact, often unsettled. Moreover, the intent of *Wood* is not to bind public administrators only when a very similar or identical case concerning the kinds of action under consideration has already been decided. Rather, the intent is for public administrators to know the law even before it has been specifically crystallized in a judicial decision. Thus, in the *Wood* case itself, the application of due process to expulsions from public schools was treated by the majority as settled law even though no single Supreme Court decision specifically on the matter was extant when the expulsions took place. Consequently, public administrators may not have to predict the future course of constitutional law, but they cannot simply wait for the courts to tell them what the law is. They must follow the case law and understand the judiciary's logic and values in an effort to determine what they can achieve through constitutional means. In a sense this is inevitable because, as Philip Kurland has remarked, ". . . the Constitution is largely a document of the imagination, but always treated as if it were real" (Kurland, 1976:7). This being the case, the courts rarely admit to creating constitutional law, but rather claim only to interpret it.

The *Wood* case created the standard that now generally governs public administrators' immunity in civil suits for damages. Although it could have been confined to school board members, it was subsequently applied by the Supreme Court to the superintendent of a state hospital and to prison administrators (*O'Connor v. Donaldson*, 1975; *Procunier v. Navarette*, 1978). Moreover, in *Butz v. Economou* (1978). the Supreme Court indicated that it would also apply to federal administrators generally, though, as noted earlier, the Court granted an absolute immunity from Bivens-style suits to federal administrators exercising judicial functions.

Although it established the current standard of public administrators' liability for their unconstitutional actions, the *Wood* case was not the last word in this area. The rights of antagonists to sue the administrative state were enhanced substantially by two related developments. First, the Supreme Court extended

*In *Youngberg v. Romeo* (1982), the Supreme Court held that a mental health professional would not be personally liable for unconstitutional or illegal treatment caused by budgetary constraints.

liability under section 1983 to municipal corporations (cities). In *Monell v. New York City Department of Social Services* (1978), the Court overruled an earlier decision, *Monroe v. Pape* (1961), by holding that cities were *persons* within the meaning of section 1983. Thus, where the policies of a city were the cause of a violation of an individual's constitutional rights, the individual could sue the city for damages. Importantly, such suits raised the prospects for recovering large sums in damages since a city would presumably have greater resources than an individual public administrator. Much of the Court's discussion in *Monell* centered on the intent of Congress in drafting the Civil Rights Act of 1871. Although its analysis was somewhat inconclusive, its desire to bolster the rights of antagonists of the administrative state was wholly clear. Indeed, in a related case, *Owen v. City of Independence* (1980), the Court removed the possibility of a city raising a qualified good-faith immunity as a defense and held specifically that ". . . a municipality will be liable for all of its injurious conduct, whether committed in good faith or not" (651).

In another expansion of the rights of antagonists, the Supreme Court clearly held for the first time that section 1983 allowed individuals to sue state administrators for breach of their rights under federal law, rather than for violation of constitutional rights alone. Thus, *Maine v. Thiboutot* (1980) considered the meaning of the words "and laws" in the Civil Rights Act of 1871 and concluded that "Given that Congress attached no modifiers to the phrase" (4), it should be read neither as a dead letter nor a provision limited to civil rights laws. Rather, it extended to the state administration of federal laws generally, specifically including violations of the Social Security Act, which was the subject of the litigation at hand. Included in the category of federal laws which might give rise to a section 1983 suit against state administrators were: the Food Stamp Act, Comprehensive Employment and Training Act, Juvenile Justice and Delinquency Prevention Act, Urban Mass Transportation Act, United States Housing Act, National School Lunch Act, and a number of statutes dealing with joint federal-state regulatory endeavors and resource management activities. Therefore, the case represented an important victory for antagonists of the administrative state. They were now able to secure forcefully their legal as well as their constitutional rights. Moreover, securing these rights was facilitated by the Court's holding that attorney's fees may be awarded to the prevailing party in such suits. If victorious, the antagonist's attorney's fees might now be paid by the losing side—a development which certainly reduces an important barrier to litigation.

Antagonists and Public Law Litigation

The application of section 1983 is not confined to individual civil suits for damages. Its language has been considered broad enough to support suits seeking injunctive relief from widespread institutional or systemic violations of constitutional rights. In fact, although the framers of the Civil Rights Act of 1871 could not have foreseen the implication of their choice of words, section 1983 has become closely associated with the particular type of suit generally referred to as *public law litigation* as discussed in Chapter 3 (Chayes, 1976). The use of the statute in this fashion has been an integral part of the judicial response to the rise of the administrative state and has enabled the federal judiciary to play a very comprehensive and forceful role in overseeing public administration.

The public law litigation model not only changes the nature of litigation itself, it also alters the relationship of the judiciary to public bureaucracy. This change has been elaborated upon by Roger Cramton (1976:552), who asks us to "consider in the context of the Leviathan [bureaucratic] State two models of judicial review of administrative action." One is "the traditional model . . . of a restrained and sober second look at what government has done that adversely affects a citizen. The controversy is bipolar in character, with two parties opposing each other; the issues are narrow and well-defined; and the relief is limited and obvious" (1976:552). Judicial review in this model is essential as a corrective to the "tunnel vision in which particular values are advanced and others are ignored" (1976:552) by administrative agencies. But, Cramton believes that this model has been deemed insufficient and too limiting a basis for judicial activity in the administrative state. Thus, he suggests there is a prevailing attitude, expressed by one federal judge, that "if there is a serious problem, and the legislature and executive don't respond, the courts have to act" (1976:554). This approach leads to

. . . a second model of judicial review that is growing in acceptance and authority. This model of the judicial role has characteristics more of general problem-solving than of dispute resolution. . . . [There is] a modern tendency to view courts as modern handymen—as jacks of all trades available to furnish the answer to whatever may trouble us. "What is life? When does death begin? How should we operate prisons and hospitals? Shall we build nuclear power plants, and if so, where? Shall the Concorde fly to our shores?" (1976:552).

It is increasingly this second model that affords antagonists of the administrative state opportunities to challenge public bureaucracies in court.

The public law litigation format is available under section 1983 to clients, public employees, and captives in the contemporary administrative state. Examples of its use in cases involving patients in public mental facilities and inmates in prisons have already been considered. But what is of particular interest about this vehicle for antagonists is that it offers a process that cuts across all areas of constitutional rights and is not specific to one role or another. Thus, public law litigation under section 1983 has been used to challenge hospital and prison systems for breaches of substantive constitutional rights, but it has also been used to challenge the denial of equal protection in public school systems and other areas. In this fashion, it has offered the judiciary a very wide opportunity to engage in the reform of public institutions and essentially to take over their administration, if need be.

The Boston public school desegregation case discussed in Chapter 3 provides an excellent example of a section 1983 suit in the public law litigation model. The nature of busing, the racial composition of individual schools, the number of schools, and several other matters, once considered primarily administrative questions, became issues for judicial resolution. When the Court's plan was met with violence, an entire school was placed under the Court's continuing and direct supervision. Although the extent of judicial intervention in public administration was highly pronounced in that case, it was not unique in terms of section 1983 suits. Similar judicial involvement has occurred in prison administration (see *Rhem v. Malcom*, 1974) and elsewhere, as has already been noted. It is evident, therefore, that such suits are a crucial aspect of the judicial response to the rise of the administrative state. They effectively accomplish two important purposes without which the judicial response would not be complete. First, they provide antagonists with a vehicle for opposing administrative *systems*, as opposed to simply bureaucratic agencies or public administrators as individuals. The operation of state or citywide schools, prisons, and hospitals can be successfully challenged in this fashion. Consequently, the antagonist is not limited to receiving compensation for past breaches of his or her constitutional or legal rights; general systemic reform can be obtained through such suits. This provides the citizen-antagonist with new and potentially very strong leverage against the administrative state. A return to prebureaucratic, constitutional democratic government has not been accomplished, but now the citizenry has another and potentially highly effective channel for protecting their fundamental rights within the administrative state.

Second, such litigation enables the judiciary to intervene directly in public administration. In the context of class action section 1983 suits for injunctive relief, the judiciary is able to move beyond the imposition of constitutional values upon public administrators; it is able to take over the tasks of administration itself. This enables judges to take control of positions of power in the administrative state and use them as they believe is constitutionally required. While this does not place the entire bureaucratic apparatus for a given function under the actual control of a judge, it does place the judge in the position of a political executive vested with extraordinary authority.

What is especially peculiar about judicial activism of the nature under discussion is that judges can operate with more authority and fewer constraints than other administrative actors. For example, if need be, judges can rely on the power to hold public officials and others in contempt of court for their obstruction of judicial decrees and orders. Moreover, unlike administrators generally, judges often possess great leverage over budgetary allocations. They may be able to confront the legislature with an all or nothing proposition such as, "either appropriate sufficient funds to operate a prison or hospital constitutionally, or close these facilities altogether." The use of receiverships* and other devices further enhances the administrative power of judges in contests with state legislatures. In addition, since it is judges who determine what the constitutional law is, sometimes they elude its very constraints. For instance, as noted in Chapter 3, it was alleged in the Boston school case that the court-imposed plan would create white flight from the public schools, thereby inevitably militating against desegregation. Both the district court and the court of appeals gave short shrift to this challenge, though there is little doubt that if a plan formulated and implemented by nonjudicial officials had the same impact, it would have been adjudged constitutionally inadequate. As a result of these conditions, judges have the potential of responding to the rise of the administrative state by becoming superadministrators with unusual authority. Thus, the public law litigation model not only enables an antagonist to bring a suit, but allows the judiciary to respond by taking direct control over public administrative systems. A more dramatic assertion of judicial power in a bureaucratized government would be difficult to imagine.

Standing

The citizen-antagonist's ability to bring law suits against the administrative state is not confined to section 1983 or *Bivens*-style actions. Rather, as part of the general judicial response to the rise of the administrative state, the federal courts have also made it easier for one who is injured by an administrative decision or policy to challenge it through litigation. This has been accomplished by reducing the barriers to standing to sue, that is, the ability to demonstrate a judicially cognizable individual or group injury stemming from governmental action.

Justice Douglas once admonished that "generalizations about standing to sue are largley worthless as such" (*Association of Data Processing Service Organizations v. Camp*, 1970:151). Nevertheless, although the process has been uneven, a liberalizing trend does seem to have taken place. For instance, in *Flast v. Cohen* (1968), the Supreme Court substantially modified a 45-year-old rule that

---

*A receivership enables a court to appoint an individual to act as caretaker of a litigant's property. See *Black's Law Dictionary* (St. Paul, Minn.: West Publishers, 1979), p. 1140.

simply paying federal taxes did not establish sufficient injury to bring suit against a federal agency. Taxpayer suits were not authorized per se, but rather would be entertained when governmental action violated specific constitutional restriction on the expenditure of funds, such as for the purpose of establishing a religion. In *U.S. v. Students Challenging Regulatory Agency Procedures* (1973), the Court found standing on the most minimal of potential injuries—the possibility that an ICC regulation would adversely affect the recycling of beverage containers and thereby increase the pollution of public parks in the Washington, D.C. area, which in turn, would diminish the ability of a few law students to enjoy these facilities. In summarizing these developments, Kenneth Culp Davis writes:

> Beginning in 1968 the Supreme Court has given the federal law of standing a new basic orientation. Many now have standing who were denied it before 1968. . . .
>   The present law of standing differs no more than slightly, if it differs at all, from the simple proposition that one who is hurt by governmental action has standing to challenge it (Davis, 1975:72).

Therefore, in this context too, the courts have enhanced the prospects of challenging the administrative state. By providing a forum for so doing, they have also expanded their role and authority in regulating the activity of public administrators.

Conclusion

The judicial response to the status of the antagonist of the administrative state has far-reaching consequences for public administration. First and foremost, the judicary has developed a mechanism which virtually assures that public administrators will be cognizant of judicial values. The nature of public administrators' liability is such that in order to perform their functions in a fashion deemed acceptable by the judiciary, they must adhere to constitutional values and give them preeminence over administrative values generally. This approach enables the judiciary fundamentally to condition the operation of the administrative state and to force it to operate more compatibly with the concepts of constitutional democracy. Inevitably, such an approach must lead to a reformulation of administrative theory and values, a matter that is discussed in the following chapter.

A second consequence of the expansion of the rights of antagonists has been to enable the judiciary to play a more active role generally in the administrative state. The courts are no longer confined to reviewing the activities of administrative agencies in a narrow fashion, nor are they limited to the creation of new rights for citizens who interact with public agencies. Rather, as a result of their development of the public law litigation model, the courts are now able to intervene directly in public administration to the extent of taking over the control of entire public administrative systems in an effort to bring them up to constitutional standards. Thus, the fates of the antagonist and the judiciary are inherently linked. Again, however, this approach will have widespread ramifications for the practice of public administration. It requires the development of a new relationship between judges and administrators and between bench and bureau generally. It is to these issues that the conclusion of this study speaks.

References

Arnold R. Douglas, 1979. *Congress and the Bureaucracy*. New Haven, Conn.: Yale University Press.

Association of Data Processing Service Organizations v. Camp, 1970. 397 U.S. 150.

Barr v. Matteo, 1959. 360 U.S. 564.

Bivens v. Six Unknown Named Federal Narcotics Agents, 1971. 403 U.S. 388.

Bivens v. Six Unknown Named Federal Narcotics Agents, 1972. 456 F2d 1339.

Brown v. Board of Education, 1954. 347 U.S. 483.

Butz v. Economou, 1978. 438 U.S. 504.

Carlson v. Green, 1980. 446 U.S. 14.

Chayes, Abram, 1976. The role of the judge in public law litigation. *Harvard Law Review* 89: 1281-1316.

Cramton, Roger, 1976. Judicial lawmaking and administration in the leviathan state. *Public Administration Review* 36: 551-555.

Davis, Kenneth C., 1975. *Administrative Law and Government*. St. Paul, Minn.: West Publishing.

Davis v. Passman, 1979. 442 U.S. 228.

Fiorina, Morris, 1977. *Congress: Keystone of the Washington Establishment*. New Haven, Conn.: Yale University Press.

Flast v. Cohen, 1968. 392 U.S. 83.

Harlow v. Fitzgerald, 1982. 50 Law Week 4815.

Harvard Law Review, 1977. Section 1983 and federalism. Vol. 90: 1133-1361.

Hummel, Ralph, 1977. *The Bureaucratic Experience*. New York: St. Martin's.

Imbler v. Patchman, 1976. 424 U.S. 409.

Kletschka v. Driver, 1969. 411 F2d 436.

Kurland, Philip, 1976. Some reflections on privacy and the Constitution. *The University of Chicago Magazine*, Vol. 69:7-13, 34-36.

Lowi, Theodore J., 1969. *The End of Liberalism*. New York: W. W. Norton.

McConnell, Grant, 1966. *Private Power and American Democracy*. New York: Knopf.

Maine v. Thiboutot, 1980. 448 U.S. 1.

Monell v. New York City Department of Social Services, 1978. 436 U.S. 658.

Monroe v. Pape, 1961. 365 U.S. 167.

Moynihan, Daniel P., 1970. *Maximum Feasible Misunderstanding*. New York: Free Press.

Nachmias, David and David H. Rosenbloom, 1978. *Bureaucratic Culture: Citizens and Administrators in Israel*. New York: St. Martin's.

O'Connor v. Donaldson, 1975. 422 U.S. 563.

Owen v. City of Independence, 1980. 445 U.S. 622.

Pierson v. Ray, 1967. 386 U.S. 547.

Procunier v. Navarette, 1978. 434 U.S. 555.

Rhem v. Malcolm, 1974. 371 F. Supp. 594.

Rosenbloom, David H., 1977. *Federal Equal Employment Opportunity*. New York: Praeger.

Scheuer v. Rhodes, 1974. 416 U.S. 232.

Shapiro, Martin, 1968. *The Supreme Court and Administrative Agencies*. New York: Free Press.

Slaughter House Cases, 1873. 83 U.S. 36.

Spalding v. Vilas, 1896. 161 U.S. 483.

Tenney v. Brandhove, 1951. 341 U.S. 367.

U.S. Congress, 1973. Senate Committee on Government Operations; Sub-Committee on Intergovernmental Relations. *Confidence and Concern: Citizens View American Government*. 93d Cong., 1st Sess., December 3.

U.S. v. Students Challenging Regulatory Agency Procedures, 1973. 412 U.S. 669.

Wood v. Strickland, 1975. 420 U.S. 308.

Wyatt v. Stickney, 1971. 325 F. Supp. 781; 334 F. Supp. 1341.

Youngberg v. Romeo, 1982. 50 Law Week 4681.

7
Conclusion: Public Administration and Public Law

The legal developments of the last three decades concerning the rights of clients, employees, captives, and antagonists of the contemporary American administrative state will have major ramifications on public administration and political life in the United States. These developments constitute nothing less than a fundamental and revolutionary change in constitutional law. A new relationship between the citizen and the bureaucratized government has been forged, as has a new relationship between the judiciary and public administrators. The importance of these new relationships is indisputable. The Bill of Rights now protects the citizenry in its interaction with public bureaucrats and public agencies. Judicial and constitutional values have become a major facet of public administration for the first time in the nation's history. Indeed, at no other time has the study of constitutional law been so necessary a part of the training of public administrators. However, recognizing the magnitude of constitutional change is relatively easy in comparison with predicting its consequences for administration and government in the future. Nevertheless, this task must be undertaken in order to integrate the discussion of individuals' civil rights and liberties in the administratve state and to appreciate the coherence of the judicial response to the rise of bureaucratic government.

Bench and Bureau in the Administrative State

At first thought the notion of a coherent judicial response to the rise of the administrative state appears improbable. The federal judiciary is highly fragmented among different courts, circuits, and hierarchical levels. Judges are highly autonomous from other elements of the political system and somewhat independent of one another. True, the Supreme Court has substantial capabilities to coordinate and supervise lower courts. But the process by which this occurs is slow and often haphazard. Under these conditions, how could a coherent judicial response to development of bureaucratic government occur? What is its underlying premise?

The answers to these questions must begin with an assessment of the judiciary's own power in the administrative state. Its formal constitutional independence and coequal status has always given the U.S. judiciary a large measure of power vis-à-vis the other branches of government. This power was solidified and enhanced when the courts' power of judicial review was first articulated and later fully accepted as a legitimate exercise of the judiciary's role in constitutional government. Armed with autonomy and judicial review, the courts served as the final arbiters of the two great relationships established by the Constitution. On the one hand, they determined the constitutional relationship among the units of government. This judicial role not only involved resolution of disputes among Congress, the president, and/or the courts themselves, but also those arising between the state and national governments. On the other hand, the courts struck an ever-changing balance between the rights and obligations of citizens and the powers and responsibilities of government.

The rise of the contemporary administrative state inevitably altered the context of these roles. First, since the Constitution makes few provisions for administrative governments, its development necessarily alters the nature of the separation of powers. An administrative branch with policy-making and regulatory authority was simply not part of the Founding Fathers's scheme, nor was a large federal bureaucracy with the ability to act directly upon individuals. Whether or not such a governmental branch is truly necessary for modern government, the fact is that it arose and required some important constitutional adjustments. Most important, administrative government as we now know it requires vast delegations of power by the legislature to the executive branch. Whereas once such delegations were considered to be breaches of the separation of powers, today they are deemed constitutionally acceptable even when accompanied only by the vaguest of legislative guidelines. In a sense, this result is necessary since under the Constitution the federal bureaucracy is established largely by exercise of congressional power but is directed under executive authority. Thus, the rise of the federal bureaucracy to the heart of American government could only be accompanied by a changing view of the requirements of the separation of powers.

This situation left the federal judiciary in a very difficult position. During the New Deal, when the American administrative state emerged in earnest, the judiciary was confronted with one of its most historically threatening moments. Based on traditional constitutional concepts of the separation of powers, it had the option of trying to resist the rise of bureaucratic government by ruling that legislative delegations of power to the administrative or executive branches were unconstitutional. And this is precisely what the Supreme Court did up to the mid-1930s. Whatever its constitutional logic—and a strong case can be made for limiting legislative delegations—politically, this approach proved to be disasterous for the judiciary. The president, legislature, and nation as a whole sought governmental action to end the Great Depression. Action in the New Deal formula demanded the creation and use of administrative agencies. Indeed, more than 60 new federal agencies were created during Roosevelt's first administration. But there stood the Supreme Court, seeking to envoke the constitutional proscription of the breach of separation of powers and thereby threatening the nation's chosen path to economic recovery. This prompted Roosevelt to introduce his court-packing plan, and the Supreme Court, presumably understanding the threat to its legitimacy, soon capitulated on the issue of administrative power under the Constitution (Pritchett, 1948). Soon after, the exercise of legislative power by administrative agencies became fully acceptable.

This development had very far-reaching political consequences, as discussed in Chapter 1. Eventually, it shifted efforts to obtain representation substantially to the federal bureaucracy and placed public administration at the heart of government and politics. It also threw the separation of powers out of balance in a way that was especially unfavorable to the judiciary. Administrative government requires administrative independence and tends to breed administrative autonomy. Nevertheless, in a formal sense the president and Congress have always retained formidable authority and power over public bureaucracy. Together, these branches create, empower, fund, staff, investigate, and seek to direct and supervise administrative agencies. The judiciary, on the other hand, traditionally exercised none of these powers or functions. Once it accepted the transformation of legislative power into administrative power, the judiciary had to develop new approaches for arbitrating the constitutionality of the activities of public agencies and for asserting its power over public administrators. The separation of powers issue being resolved in favor of administrative government, the courts, perhaps inevitably, began to focus on the second great relationship established by the Constitution: in this context, the relationship between administrative agencies and individuals' civil rights and liberties.

In retrospect, this refocusing of attention did not take long for a constitutional change of such great magnitude. Indeed, within two decades of the Supreme Court's greatest effort to envoke the separation of powers against administrative power, the doctrine of privilege was being substantially weakened in its hold over relationships between public agencies and their employees and clients. For the most part, the delay in using the Bill of Rights as a constraint on administrative power can probably be traced to the courts' desire to pay deference to administrative expertise and its effort to avoid reopening the issues (and wounds) of the New Deal era. The administrative branch was accepted as a full-fledged partner in government. Judge David Bazelon, an activist in seeking to constrain administrative power over individuals, observed that until the 1970s, "The court's role was to assure simply that the agency functioned fairly and treated all interests with decency. Agencies were to proceed in a manner designed to ensure that the parties, the public, and the reviewing courts knew the basis of their decision and so that the courts could review their reasoning in the light of the evidence" (1976:103). However, the acquiescent approach began to lose force as the judiciary came to recognize a tension between the growth of administrative power and the maintenance of individual civil rights and liberties. If Congress wanted to give its power to the administrative branch, that was one matter; the individual citizen never sought to surrender his or her rights and liberties to unelected and seemingly unrepresentative bureaucratic agencies. By the 1970s, then, the issue of bureaucratic power over individuals had been placed squarely before the judiciary.

Its response has been based on at least two premises. First, there is a recognition that bureaucratic power over individuals can be formidable, may be unchecked by the legislature or the political executive, and ultimately may destroy the quality of democratic citizenship. Second, and a related premise, there is a recognition that a proper and natural judicial role in the administrative state is to assure that bureaucratic power over individuals is exercised in a fashion that is compatible with the Bill of Rights. Together, these premises amount to the proposition that the judiciary has an important constitutional role in checking public bureaucracy by forcing it to respond to constitutional values. Indeed, the judiciary has sought to maintain its position of coequality with the legislature and the elected executive by fashioning a supervisory role for itself over public bureaucracy—a role that is a rough counterpart of the supervisory roles of the two other branches of government. In a bureaucratic government, power is directly related to the authority and ability to control or influence public agencies. At least one very influential judge, Judge Bazelon, has expressed these premises and thoughts in a call for the forging of a "partnership" between judges and bureaucrats, with the judges being the senior partners.

> Administrators are not always happy about judges meddling in their affairs; judges are not always happy with the administrative responses to their meddling. Under the circumstances, a certain amount of disappointment and frustration on both sides is entirely natural. As the Constitutional right to due process of law expands, more and more administrators will find themselves locked into involuntary partnerships with the courts. Therefore, efforts should be made to forge a better relationship between the partners (Bazelon, 1976:104–105).

The notion of a partnership of this nature between judges and bureaucrats is remarkable. A few decades ago it would have been unthinkable. But today, as a result of a certain coherence to the judicial response to the rise of the administrative state, it is an evermore visible reality.

A concern with the power of public agencies over individual citizens and a desire to develop a more forceful role in overseeing the administrative state constitute the bases of the judicial response to the rise of bureaucratic government. Though often unarticulated in any given judicial decision, the overall record and the statements of several leading members of the federal judiciary leave little doubt that these elements are frequently at the root of the courts' action vis-à-vis public bureaucracies. Consequently, even though the judicial decisions that constitute the judicial response under consideration often deal with disparate issues and rights, there is a potential coherence or interrelated quality to them. Ultimately, they have been effectively integrated into a fundamentally new relationship between public law and public administration by the Supreme Court's action in cases involving the rights of antagonists to sue public agencies and public administrators. This development can be explained more concretely in terms of the findings of the body of this book.

A major advantage of focusing the discussion of legal/constitutional developments on the ways in which individuals come into contact with public agencies is to place the creation of new constitutional rights in a particular context that makes them readily understandable. Using this approach leaves no doubt that over the past two or three decades the federal judiciary has massively expanded the rights of clients, employees, and captives of administrative agencies. The procedural and substantive rights of individuals who fall into any of these categories have been strengthened immensely. In fact, whole new rights, such as the constitutional rights to treatment and habilitation, have been proclaimed. As the doctrine of privilege met its demise, procedural due process was afforded to clients and public employees in a wide variety of circumstances. The citizenry's freedoms of speech, association, and thought were also given greater protections against bureaucratic encroachments. The protection against cruel and unusual punishment was strengthened. In sum, the judicary forged what amounts to a bill of rights for the citizen of the contemporary American administrative state.

The creation of these new rights and the expansion of older ones was in itself an exercise of judicial authority over public adminstration. Typically, the expansion of individuals' rights vis-à-vis bureaucratic agencies is synonymous with the imposition of constraints on the traditional public administrative way of doing business. For example, the expansion of the due process rights of clients or public employees represents a limitation on the exercise of discretion by public bureaucrats. The same is true of substantive rights. Consequently, this aspect of the judicial response to the rise of the administrative state has the impact of reducing bureaucratic discretion and power over the citizenry. In this fashion, the courts have sought to force public administrators to adhere to the

judicial interpretation of the Constitution. Thus, through the expansion of
individuals' rights, the judiciary emerges as a broad overseer of public administration in the United States. Hence, in effect the judiciary enhances its own
power within the framework of the administrative state, taking a position
related to those of Congress and the president in overseeing the administrative
branch.

But oversight in this sense is almost by definition after the fact. It does not
enable the judiciary to be proactive in its relationships with public adminstrators. This is why the judiciary's resurrection of the section 1983 suit and the
creation of the *Bivens* (1971) remedy is so important. These legal processes
follow naturally from the expansion of individual substantive and procedural
rights within the administrative state because they provide a mechanism by which
a client, public employee, or captive can seek to vindicate breaches of his or her
constitutional and/or legal rights. On one level, the expansion of the bureaucratic citizen's rights and the forging of an effective legal mechanism by which
individuals can seek to assure enforcement of their new rights has a coherence
that cannot be denied. Indeed, it is not too much to say that the creation of
rights for antagonists was a necessary part of the expansion of the rights of
clients, employees, and captives. For without the one, the other has far less
meaning.

But there is a deeper level as well, and one that speaks directly to the issue
of judicial power in the administrative state. The Supreme Court's interpretation of the section 1983 and *Bivens*-style suits affords the judiciary a proactive
means of supervising the broad ways in which public administrators act upon
individual citizens. By holding that public bureaucrats, in general, are liable for
their unconstitutional or illegal encroachments upon the rights of individuals,
if they knew or reasonably should have known that their actions would have
this effect, the Supreme Court has forced public administrators to be fully
cognizant of the law. Consequently, knowledge of the law, and especially
constitutional law, becomes a positive job requirement for the public bureaucrat
who acts upon individuals and seeks to avoid losing a civil suit for damages.
But at noted earlier, since "the constitutional law is what the courts say it is,"
this new job requirement is really one of adhering to judicial values even though
they may stand in opposition to administrative values. Consequently, a major
ramification of the establishment of new rights for the antagonist of the administrative state is to enable the judiciary to play a far greater role in determining the
values to which public administrators must be responsive. This, in turn, as Judge
Bazelon (1976) suggests, places the judiciary in the role of senior "partner" of
public administrators. And this is very much a role that enables the judiciary
to assert some control over public administration and, therefore, also to
strengthen its own power in the administrative state. Again, it is evident that the
reactive approach of creating new procedural and substantive rights for the

citizenry goes hand in hand with the proactive approach embodied in the judiciary's drastic expansion of the liability of public administrators and of public agencies. Standing alone, neither approach would afford as much protection to the citizenry or enable the judiciary to assert so much power over contemporary public administration. Therein lies the fundamental coherence of the judicial response to the rise of the administrative state.

Indeed, the assertion of judicial power becomes complete when, in order to protect the newly established rights of individuals, the courts take over direction of the actual operation of a governmental institution or agency, such as a prison or school system. This is a revolutionary development that even a decade ago few would have thought so generally possible. The idea of the judiciary directing public bureaucrats appears antithetical to the principle of the separation of powers. But as noted previously, the rise of a large federal bureaucracy places great strains on the concept of the separation of powers and it cannot be stressed too frequently that in an administrative state power lies with those who can direct the public bureaucracy. To the extent that the judiciary seeks to maintain its historic place in the separation of powers, that is, to be coequal to the legislature and the elected executive, it must develop powers equivalent to those of the other branches to direct, oversee, and constrain the actions of public administrators. That the judiciary has been largely able to accomplish this end is a remarkable testimony to the governmental flexibility allowed by the Constitution. In essence, the judiciary has managed to adapt the Constitution *itself* to the rise of the administrative state by creating new rights for the citizenry and a new role for the courts vis-à-vis public administrators. From this perspective, the judicial response to the rise of the administrative state has a historical coherence that surpasses its immediate logical coherence. Yet, many important questions remain. Fortunately, understanding the origins and coherence of the judicial response provides a valuable perspective that enables the identification of several of its possible ramifications.

Public Bureaucracy

The judicial response to the rise of the administrative state is based upon a concern for individual rights and for judicial power. It does not emphasize effective or efficient public administration as traditionally conceived. Consequently, there is every reason to believe that the judicial response will make public administration more compatible with constitutional and judicial values, but little reason to believe that it will promote the organizational desiderata generally sought in classical public administration. In fact, the judiciary's constitutionally coherent approach may make public administration less organizationally coherent. Since most public administration in the United States is carried out by bureaucratic organizations, an assessment of the impact of the judicial response on the structure of bureaucracy will conveniently serve to illustrate the point.

According to Max Weber (1958) and many others, including classical American theorists of public administration, public bureaucracies are highly efficient forms of organizations. Their efficiency stems from their organizational characteristics which create an integrated organizational form that is especially effective in processing a multitude of routine cases. Generally, the key organizational characteristics of bureaucracy are identified as hierarchy, specialization, formalization, impersonality, a merit-oriented personnel system, and a large size* (Weber, 1958; Downs, 1967; Nachmias and Rosenbloom, 1980). Where all of these characteristics are strengthened at once, organizations will become more bureaucratic and, at least according to classical theory, more efficient and effective as well. Conversely, weakening these characteristics should have the opposite effect. However, what if some characteristics of bureaucracy are strengthened while others are simultaneously reduced? What kind of organizational form will then emerge, and what will be *its* strengths and weaknesses? Contemporary organization theory is loaded with alternatives to bureaucracy (e.g., Bennis, 1965), but none convincingly addresses this issue in a precise fashion. Yet, this emerges as a central issue because there is every reason to believe that an important impact of the judiciary's current approach will be the development of such an organizational form. More specifically, the judicial response seems likely to have the following impacts on the characteristics of public bureaucracy.

1. *Hierarchy* will be substantially undercut in three ways. (1) The section 1983 and *Bivens*-style suits reduce hierarchy by personalizing responsibility for unconstitutional and/or illegal actions. A public bureaucrat becomes responsible to the law, rather than simply to a superordinate. For instance, in at least one case, *Parrish v. Civil Service Commission* (1967), an employee dismissed for refusing to engage in an unconstitutional raid on the homes of welfare recipients was subsequently reinstated by judicial order. Conversely, an employee's defense of unconstitutional action based on the directives of superordinates is not likely to be successful. (2) The cases dealing with the rights of public employees obviously reduce the ability of superordinates to control their subordinates. Public employees are allowed to organize trade unions and to speak out on political and policy issues. They cannot easily be dismissed for the exercise of their newly found constitutional rights without a substantial measure of due process, nor can they ordinarily be dismissed as part of a patronage system. Other negative sanctions, such as demotions, can also be constitutionally encumbered. Hence, the public manager can no longer rely on a hierarchy of authority or the concept of "I'm the boss" in public personnel matters. This

---

*Nonmarketable output is another, as discussed in Chapter 1.

reduces the efficacy of traditional approaches to public management relying upon negative sanctions, though it may allow for the operation of hierarchy based upon positive inducements to cooperation and performance. (3) The broadening of the applicability of due process diminishes hierarchy because it often requires that decisions concerning the eligibility of clients or the personnel status of public employees be determined by an independent hearing examiner who is outside the hierarchical structure of command within an organization. To the extent that authority lies within such hands, hierarchy is by definition reduced.

2. *Impersonality* is also diminished in at least three ways. (1) The requirement of due process creates the right of an individual to present his or her personal situation and to be judged on that personalized set of circumstances. It is a judicialized process that by its very nature turns on issues of personalized motives, actions, and fact patterns. Indeed, the very purpose of due process is to explore the personal circumstances of individuals by giving them a right to be heard. (2) The constitutional rights to treatment of the publicly confined mentally ill and habilitation of the publicly confined retarded strongly militate against impersonality by requiring that individualized treatment plans be developed. According to *Wyatt v. Stickney* (1971), these must be geared to the personal condition of the individual patient in order to satisfy the constitutional requirement. (3) The case-by-case approach to the rights of public employees demands a personalized assessment of an individual's ability to perform in a specific job. This requirement has been most notable in the Supreme Court's decisions on mandatory maternity leaves for pregnant school teachers, which now require an individualized medical determination of the teacher's ability to continue in her job. In addition, the Court's decisions on patronage dismissals promote an individualized determination of the nature of the position, as is also true of its holdings on the issue of whether aliens can be banned from public service positions.

3. *Specialization* is enhanced through the requirement of due process, which requires the creation of quasijudicial roles such as hearing examiner. Eventually, as the use of hearings leads to the development of a body of decisions having a distinctive legal flavor, these quasijudicial roles may become highly specialized and require substantial training. It is interesting to note, in this context, that in *Butz v. Economou* (1978), the Supreme Court recognized the specialized nature of these roles by affording public administrators with judicial functions an absolute immunity from constitutionally based civil suits for damages. Presumably, the same immunity would exist for similar state officials faced with section 1983 suits. Specialization may also be promoted through the application of the equal protection clause of the Fourteenth Amendment to public personnel examinations. To the extent that merit exams must actually be validated against on-the-job performance, it is likely that position classification will become even more elaborately specialized than it already is (Shafritz et al., 1981).

Highly specialized position descriptions and classifications will facilitate the specific evaluation of different categories of public employees. Thus, whereas much of the literature on *job design* argues in favor of broader tasks and responsibilites, the validation of examinations tends to be very difficult and generally unconvincing under such conditions.

4. *Formalization* will be enhanced in several ways already alluded to. (1) Due process promotes formalization because it introduces what is often an elaborate judicial process into public management. Notice, the opportunity to be heard, and the right to know the reasons why an action is being taken are all governed by formal procedures and strongly tend to promote further formalization. Moreover, records must be kept, investigations undertaken, witnesses heard, and statements must often be in writing if cases are to be won. (2) The section 1983 and *Bivens*-style suits may also promote formalization by requiring that clear lines of responsibility and discretion be established. Neither subordinates nor superordinates want to suffer personal damages for the actions of the other. In addition, as a potential defense against such suits, many public employees will seek written opinions from agency lawyers before taking official action on clients, other employees, or captives. (3) As suggested previously, the application of the requirement of equal protection in public personnel examinations may result in more formalized examination, evaluation, and position classification processes.

5. *Merit-oriented public personnel administration* will also be strengthened. (1) Judicial decisions require that personnel examinations having a harsh racial impact be valid predictors of on-the-job performance. Otherwise, they run afoul of the Constitution or laws. In other words, if an examination tends to have a harsh racial impact, it must be an adequate predictor of merit. Since so many examinations do manifest such an impact, this requirement serves to assure that merit exams really do measure merit. (2) The cases dealing with patronage dismissals go even further in virtually constitutionalizing the merit system. For the most part, patronage appointments are now unconstitutional. Thus, what was a matter of intense political controversy in 1829, when the spoils system got underway in earnest at the federal level, and again in 1883, when civil service reform was introduced, has now become a matter of constitutional law. Of course, the banning of patronage does not automatically result in the institution of a merit system, but merit has been the historical alternative.

6. *The size of public bureaucracies is likely to grow larger.* This is most evident in three contexts, but is also probably inherent in much of what the courts have required of public administration: (1) Due process requires the appointment of hearing examiners, transcribers, lawyers, and investigators. All of these personnel may require some additional support staff. (2) The rights to treatment and habilitation have been accompanied by increased staffing requirements. These are sometimes directly imposed by the judiciary. (3) The

Eighth Amendment cases promote the same tendency. More guards, medical personnel, and other prison employees are sometimes required to alleviate conditions of cruel and unusual punishment.

In sum, it can be observed that rather than all the central organizational characteristics of bureaucracy being promoted or weakened at the same time, hierarchy and impersonality are diminished while specialization, formalization, merit-oriented personnel procedures, and large size are enhanced. Thus, the judicial response to the rise of the administrative state is not antibureaucracy per se, but rather selectively so in terms of certain organizational characteristics. This being the case, there is no reason to believe that the judiciary's impact on public agencies will promote organizational coherence. Clearly, such coherence has been of only secondary concern to the judiciary, and it is difficult to see how public administration can operate efficiently and effectively under these new organizational conditions.

Two examples will serve to illustrate the problem further. First, the simultaneous reduction of hierarchy and the increasing of specialization seems certain to promote problems of coordination. As Blau and Meyer observe, "A high degree of specialization creates a need for a complex system of coordination. . . . Managerial responsibility, therefore, is exercised through a hierarchy of authority, which furnishes lines of communication between top management and every employee for obtaining information on operations and transmitting operating directives" (1971:8). However, the nature of the specialization promoted by the judiciary is such that coordination through hierarchy is particularly inappropriate. For instance, any effort of hierarchical authorities to compromise the independence of hearing examiners is certain to raise an issue of breach of due process. Yet, since among other issues hearing examiners determine clients' eligibility for benefits, they frequently make policy that affects the agency as a whole, and they render decisions that can have important budgetary consequences. Whether their decisions can be coordinated or whether an agency can plan under these conditions remains to be seen.

Impersonality and formalization present another example. It will be recalled that Max Weber (1958) referred to dehumanization (impersonality) as the "special virtue" of bureaucracy because it eliminated human emotions from on-the-job performance. This turned employees into "cogs" who worked with great efficiency in processing numerous cases with very little deviation in routine. Blau and Meyer echo this approach: "For the operations of hundreds of employees to be coordinated, each individual must conform to prescribed standards even in situations where a different course of action appears to him to be the most rationale. . . . Efficiency also suffers when emotions or personal considerations influence administrative decisions" (1971:9). Thus, formalization is used to promote impersonality. Formalized rules specify what each bureaucrat must do in each situation. Human judgment and emotion are to be eliminated for the sake of even treatment and coordination. Consequently, impersonality and formalization depend upon each other to a considerable extent. Increasing formalization while decreasing impersonality appears antithetical to the purposes of each. If bureaucrats are supposed to take personal factors into account, then coordination through formalization can be procedural at best, rather than substantive. Where decisions are personalized, public administrators will often be unable to exclude their emotions in making their choices. For instance, under conditions of limited resources, a determination of the nature of an individualized treatment plan for a mentally ill patient may inevitably rest partially upon an assessment of the patient's potential to make useful contributions to society.

Thus, we are left with the question of whether the bureaucratic model of public administration can work well under these new constitutional/legal conditions. Presumably, if Weber and classical organization theory are correct, any diminution of the characteristics of bureaucracy will lead to less efficient and less effective organizations. Although it is easy enough to dismiss efficiency and effectiveness as unimportant ends for democratic government, it must also be recognized that less efficient and less effective organizations cost more money to operate. Consequently, the judiciary's impact on the organizational characteristics of public agencies may ultimately require an increase in administrative costs or a corresponding reduction in the level of activity provided. Making government more expensive may require that government do less. This, in turn, raises the issues of values, or the question of public administration for what?

Administrative Values and Constitutional Democracy

Traditional public administration has stressed the need for efficiency above all else. In the view of the classical approach, efficiency is "axiom number one in the value scale of administration" and, consequently, "This brings administration into apparent conflict with the value scale of politics. . . ." (Gulick and Urwick, 1937:192). Thus, politics may want one thing from public administration, whereas public administration may want another. Clearly, in a constitutional democracy such as the United States, the polity may prefer that public administration promote justice and freedom more than efficiency. Therefore, it is not surprising that when the federal judiciary began to force its values upon contemporary public administration, it promoted constitutional concerns as opposed to the administrative concerns with efficiency.

In general, the emergent conflict between judicial values and administrative values can be understood best in terms of diversity versus uniformity. As stressed throughout this book, public administration and bureaucracy place great stress upon uniformity. Public employees are turned into cogs to promote efficiency and effective management. Clients are turned into cases that can be readily processed. Captives are dehumanized to reduce the costs of handling them. On the other hand, constitutional law and the judiciary place greater stress upon the diversity that stems from an appreciation of individuality. To a large extent, this value is ingrained in the constitutional approach to government, which attempts to promote and profit from diversity among the population. Federalism, the different constituencies of the elected branches of government, and the different powers and terms of offices of elected officials are all efforts to bring a substantial measure of diversity of opinion into government. Indeed, the scheme of checks and balances would be undermined by dominant consensus in government. The Bill of Rights is also an effort to protect and promote diversity among the citizenry. But the judiciary's appreciation for diversity and individuality is also ingrained in the case method and adversary proceeding. The judicial approach to decision making requires that an individual be allowed to state his or her own personal case before the courts. Social scientific generalizations may be used, but ultimately judicial decisions turn on the facts presented in individual, idiographic circumstances, sometimes affecting only one or a few people directly. In this fashion, great principles of constitutional law and judicial policy making may spring from circumstances involving such seemingly minor incidents as high school pranks. Indeed, the courts generally rely upon individuals to bring out not only the facts of an incident, but also the legal principles they believe should govern its resolution. Such a method demands a great appreciation of individual worth and the devotion of attention to the diverse claims of individuals.

Again, however, there is a problem. Public administration has tended to turn people into cogs and cases less out of inhumanity than from the need to provide services and regulatory functions in an efficient and effective manner. As judicial values become more predominant in public administration, the cogs and cases will be turned back into human beings. This is best illustrated by the application of due process to administrative decisions adversely affecting individuals. But can public administrative organizations efficiently and effectively deal with human beings in a personalized fashion that weighs their individual and diverse claims? Probably not as we know such organizations and, therefore, it can be seen that the judicial approach to public administration requires organizational change in this context as well.

From these perspectives, the judicial response to the rise of the administrative state is but one of several forces demanding widespread reform of public administration. Thus, organizational theorists have long been concerned that traditional concepts of public administration and bureaucracy are now out of date. Indeed, even Max Weber eventually came to condemn the growing passion for bureaucracy. Others, such as Warren Bennis (1965) have been concerned with moving us "beyond bureaucracy" to some new form of organization that will be more appreciative of human needs and less reliant upon hierarchy, specialization, and formalization. Similarly, Frederick Thayer (1973) has called for *"An End to Hierarchy! An End to Competition!"* In the same vein, the call for a "new public administration" has stressed the need for public organizations to be concerned with equity and to promote constitutional democratic government (Marini, 1971).

Elected officials have also demanded reform of contemporary public administration. A political campaign can hardly be waged now without an obligatory condemnation of public bureaucracy. Indeed, in 1968, when U.S. cities were in the flames of race riots and the nation's troops were mired in a disasterous war in Southeast Asia, candidate Nixon demurred that "The chief revolt in America is against 'an increasingly impersonal' Federal bureaucracy that saps individual initiative" (*New York Times*, 1968:1). President Carter was even more vocal in condemnation of bureaucracy and called the Civil Service Reform Act of 1978 the "centerpiece" of his program to make the federal government more efficient and effective (*New York Times*, 1978:1). In fact, today it would be surprising if a candidate for an executive branch position did not have a program to reform public budgeting, personnel, or management.

The public also seems to be growing dissatisfied with public bureaucracy, especially its costs. Thus, several tax-cutting proposals, such as California's Proposition 13 have been enacted across the nation in an effort to reduce the size of public bureaucracies. As noted earlier, public opinion polls also indicate public dissatisfaction with governmental bureaucracy.

However, one of the consequences of the fragmentation of American government is that the demands for change voiced by one branch of government are not always compatible with those advocated by another. This is partly true of the judiciary's demands for public administrative reform, especially in the areas of public personnel management and the costs of providing services. For instance, at the same time that executives are trying to gain greater flexibility in appointing and dismissing public personnel, several judicial decisions, such as those involving free speech and patronage, serve to limit executive authority. Judicial decisions concerning the status of captives are the clearest examples of the tendency of the courts to increase the costs of public administration while the society as a whole is trying to reduce them. Consequently, whatever its merits—and they are considerable—the judicial response to the rise of the administrative state is not fully compatible with the reforms of public administration being promoted elsewhere in the political system. This raises the very fundamental issue of the relationship of the judicial response to the separation of powers.

Separation of Powers

The judicial response to the rise of the administrative state stems largely from a concern that the courts maintain their historic coequal status in the separation of powers despite the development of bureaucratic government. However, the issue of whether the judiciary has gone too far in attempting to regulate public administration is unavoidably raised. Is jurocracy (i.e., rule by judges) being substituted for bureaucracy? Are the courts well equipped to supervise or to manage public administration?

Another way of looking at the judicial response to the rise of the administrative state is to appreciate the extent to which public bureaucracy has been judicialized by court decisions. Again, this is especially evident in terms of the application of due process to administrative decisions, but it also flows from the courts' requirement that public adminstrators be cognizant of constitutional law. Leaving aside the question of whether these approaches are organizationally desirable, there is the issue of whether they place the courts in a position of supremacy in the administrative state. Perhaps the problem can be best illustrated in terms of captives.

On their face, judicial decisions concerning the rights of captives do not violate any notions of the separation of powers. No court has required that the government establish a program for the care of the mentally ill, nor has the judiciary required that governments imprison people. Rather, what is required is that when a government elects to hold people in captivity, the captives' constitutional rights be afforded protection. But this interpretation is somewhat too facile. No government is actually likely to abandon the function of incarceration, and few will close down their mental health services. Consequently, when a court requires reforms of such facilities, in essence it may be requiring that money be appropriated for their implementation. This is essentially a legislative function. Similarly, when a court establishes staffing ratios or requires better management, it is engaging in an executive function. In such cases, therefore, courts may emerge as legislator, executive, and judge.

Although there are substantial checks that can be exercised against the judiciary, they are politically difficult to implement no matter how unpopular a particular judicial decision may be. Consequently, it remains to be seen whether the other branches of government will act to restrain efforts by the judiciary to establish its superiority over facets of public administration. To a large extent, the question may ultimately turn on the judiciary's competence in the administrative realm. For, if the courts fail to establish the conditions they seek and if they nevertheless alienate bureaucrats, legislators, political executives, and the public, substantial pressures will be directed at the judiciary to play a less active role in public administration.

However, it is still too early to develop a comprehensive assessment of the judiciary's success in intervening in public administration. At best, some broad considerations can be addressed. First, there is the issue of judicial expertise. Legal training and expertise in law does not automatically enhance the ability to deal with the issues presented by public administration. Thus, it is not to be expected that judges generally have expertise in questions of mental health treatment, education, or management. Although they can summon experts to serve as advisors, masters, and so forth, ultimately judges' knowledge of some areas will necessarily be secondhand. This stands in marked contrast to the expertise of public administrators in the areas of their own specializations. To the extent that judges lack expertise, they may make and seek to implement poor policy decisions. However, the issue goes somewhat beyond the question of who is best suited for policy making. Inexpertness on the part of the courts may tend to diminish the judiciary's legitimacy in government.

Second, the judicial process has evolved to investigate and establish what can variously be called *historical facts, adjudicative facts*, or *legislative facts*. These ". . . are the events that have transpired between the parties to a lawsuit" (Horowitz, 1977:45). Historical facts provide the basis for the vast bulk of the day-to-day decisions rendered by the nation's courts. However, public law litigation turns less on historical facts than on social facts. Horowitz (1977) defines these as ". . . the recurrent patterns of behavior on which policy must be based" (45). He further observes that "two different kinds of fact-finding processes are required for these two different functions. The adversary system of presentation and the rules of evidence were both developed for the [determination of historical facts], and they leave much to be desired for the [determination of social facts]" (47). Moreover, judges may be ill-trained in social science; they may fail to understand the nature of social scientific generalizations and statistical techniques. They may also have a tendency to search for single-factor explanations of complex social phenomena. To the extent that this is true, the courts will be guilty of poor social science, and their efforts at policy making will suffer accordingly. Of course, this situation can be mitigated by the courts' reliance on experts, but the fundamental problem of the incompatibility between the judicial process and the discovery of social facts is likely to remain.

Third, and a related factor, the judges seem to have substantial difficulties in anticipating the consequences of their decisions on matters of public administration. For instance, in *Wyatt v. Stickney* (1971), the court failed to anticipate that administrators might attempt to reduce costs by dumping patients in the community. Nor have school desegregation decisions been notable in establishing equal educational opportunity for minorities. More generally, as discussed previously, the judicial intervention in public administration may reduce the organizational coherence and effectiveness of public agencies while raising their costs to the extent that less service will be provided. Indeed, one response to desegregation decisions—and one that the courts refused to tolerate—was to stop providing public education (*Griffin v. County School Board of Prince Edward County*, 1964). Since it is unlikely that governments will stop incarcerating people or completely stop trying to accommodate the mentally ill or retarded, raising the costs of these functions may reduce the resources available for others. Yet, it is not at all clear that the judiciary is cognizant of this, or that such a process represents any consistent view of how the society ought to operate.

Fourth, as judges become active in public administration they are almost certain to lose their cloak of neutrality. A judge seeking to implement mental hospital or prison reform becomes a partisan of the changes being advocated. He or she is no longer a referee in a contest between private or public parties, but rather is aligned on one side or the other. A loss of neutrality can be particularly damaging to the judiciary's legitimacy.

A fifth problem is that coordination among the judiciary is often difficult. Different courts have come to different conclusions. Different circuits may be governed by different interpretations of the law. Ultimately, these disparities can be rectified by the Supreme Court. However, this takes time. Moreover, the Supreme Court is generally dependent upon the lower courts to carry out its will, but these may remain recalcitrant for some time.

Finally, anytime the judiciary enters overtly into the policy making arena, the issue of representative government arises. Generally speaking, the courts are a highly unrepresentative branch of government. The social origins of judges are considerably higher than those of the average citizen. Their political views are presumably different from those of the population as well, stressing the need for civil rights, civil liberties, and due process. At the federal level, judges are not elected. They hold their positions during "good behavior," which may mean for life. Hence, they are largely unaccountable to the rest of the political system. Impeachment is a possibility, but one rarely undertaken with success (Goldman and Jahnige, 1971). Interestingly, this lack of accountability is enhanced by the fact that judges are immune from civil suits for damages arising out of the exercise of their official functions. Thus, even when egregiously wrong in deciding matters, the individual harmed has no recourse through such a suit (see *Stump v. Sparkman*, 1978).

In sum, the judicial response to the rise of the administrative state carries with it a substantial threat to the separation of powers. The courts have tended to establish their supremacy in some areas of public administration. They have certainly secured the potential to force the administrative state to respond to their values. In some cases, they have taken on legislative and executive functions, as well as exercised their traditional judicial ones. There remains a substantial issue of the propriety of these activities, and of the courts' ability to undertake them successfully. Moreover, although such judicial activism in the realm of public administration serves to protect individuals' rights, it may nevertheless weaken constitutional democracy by allowing increasing power to be exercised by an unrepresentative, unelected, and largely unaccountable branch of the government. As opposition to the judicial response to the rise of the administrative state develops and crystallizes, the judiciary's legitimacy in engaging in the regulation and supervision of public administration will inevitably be called into question. If history serves as a guide, the courts will sense this and may curtail their activist stance. A different balance between judicial review and judicial restraint will be struck. This, after all, is precisely how the system of checks and balances operates: the power of one branch may be dominant for a time or out of harmony with that of the others, but eventually the latter will exercise their ability to limit the former.

The Future

The future of the judicial response to the rise of the administrative state remains unclear. It is uncertain whether the courts will continue to expand their control over public administration. In some areas, the Supreme Court seems to have signaled a call for greater judicial restraint toward public administration. This is true, for example, in the realm of cases involving the due process rights of public employees, as can be seen from the Court's holding in *Bishop v. Wood* (1976). The Court's decision in *Pennhurst State School v. Halderman* (1981) suggests it is not enthusiastic about embracing either a statutory or constitutional right to treatment *in the least restrictive environment*, though this will undoubtedly be clarified in further litigation. On the other hand, judicial intervention in public administration concerning the First Amendment rights of public employees, the rights of prisoners, and those of antagonists continues unabated with strong support from the Supreme Court.

A great deal of weight should not be placed on these contradictory tendencies. Judicial decisions often turn on the precise wording of a statute or the precise circumstances of a particular case. Predicting the future from one or two decisions is likely to be a fruitless endeavor. Rather, prediction must be based on some more lasting set of historical and political circumstances. These would strongly suggest that the judiciary will maintain its current level of intervention in public administration. The fundamental consequence of its response to the rise of the administrative state has been to assert its coequality with the legislative and executive branches in the face of the bureaucratization of government. The judiciary has sought to establish a forceful role for itself in the administrative state and has been successful in doing so. It is not likely to relinquish its influence in wholesale fashion in the future, though some backing and filling is inevitable.

From this perspective, a new and heavy burden is placed upon public administrators. They must know constitutional law as it affects their activities, and they must act in accordance with it. Consequently, the study of these aspects of law should become part of the training of civil servants. The purpose of this book has been to begin that process. But it is only a beginning. The law is ever changing and often ambiguous. The public administrator would be wise to assess its spirit as well as its narrower precedents. Above all, the public administrator should recognize that the judicial response to the rise of the administrative state creates both new opportunities and new challenges—opportunities to bring public administration into greater harmony with our political institutions and challenges to do so with organizational efficiency and effectiveness. Ultimately, then, we must continue upon the course established by Woodrow Wilson in the 1880s; namely, to recognize that "The principles on which to base a science of administration for America must be principles which have a democratic policy very much at heart" (Wilson, 1941:504).

References

Bazelon, David L., 1976. The impact of the courts on public administration. *Indiana Law Journal* 52: 101-110.

Bennis, Warren, 1965. Beyond bureaucracy. *Transaction* 2: 31-35.

Bishop v. Wood, 1976. 426 U.S. 341.

Bivens v. Six Unknown Named Federal Narcotics Agents, 1971. 403 U.S. 388.

Blau, Peter and Marshall Meyer, 1971. *Bureaucracy in Modern Society*, 2nd ed. New York: Random House.

Butz v. Economou, 1978. 438 U.S. 504.

Downs, Anthony, 1967. *Inside Bureaucracy*. Boston: Little, Brown.

Goldman, Sheldon and Thomas Jahnige, 1971. *The Courts as a Political System*. New York: Harper and Row.

Griffin v. County School Board of Prince Edward County, 1964. 377 U.S. 218.

Gulick, Luther and L. Urwick, eds., 1937. *Papers on the Science of Administration*. New York: Institute of Public Administration.

Horowitz, Donald, 1977. *The Courts and Social Policy*. Washington, D.C.: Brookings Institution.

Marini, Frank, ed., 1971. *Toward a New Public Administration*. New York: Intext.

Nachmias, David and David H. Rosenbloom, 1980. *Bureaucratic Government, USA*. New York: St. Martin's.

New York Times, 1968. October 7.

New York Times, 1978. March 3.

Parrish v. Civil Service Commission, 1967. 425 P2d 233.

Pennhurst State School v. Halderman, 1981. 49 Law Week 4363.

Pritchett, C. Herman, 1948. *The Roosevelt Court*. New York: Macmillan.

Shafritz, Jay, Albert Hyde, and David H. Rosenbloom, 1981. *Personnel Management in Government*. New York: Marcel Dekker.

Stump v. Sparkman, 1978. 435 U.S. 349.

Thayer, Frederick, 1973. *An End to Hierarchy! An End to Competition!* New York: New Viewpoints.

Weber, Max, 1958. *From Max Weber: Essays in Sociology*. Translated and
   edited by H. H. Gerth and C. W. Mills. New York: Oxford University Press.
Wilson, Woodrow, 1941. The study of administration. *Political Science
   Quarterly* 56(December), 481–506. Originally written in 1887.
Wyatt v. Stickney, 1971. 325 F. Supp. 781; 334 F. Supp. 1341.

Index

L 35203/

DATE DUE

		NOV 8 6 1992	
DEC 1 6 1986			
DEC 31 1987			
MAY 31 1988			
AUG 31 1988			
AUG 3 1 1988			
NOV 06 1988			
NOV 6 1988			
NOV 27 1988			
DEC 5 1988			
APR 20 1989			
MAY 0 1989			
DEC 1 5 1992			
GAYLORD		PRINTED IN U.S.A.